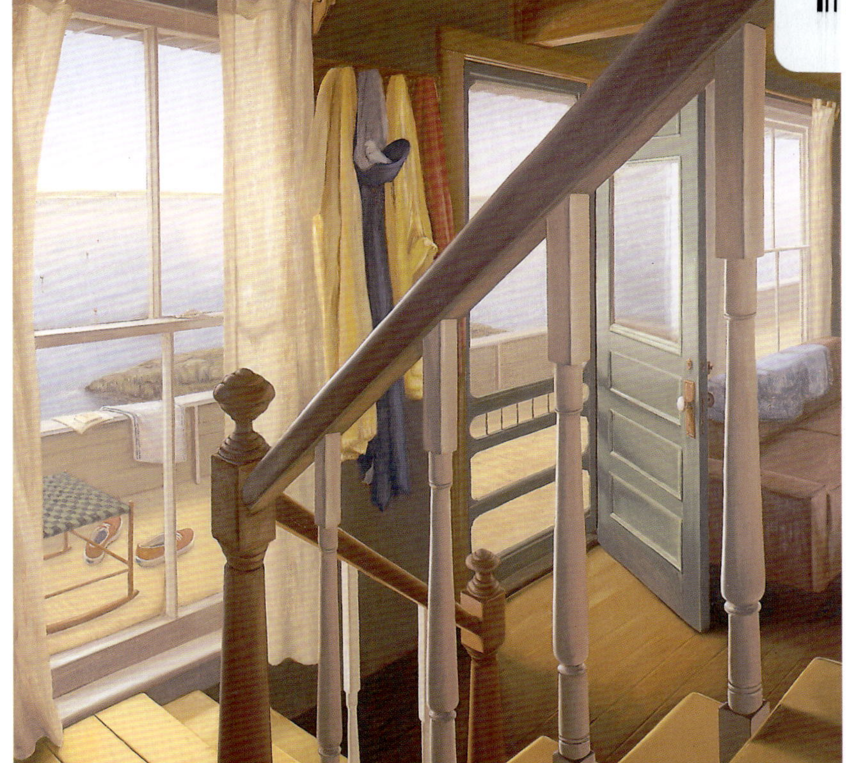

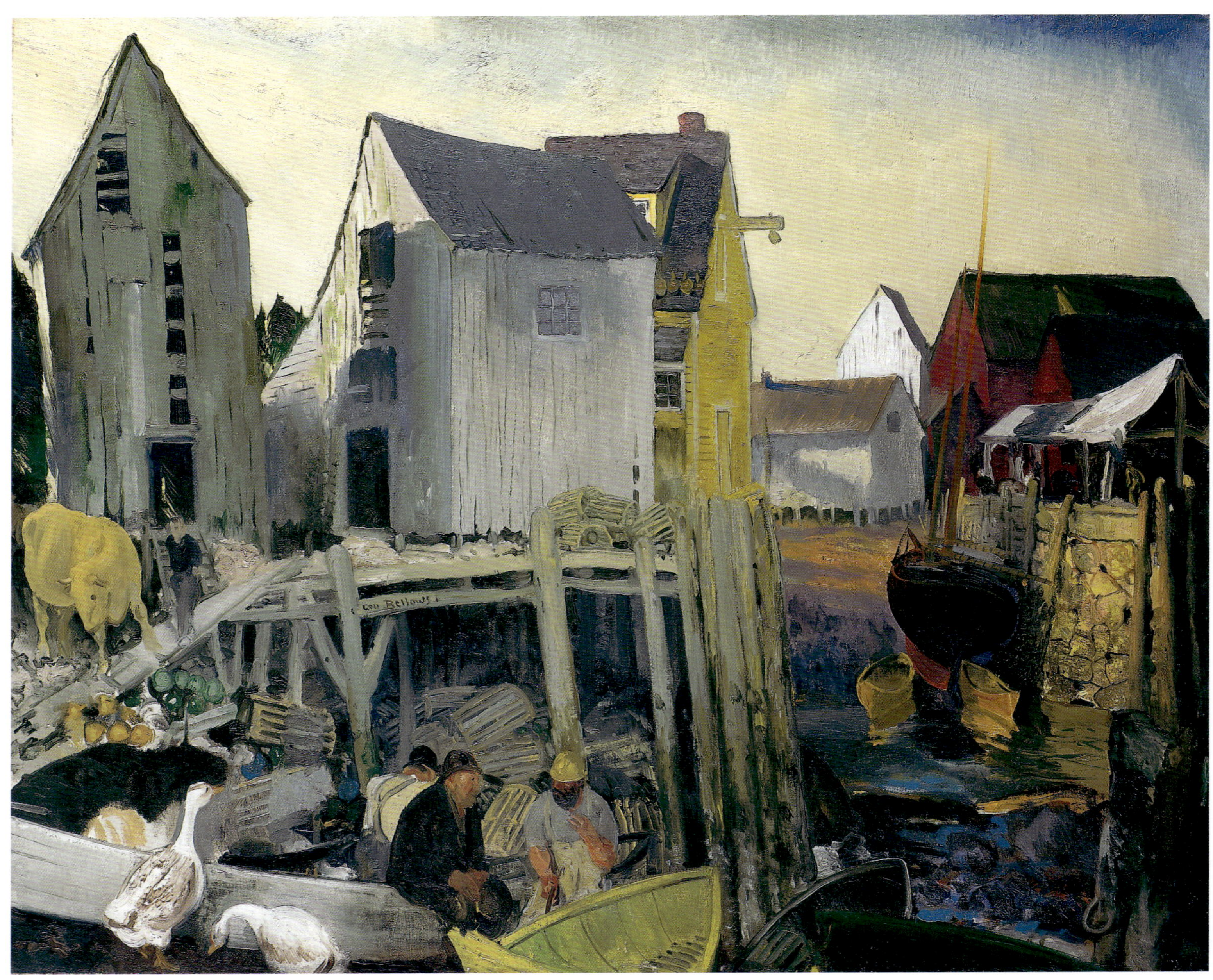
Geo Bellows

Paintings of Maine

A New Collection Selected by Carl Little

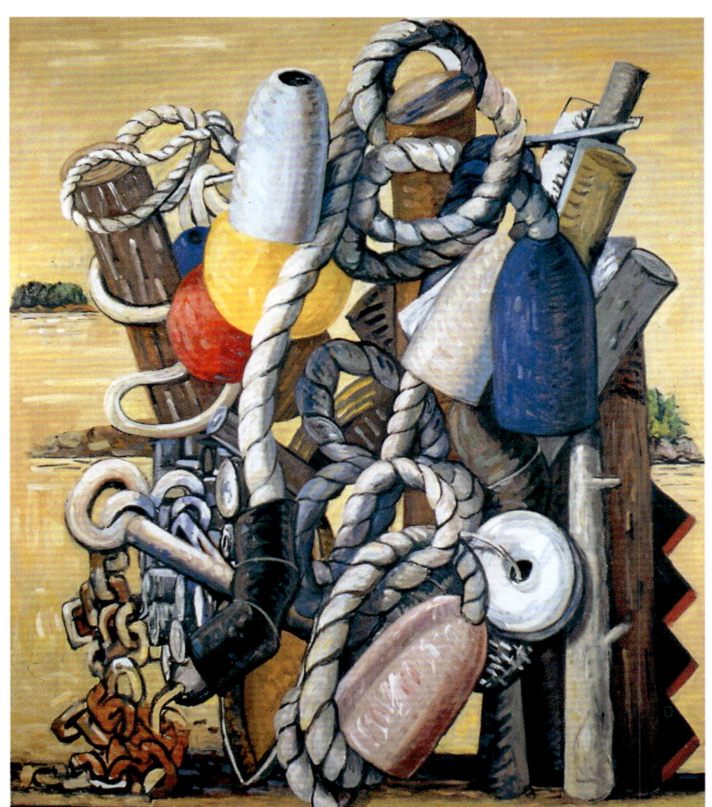

text by *Carl Little* picture editor *Arnold Skolnick*

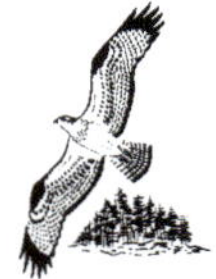

DOWN EAST BOOKS, CAMDEN, MAINE, 2006

A Chameleon Book

Published by Down East Books
Camden, Maine
A division of Down East Enterprise, Inc.
Publisher of *Down East, the Magazine of Maine*
Book Orders: 800-685-7962
www.downeastbooks.com

Produced by Chameleon Books, Inc.
Chesterfield, MA 01012
chambooks@earthlink.net

Designer/Picture Editor: Arnold Skolnick
Copy Editor: Jamie Nan Thaman
Design Assistant: KC Scott

Printed in China

ISBN: 0-89272-712-8
ISBN 13: 978-0-89272-712-4

Library of Congress Cataloging-in-Publication Data

Little, Carl.
Paintings of Maine : a new collection selected by Carl Little / Carl Little ; Arnold Skolnick, picture editor.
p. cm.
Includes bibliographical references and index.
ISBN-13: 978-0-89272-712-4 (trade pbk. : alk. paper)
ISBN-10: 0-89272-712-8
1. Painting, American--Maine. 2. Maine--In art. I. Skolnick, Arnold. II. Title.
ND230.M2L58 2006
758'.1741--dc22

2006012770

Distributed to the Trade by National Book Network

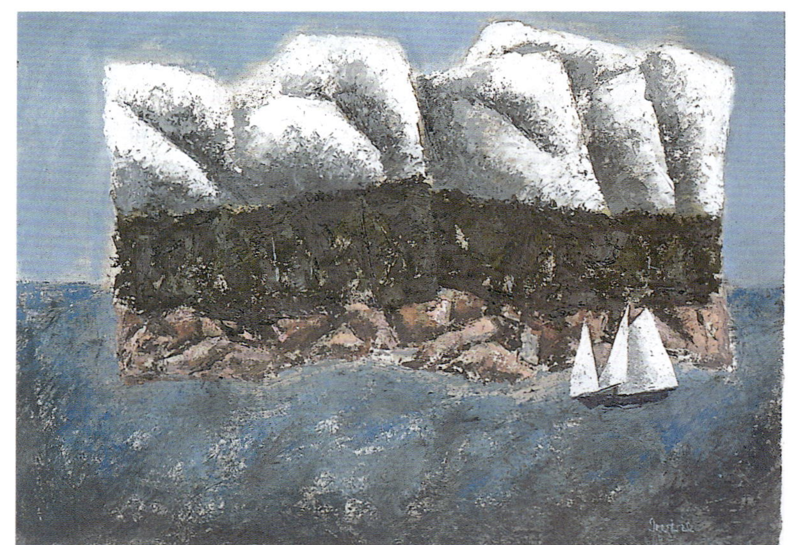

William Irvine, *Clouds over Pike Island,* 2002
Oil on board, 30 x 40 in., collection of Anne Stroud

(HALF TITLE)
Alison Rector, *Eavesdropping,* 2005
Oil on linen, 50 x 50 in., private collection

(FRONTISPIECE)
George Bellows, *Matinicus,* 1916
Oil on canvas, 32 x 40 in.
Portland Museum of Art, Maine
Bequest of Elizabeth B. Noyce, 1996.38.1

(TITLE PAGE)
Jon Imber, *Peter's Boat Gear I,* 1993
Oil on canvas, 68 x 60 in., courtesy Nielsen Gallery

For my family—that would be Peggy, Emily and James, and the rest of the kin and caboodle

And for Neil Welliver (1929–2005) and Donelson Hoopes (1932–2006)—Mainers of art and history

Acknowledgments

The author and picture editor extend special thanks to all the artists who provided slides, transparencies and jpegs. And a tip of the brush to Earle Shettleworth, Maine Historic Preservation Commission; Sandra Richardson, Barridoff Galleries; Liz Sheehan, Bates College Museum of Art; Laura J. Latman, Bowdoin College Museum of Art; Wally Mason, University of Maine Museum of Art; Hugh French, Tides Institute and Museum of Art; Bob Roth, *Chicago Reader;* John Hanson, *Maine Boats, Homes & Harbors;* Suzette McAvoy, Farnsworth Museum of Art; Jessica Skwire Routhier and Stephanie Doben, Portland Museum of Art; Deanna Bonner Ganter, Maine State Museum; April Brown, Morse Museum of Art; James M. Sousa, Addison Gallery of American Art; Amber Woods, Wadsworth Atheneum; Laurie Sims, Sheldon Museum Art Gallery; Toni Liquori, Montclair Art Museum; and Edward Deci, Monhegan Museum.

We also had great help from a number of galleries, including Alexandre Gallery; Caldbeck Gallery; Gleason Fine Art; Islesford Artists Gallery; Watson Gallery; Wiscasset Bay Gallery; Ten High Street; Veilleux Gallery; Turtle Gallery; Redfield Gallery; Firehouse Gallery; Brock & Co.; The Clown; Nan Mulford Gallery; Curtis Galleries; Mathias Fine Arts; Greenhut Galleries; Jameson Gallery; Clark House Gallery; D.C. Moore Gallery; Spanierman Gallery; Berry-Hill Galleries; Kraushaar Galleries; Marlborough Gallery; Hackett-Freedman Gallery; Eclectic Art Objects Gallery; Nancy Hoffman Gallery; Owen Gallery; and Katharina Rich Perlow Gallery. Thanks also to John Wilmerding, Remak Ramsay, John Arthur, Martha Hoppin, Sunne Savage, Linda Bean, the Cawley family, Mr. and Mrs. Graham Gund, Robert and Carol Stahl, and the staff of the Ellsworth Library.

The author is grateful to these individuals for their advice and support: Janice Coates, Port in a Storm Bookstore; Neale Sweet, Down East Books; and Arnold Skolnick, Chameleon Books. He offers special thanks to his colleagues at the Maine Community Foundation, who have helped expand his vision of his adopted state.

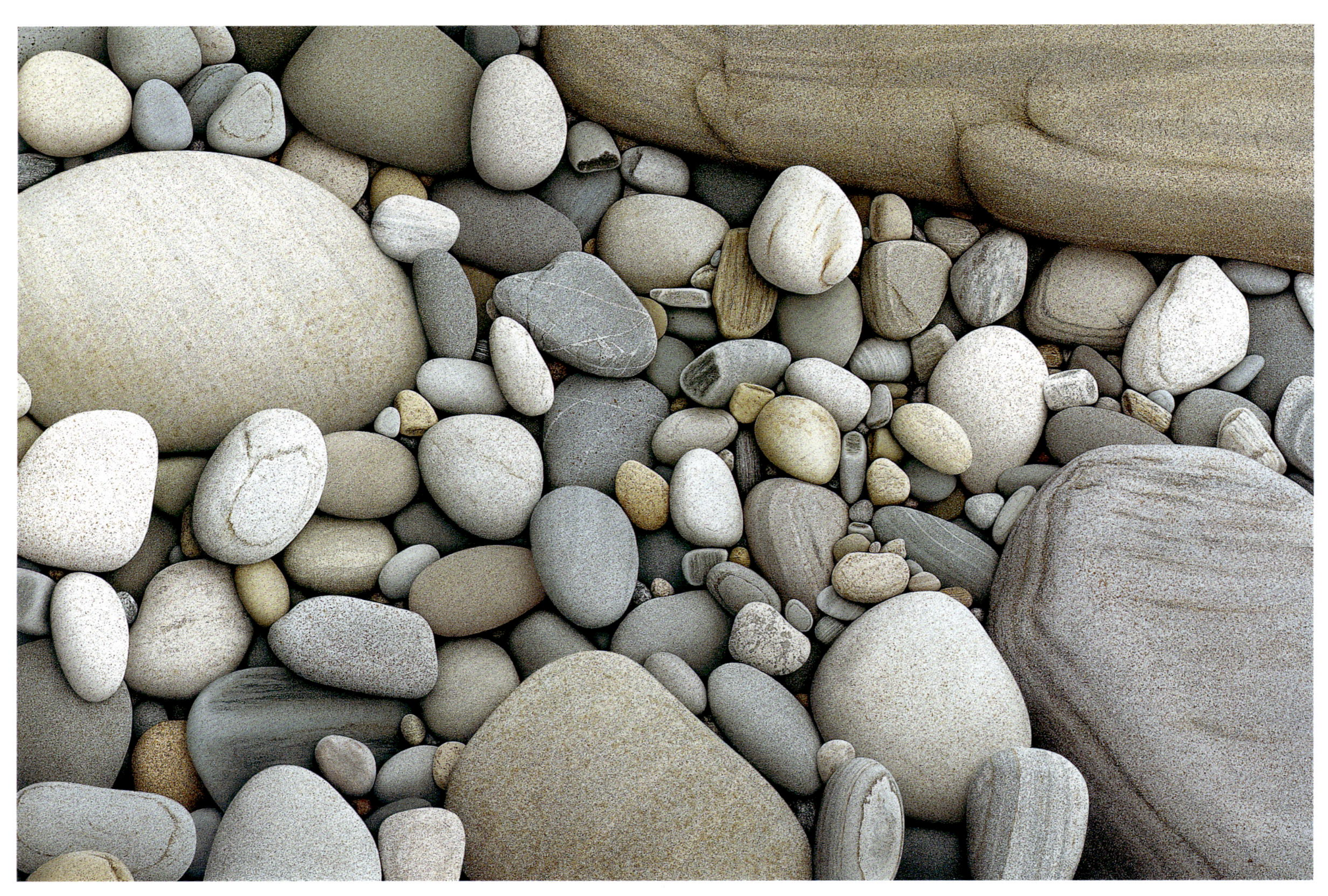

Alan Magee, *Casting of Runes*, 1984, acrylic on canvas, 48 x 72 in., private collection

Foreword

Fifteen years ago, not long after moving to Mount Desert Island, I was contacted by book designer Arnold Skolnick about writing a book called *Paintings of Maine*. I knew something about the subject. My uncle, William Kienbusch, was a Maine painter, and I had written reviews of a number of artists with ties to the state. Still, there was a lot for me to learn about who had painted in Maine—and when and where—and in the course of working on that project, my knowledge grew, and it continues to do so to this day.

Since *Paintings of Maine* appeared in 1991, I have acquainted myself with literally hundreds more painters who have been swayed by the state's landscape graces. The work of some of these artists has appeared in subsequent books, including *Art of the Maine Islands*, *Paintings of New England*, *The Art of Maine in Winter* and *The Art of Monhegan Island*. Even so, more than fifty of the artists represented in the present volume have never before appeared in one of my books—a testament to the wealth and ongoing dynamic legacy of Maine art.

The aforementioned Skolnick and I face the same challenge every time we assemble a book, and this, our eleventh collaboration, has proven no different. We started out with way too much material, more than one thousand images for a book with room for just over one hundred. The sheer bounty threatened to overwhelm us, but we gritted our teeth and made the difficult but necessary decisions.

The result is the collection you hold in your hands, more than one hundred Maine paintings by more than one hundred artists. As has been our modus operandi, Skolnick and I have mixed the old and the new, the classic and the contemporary—from Codman to Cornell, from Homer to Hardy, from Woodbury to Welliver.

We thank all the artists who submitted work for consideration. Our greatest hope is that the opportunity will once again arise to bring light to many other painters who have fallen under Maine's mighty spell.

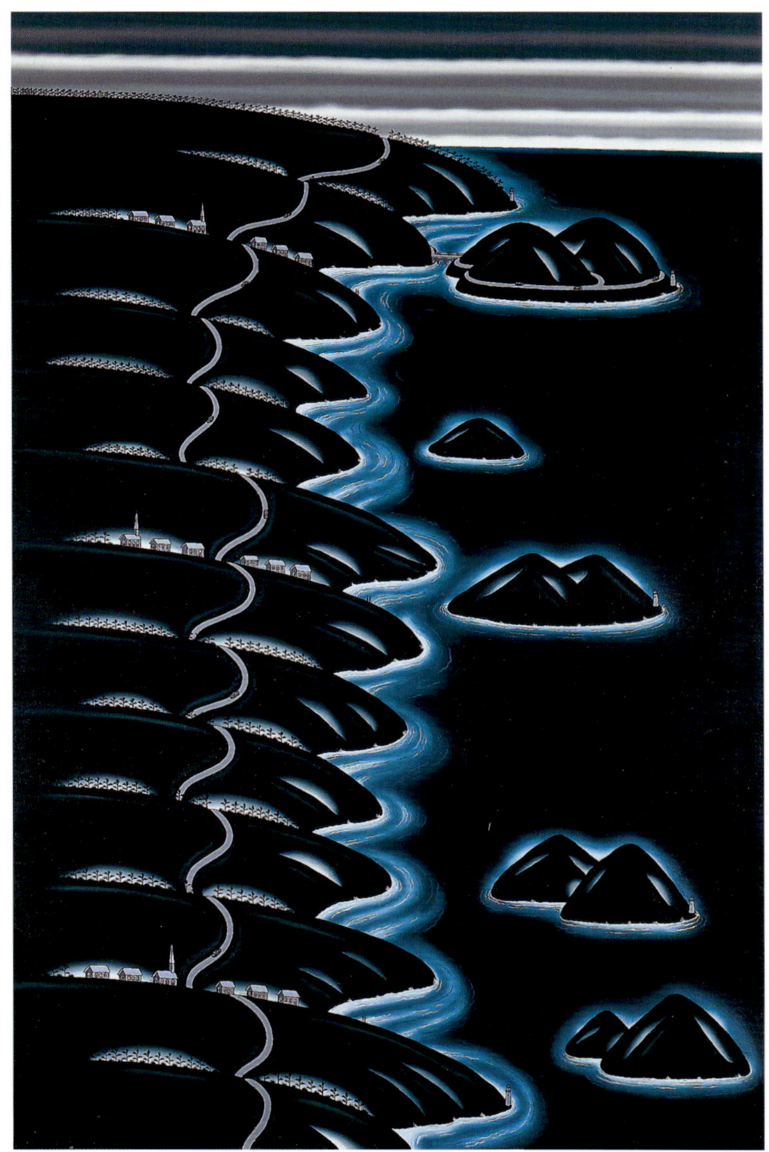

Roger Brown, *The Coast of Maine,* 1986, oil on canvas, 72 x 48 in.
© The School of the Art Institute of Chicago and the Brown family

Introduction

Places come into us lastingly; once having been in a particular place for any considerable time—or even briefly, if our experience there has been intense—we are forever marked by that place, which lingers in us indefinitely and in a thousand ways, many too subtle for us to name.

—Edward C. Casey

If you ask a Mainer, resident or visitor, for his or her favorite spot, you might hear about the "big city," which might mean Lewiston or Portland, Bangor or Augusta, or even Ellsworth, if you're living in a downeast hamlet. You might also hear mention of rural places, such as Sebago Lake, Donnell Pond and Baxter State Park.

Maine is made up of hundreds of special places—maybe thousands. Aroostook farmland, the western mountains, the Androscoggin River, the islands of Penobscot Bay—the inventory of this state's landscape treasures is broad, diverse and extraordinary, from the scruffy to the sublime, from the scenic to the downright spectacular.

Painters have a similar list of favorite places. They, too, are drawn to urban skyline and mountain solitude, sweep of road and turn of river, island edge and lake expanse. Some specialize in a particular place, such as Monhegan Island; others paint all over the state. Some take to the air to capture a special perspective; others find their muse at the edge of the sea or in the deep woods.

A number of places in Maine have had entire books devoted to the art they have inspired: Ogunquit, Monhegan, Mount Desert Island. Other locales would easily fill an album: Portland, Boothbay Harbor, Stonington, Mount Katahdin. All of these favored painters' destinations are represented here, with many distinctive spots great and small in between.

Throughout this book, artists express their passion for place through paint—oil, watercolor, acrylic, gouache, casein—with other mediums thrown in for good measure. Covering about 150 years of artistic activity, this book demonstrates the evolution of palette, from the earthier pigments of the nineteenth century to the brighter colors of recent decades.

Some of the earliest artists to paint Maine's grandeur were homegrown. Portland native Harrison Bird Brown (1831–1915) explored Maine's inland and coastal regions, seeking the sublime that ties his aesthetic to that of the Hudson River school. In his painting of Rangeley Lake, the sky is suffused with the glow of nineteenth-century luminism, the romanticism of this wilderness vista heightened to a point of transcendence.

Today, artists may arrive in Maine from a great distance. Painter Paul Alexandre John (b. 1952) lives in Eastbrook, but started out life in Calcutta, the son of Armenian parents. His rendering of the Blue Hill Fair (made famous in E. B. White's *Charlotte's Web*) is a wonderfully complex design of people and animals and exhibits, with noble Blue Hill at its center. When he isn't painting, John plays classical Indian flute, performing statewide and around the country.

Many of the contemporary artists in this book are committed to Maine, either living as full-time residents or spending extended parts of the year in the state. Some people believe that this kind of dedication is requisite to being considered a "Maine artist," giving short shrift to those who come and go as fair-weather painters. While it's true that some visitors may not "get" the place as much as those immersed in it might, there are too many exceptions to make it a rule.

A favorite example is Roger Brown (1941–1997), the eminent Chicago Imagist artist. His darkly luminous *Coast of Maine,* 1986, is comic in its scale, the whole three-thousand-plus miles of coastline reduced to a series of indentations and atoll-looking islands. Although this is an imaginary Maine, it is no less an authentic response to place.

Earlier views of Maine often offer modern-day viewers revelations about the way in which the landscape has

Neil Welliver, *Study for Islands Allagash,* 1990, oil on canvas, 24 x 24 in., photo: Alexandre Gallery, New York

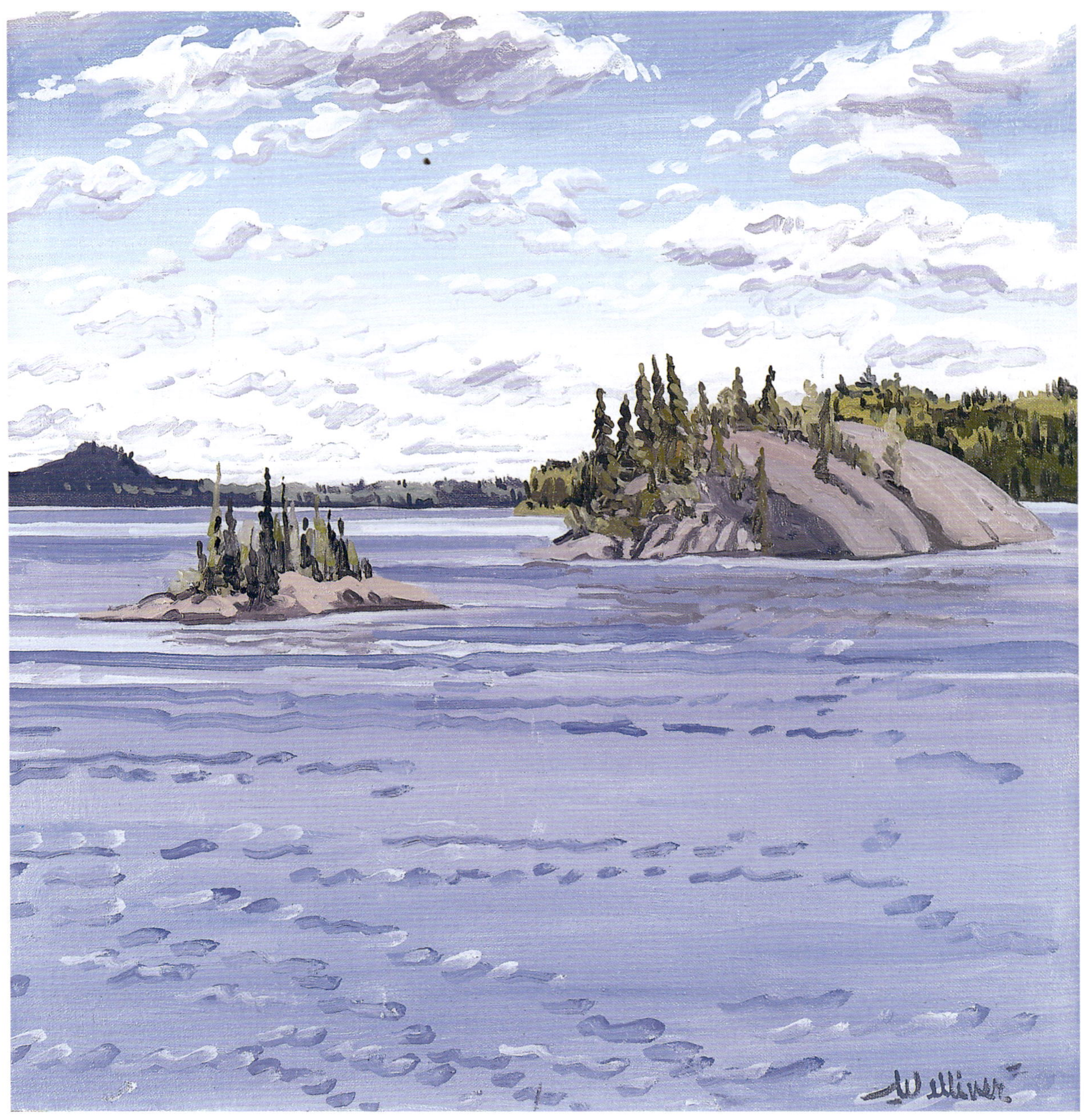

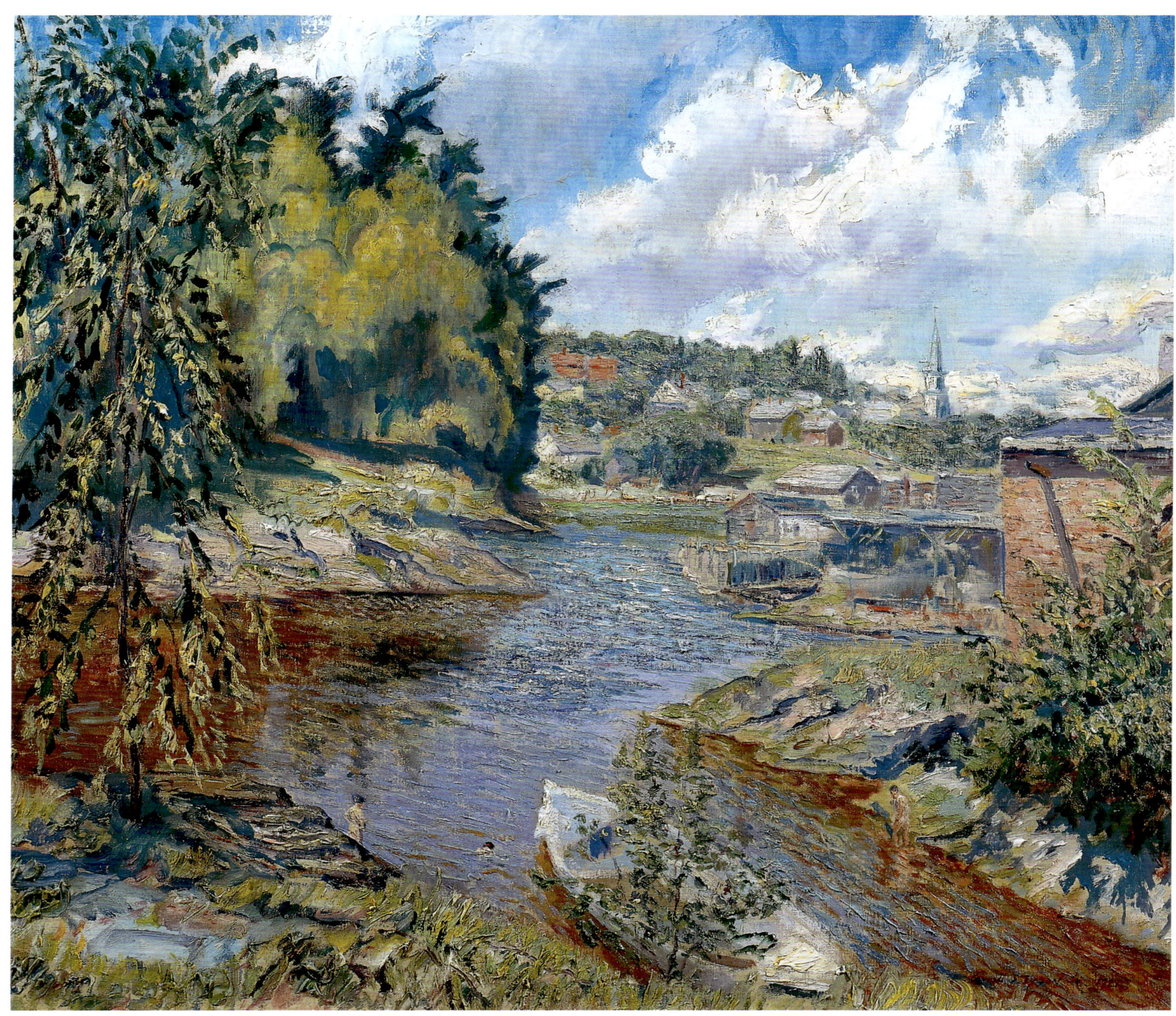

changed. A case in point is Charles Codman's painting of the State House in Augusta from 1836. Codman (c. 1800–1842)—called "Maine's first resident professional landscape artist"—pictures the grand building, designed by renowned Boston architect Charles Bulfinch, standing somewhat surreally in the rural landscape that includes grazing livestock and tree stumps, the latter testifying to the transformation under way.

Another example of change can be found in a view of Ellsworth by Carroll Sargent Tyson (1878–1956). When considering this small downeast city, many of us picture big box stores and the retail strip that leads to Mount Desert Island. In the hands of the American Impressionist Tyson, however, a view of the Union River at Ellsworth recalls the Giverny countryside of Claude Monet.

Place can be represented by a sublime configuration of beach stones painted by Alan Magee (b. 1947), or by a bright clutch of boat gear painted by Jon Imber (b. 1950). Magee, who lives in Cushing, found his subject at Pemaquid Point back in the 1980s; the splendid stones have spoken to him—and us—ever since. Residing on the outskirts of Boston, Imber spends as much time as possible in Stonington, responding to the tidal reaches and working harbor.

Even a single tree can transport you to a specific spot. Anyone who has driven picturesque Sargent Drive, which follows the shore of Somes Sound on Mount Desert Island, will recognize the pine tree in Sam Cady's painting, its windswept boughs catching the sunlight. Cady (b. 1943), a Boothbay Harbor native now living in Friendship, is especially adept at singling out landscape elements for special attention.

Carolyn Brady's lovely still life conjures a summer refuge on a Maine island. Vinalhaven in Penobscot Bay sustained Brady (1937–2005) for decades, and her brilliant watercolors reflect the light-filled ambience of her tiny cottage. "During the winter I dream of being in Maine," Brady once wrote. Life on a granite island, "surrounded by a lens of light," was tonic to the city artist, a place where one could be "restored by the sea air."

The simple thoroughfare in Kevin Beers' painting of Monhegan represents an inviting, back-to-basics island world. Turning away from the island's renowned dramatic headlands and crashing surf, Beers (b. 1952) chose to paint a quiet lane following the curving contours of this "sea-girt" isle, favored by artists for almost two centuries.

Another Maine is represented in Robert Shillady's engaging three-season triptych of his hometown of Brooklin on the Blue Hill peninsula. Shillady captures the breadth of activity, from kayaking to lobstering to riding an all-terrain vehicle. Man and animal—dolphin, fox, seal—seem to co-exist seamlessly.

Some artists are happy to paint their backyard. David Driskell's painting of the view from his home in Falmouth consists of a Cézanne-like rendering of a line of trees. Driskell (b. 1931), whose collection of African American art is one of the most significant in the nation, was introduced to Maine through the Skowhegan School of Painting and Sculpture, which he attended in 1953.

Maine's industrial landscapes also have their visual appeal. With its living legacy of shipbuilding, Bath Iron Works, commonly known as BIW, is a colossus of hulls in Carroll Thayer Berry's 1941 oil. Berry (1886–1978) was commissioned by the government to document the naval construction at BIW. The busy shipyard was the perfect subject for someone who, in the words of writer Lew Dietz, "thought like an engineer and dreamed like an artist."

More recently, the decaying American Can sardine plant in Eastport, one of the last of its kind on the coast of Maine, caught the eye of Tim Gaydos. The New Jersey-based painter, who has a second home in Lubec, was drawn to these ruins much as an eighteenth-century painter might be captivated by the remnants of a Greek temple. (The plant was razed two years after Gaydos painted it.)

The people of Maine are represented here too. Charles

Carroll Sargent Tyson, *Union River at Ellsworth, Maine,* 1921
Oil on canvas, 25 x 30 1/4 in., private collection; photograph courtesy Sunne Savage

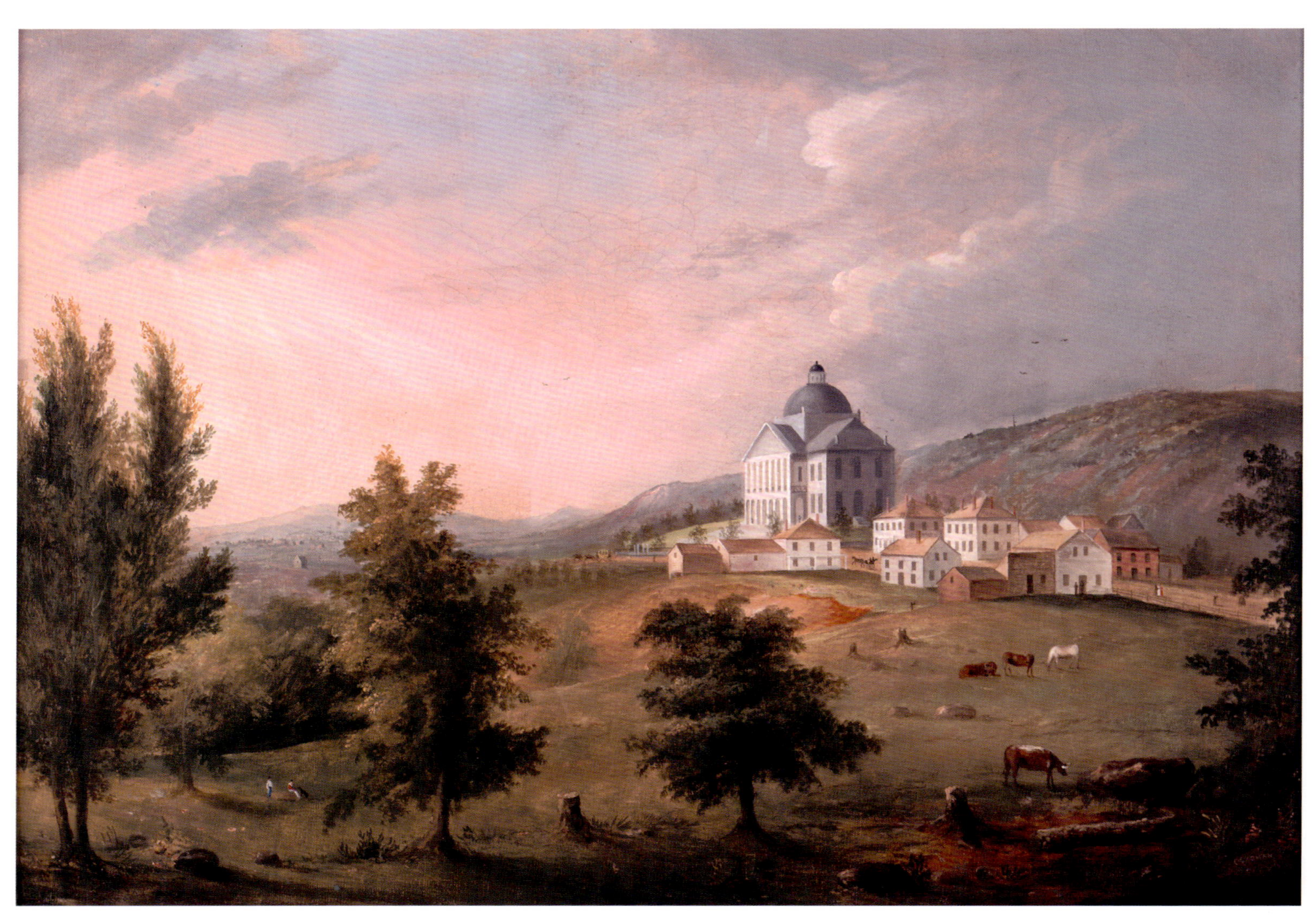

 Charles Codman, *View of the Original State House, Augusta,* 1836, oil on canvas, 23 x 34 in., Maine State Museum, Augusta, Maine

A few miles ahead, my mother was in a suppressed state of youthful excitement. They were almost there, now—in a few moments she would see the lake. . . All those who went into Rangeley that morning sixty years ago were filled with that wonderful suspense which is a combination of months of anticipation and the charm of the unknown. I doubt if we go into the woods with quite the same emotion nowadays; perhaps it is too easy to get there. But I do know this: we still come over that last hill on that road to Rangeley with a surge of emotion.

—Elizabeth Foster, from *The Islanders,* 1946

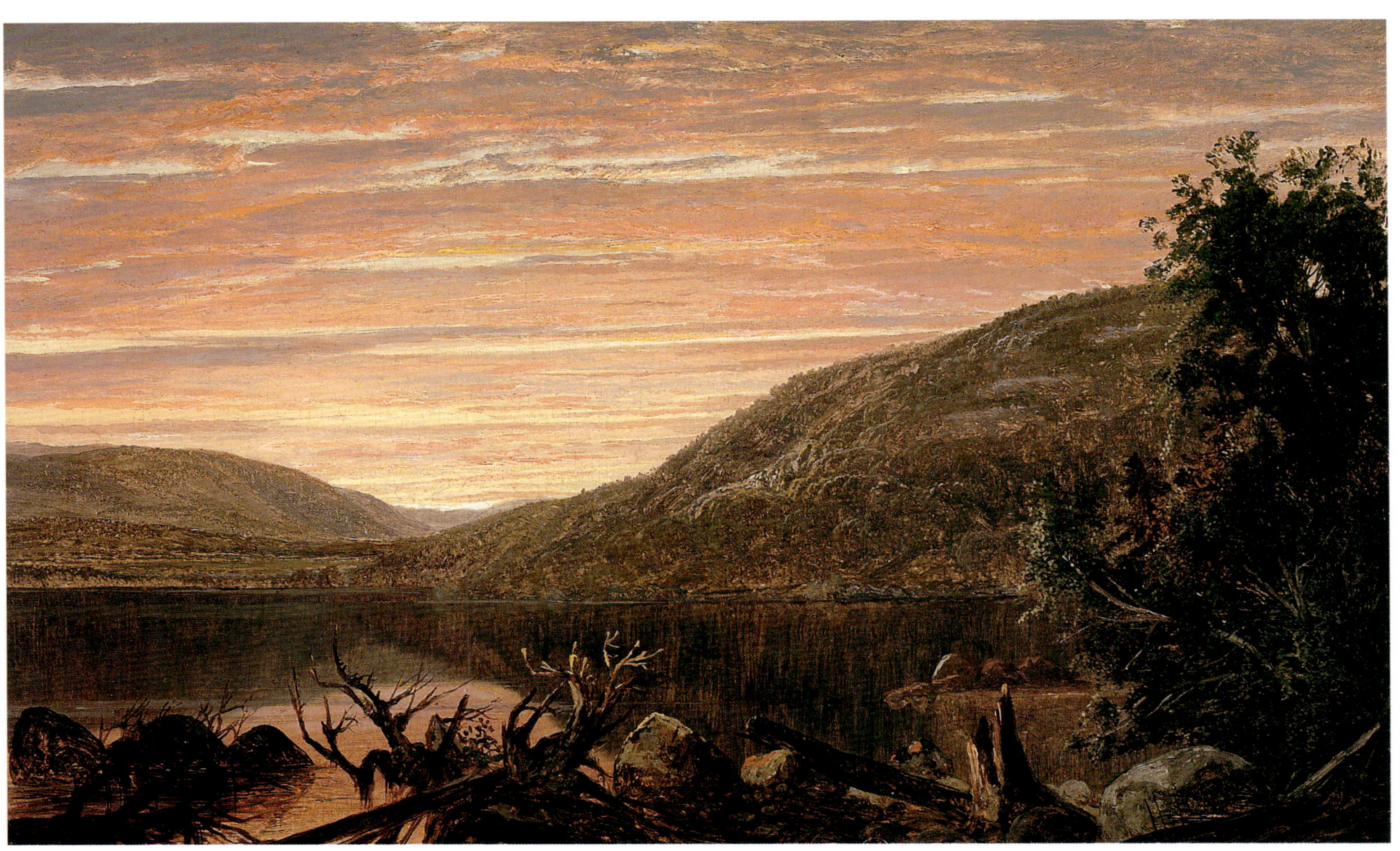

Harrison Bird Brown, *Rangeley Lakes, Maine,* n.d., oil on canvas, 13 x 22 in.
Private collection, photograph courtesy Barridoff Galleries, Portland, Maine

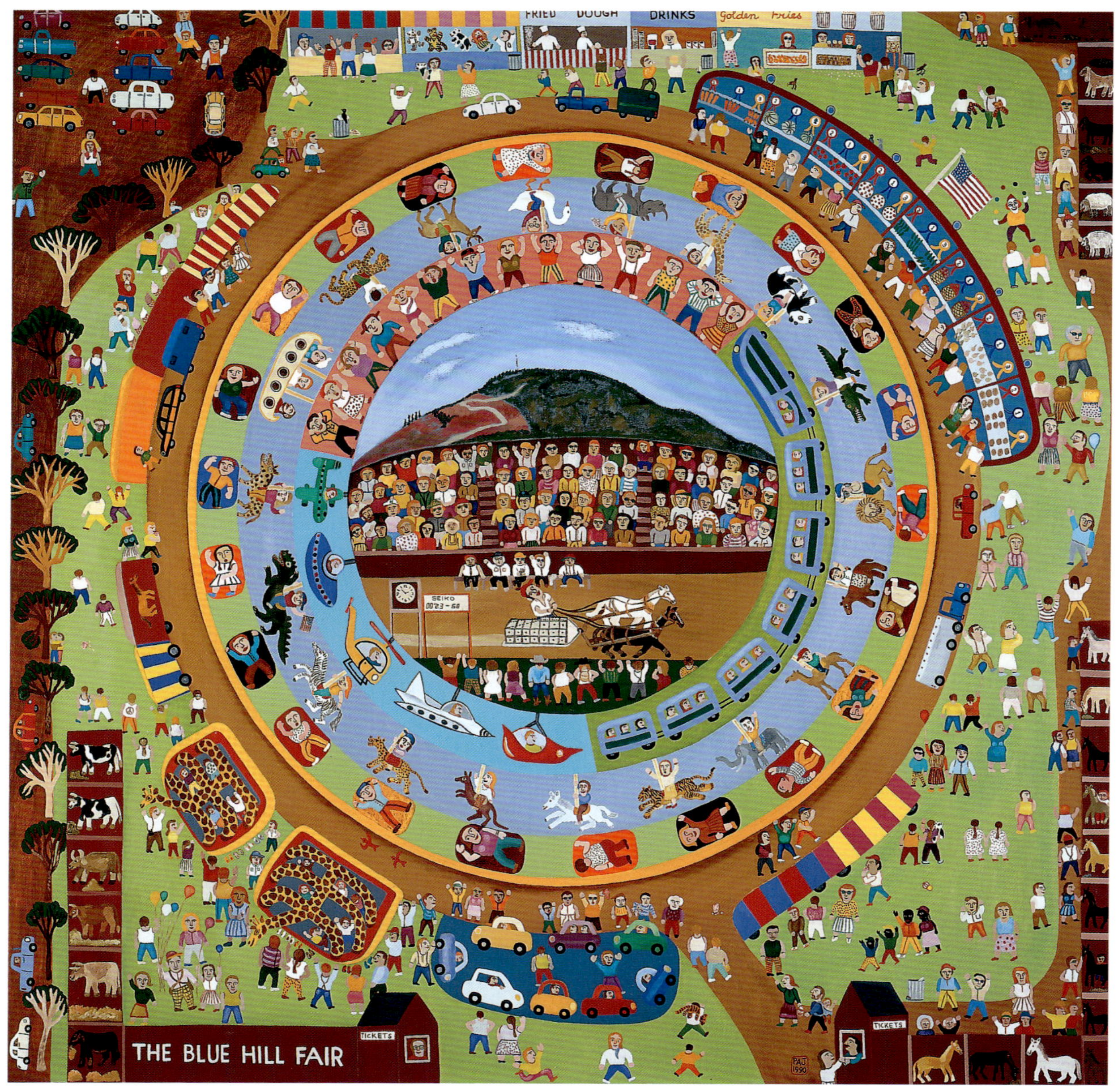

Paul Alexandre John, *Blue Hill Fair,* 1991, oil on canvas, 56 x 54 in., collection of the artist

Lewis Fox's 1892 painting of men working in a quarry reflects the Portland-born painter's empathy for the working class. Fox (1854–1927), who ran twice (unsuccessfully) for governor of Maine as the Socialist Labor Party candidate, championed a "socialist scheme of economic life" in both his actions and his art.

Nearly a century later, Thomas Cornell (b. 1937) expresses a kindred compassion in his haunting and heroic depiction of a long-haired clam digger working the mud at Barnes Point near Harpswell. Looking at this painting, some lines from Richard Eberhart's poem "The Clam Diggers and Diggers of Sea Worms" come to mind:

I watch the heavy scene,
The slow, mute progress
Of torso, arm, leg and rake
As seeing a dark core
And sombre purpose of life,
Primitive simplicity,
Dignity beyond speech.

When Neil Welliver (1929–2005) moved to Lincolnville in the 1960s, he did an about-face, ignoring the nearby coast to focus on the wild interior. He developed a special relationship with the Allagash River—this "fragile strip" that symbolizes, in conservationist Dean Bennett's words, "the value of America's diminishing wilderness."

People are so attached to places that they will fight to preserve them, to keep them open to exploration and enjoyment. In recent years, efforts to protect working waterfront, to revitalize downtowns and to preserve forest, lakes and

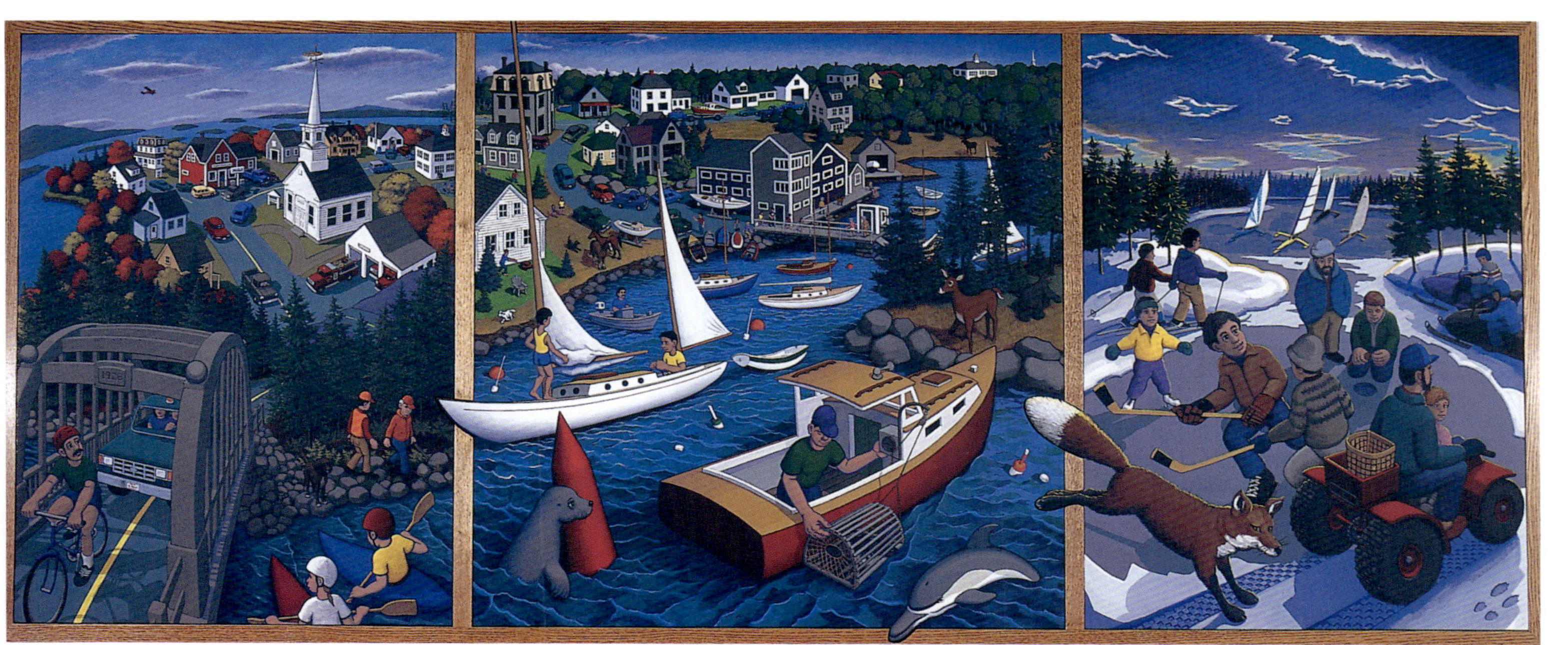

Robert Shillady, *Brooklin, 1995,* 1995, acrylic on masonite, 50 x 124 in.
The Brooklin School, Brooklin, Maine; commissioned through Maine Percent for Art

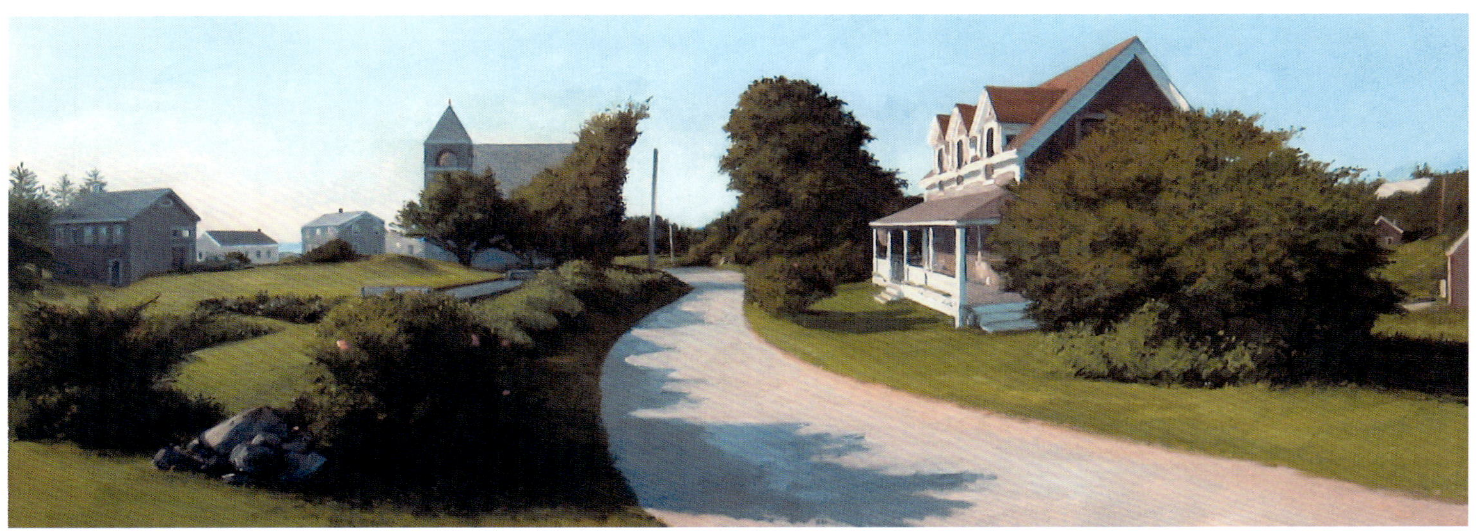

rivers have redoubled in Maine. Attachment to place is a passion, and this commitment inspires the best kind of stewardship: thoughtful, conscious of heritage and long term.

By the very nature of their enterprise, landscape painters have a conservation ethic; after all, in the act of painting a place, they are preserving it. As painter and environmental activist Alan Gussow pointed out in his landmark *A Sense of Place: The Artist and the American Land* (1971), the stakes are far greater today. "Nineteenth-century painters went out into the wilderness to bring back reports about a land we did not know," he wrote; "painters now report about a land we risk forgetting."

"Maine's beauty," John Cole once wrote, "is draped like a fine cape across the entire body of the state." Every year, artists discover a new motif somewhere within Maine's broad and diverse reaches, or simply revisit Stonington Harbor or the headlands of Monhegan or exalted Mount Katahdin—among the most painted motifs in the state—happy to drink in a familiar scene. They draw energy from the landscape. We, in turn, derive pleasure from their paintings.

Kevin Beers, *View Past Lexi's II,* 2005, oil on canvas, 22 x 60 in., private collection; photograph courtesy Gleason Fine Art

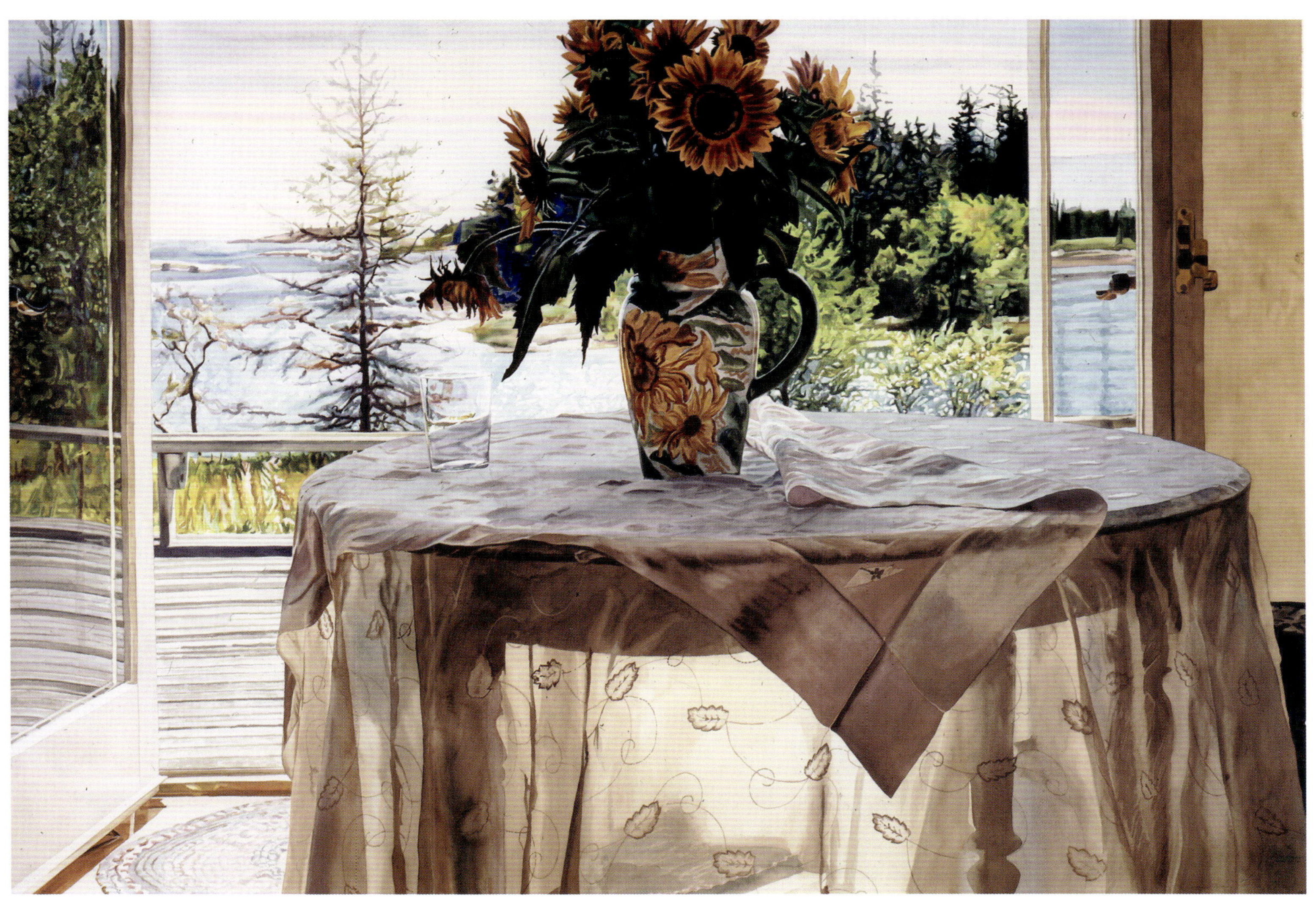

Carolyn Brady, *Inlet,* 1999, watercolor on paper, 45 x 66 1/2 in., courtesy Nancy Hoffman Gallery

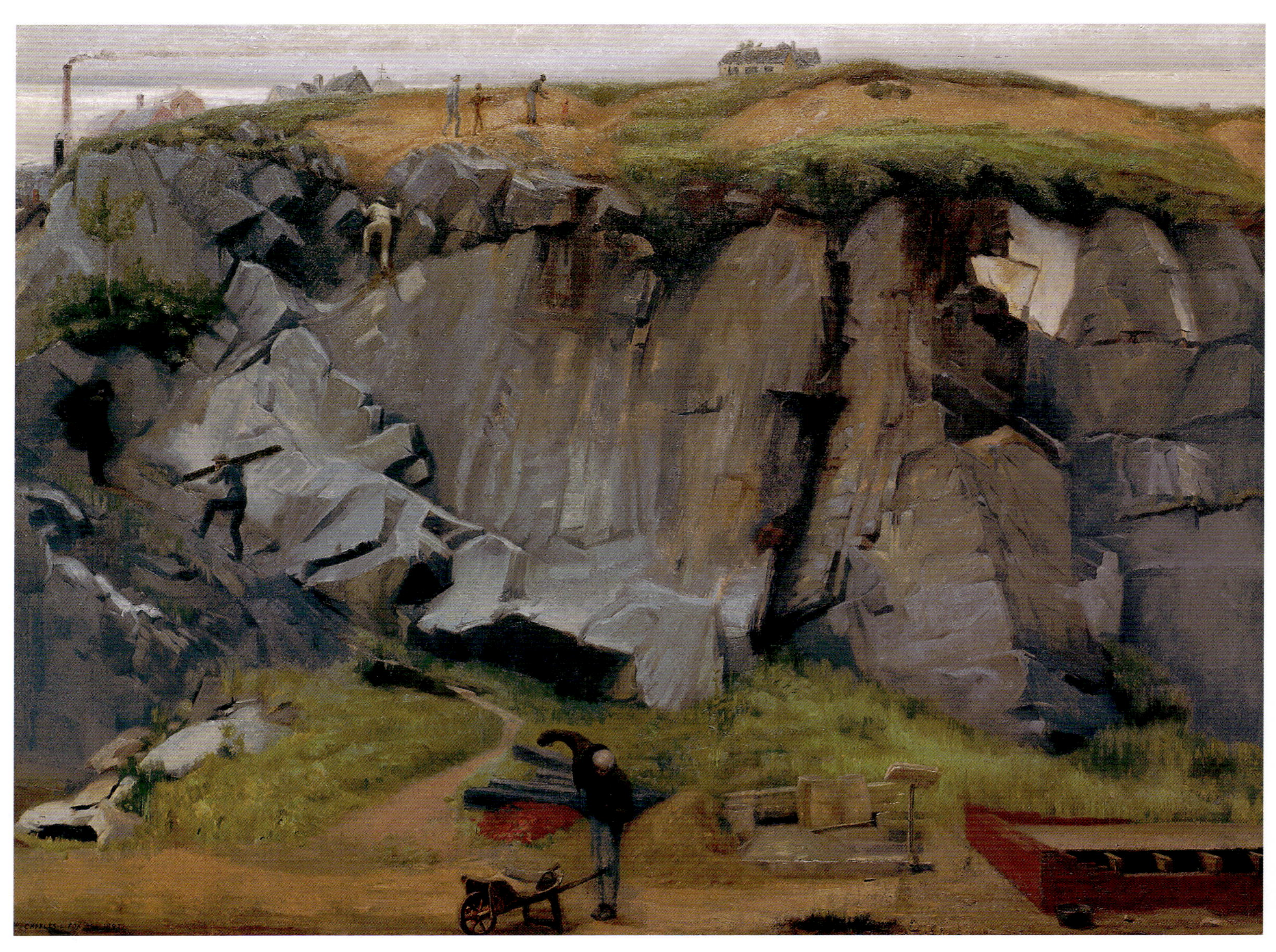

 Charles L. Fox, *Paths of the City Working Man, Portland,* 1892, oil on canvas, 22 1/4 x 30 1/4 in., courtesy Brock & Co.

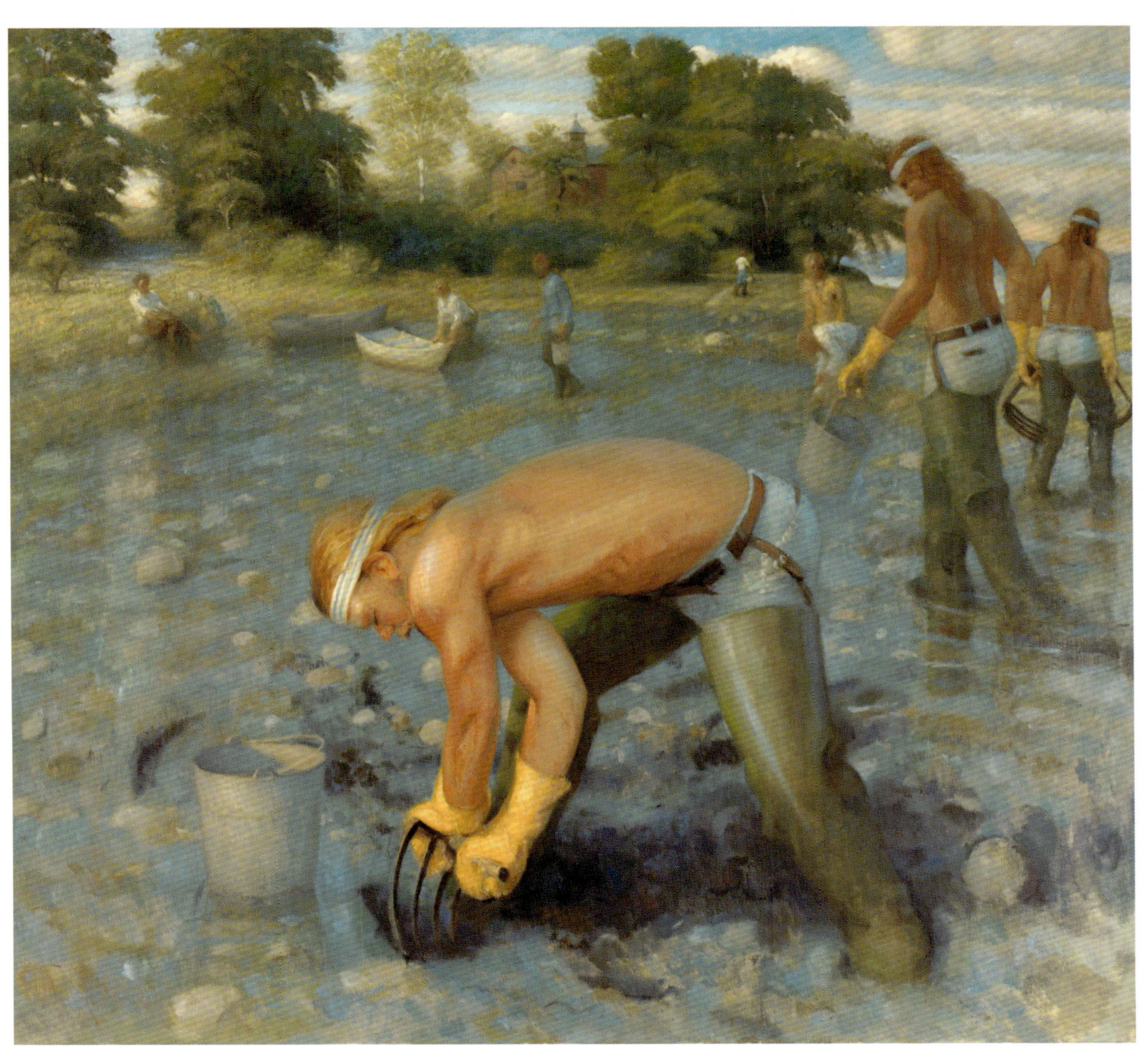

Thomas Cornell, *Clamdigger,* 1989–2004, oil on canvas, 54 x 60 in., collection of the artist

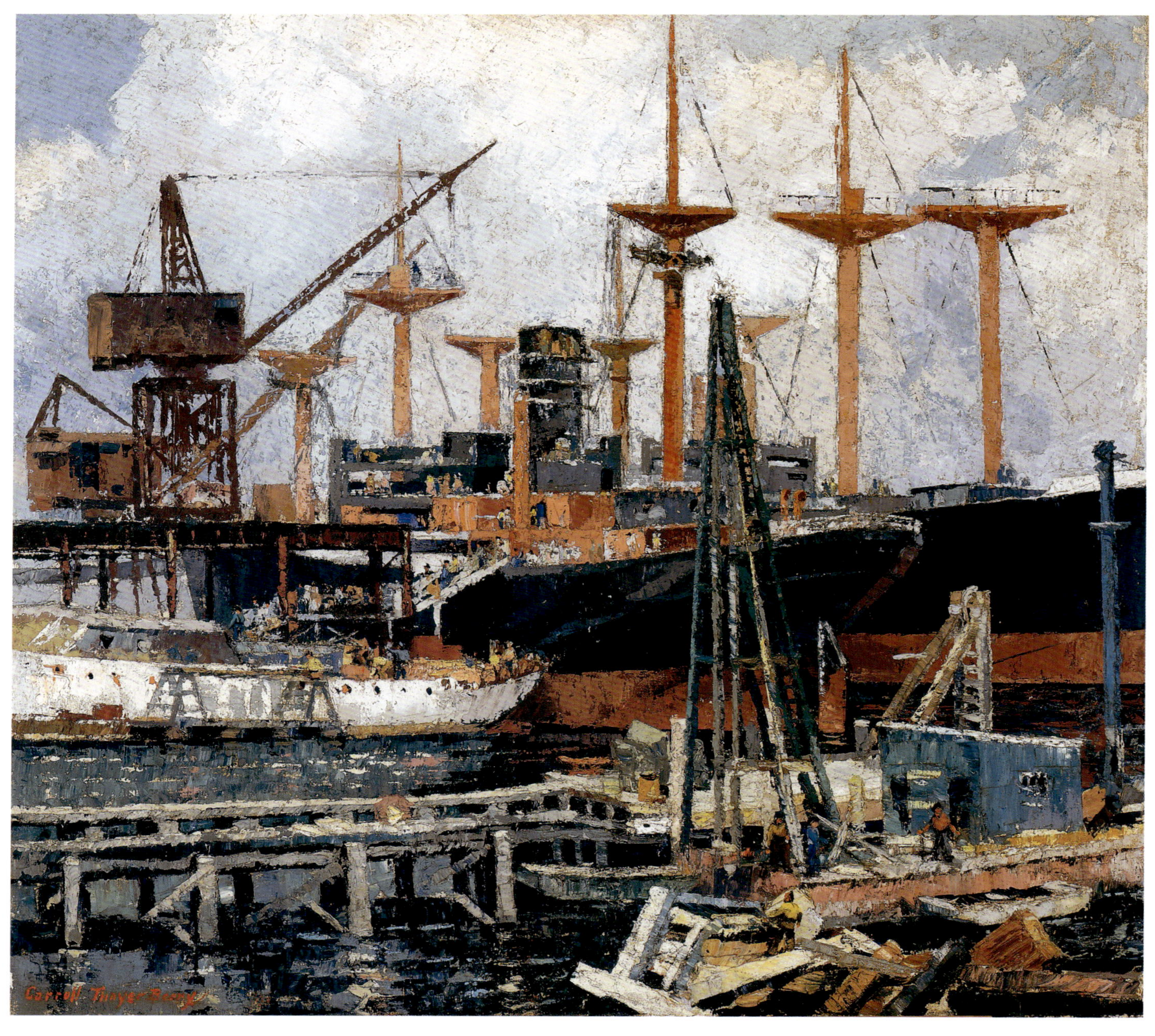

Carroll Thayer Berry, *Bath Iron Works, World War II,* 1941, oil on canvas, 32 1/4 x 36 1/8 in.
Collection of the Farnsworth Art Museum, Museum purchase (Elmer C. and Alice L. Davis Fund), 197, 72.1847

You smile sardines.
The crease these scissors have worn
moves into your palm like a lifeline.
And more, your apron full of the stench
of fish, the torsos
packed into oil and canned,
bears your body home,
smothered in scales of pearls.

—KATHLEEN ELLIS, FROM "IN THE SARDINE FACTORY"

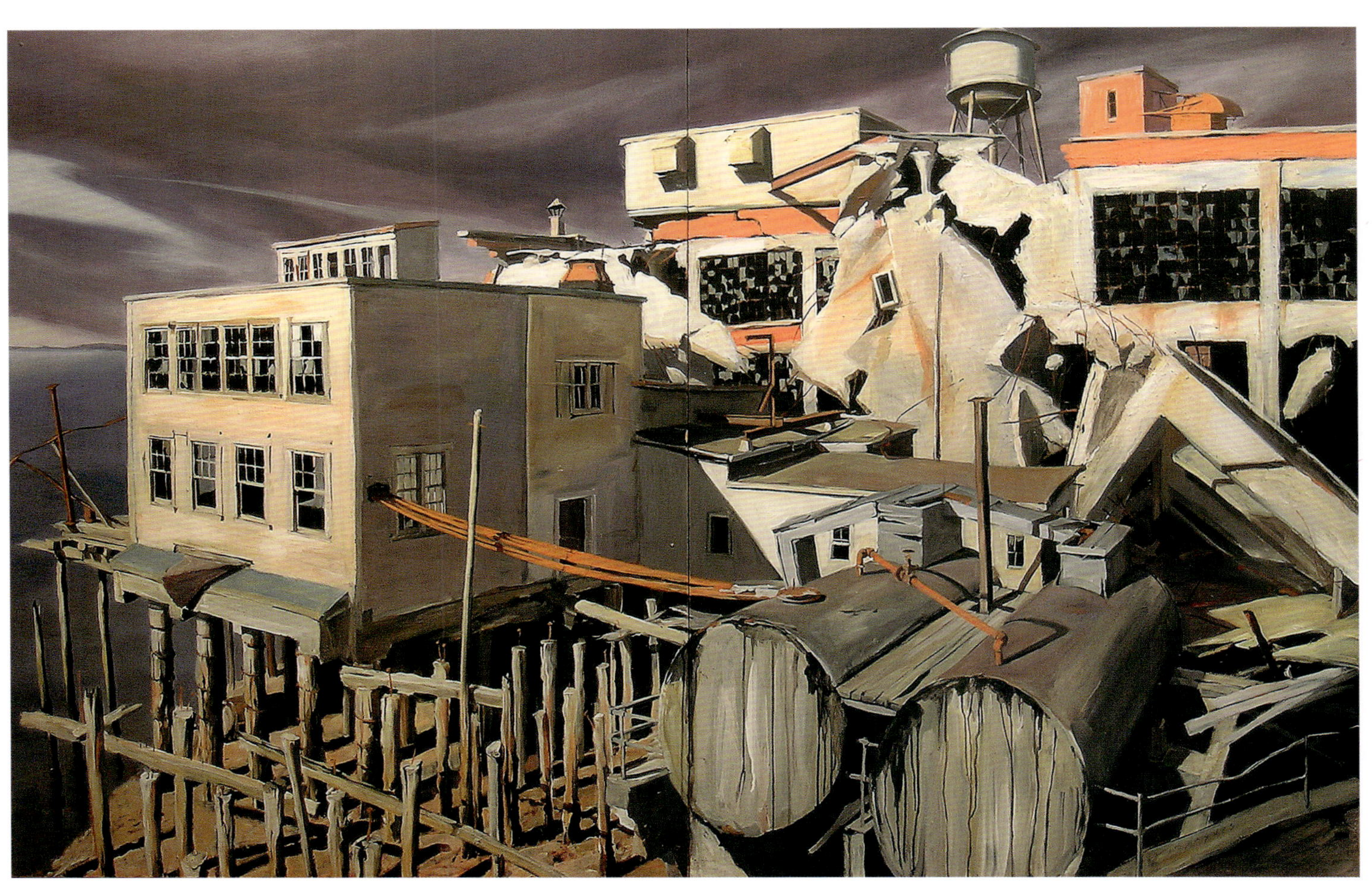

Tim Gaydos, *Approaching Storm [American Can Plant, Lubec, Maine],* 1993, acrylic on masonite, 60 x 96 in.
Tides Institute & Museum of Art, Eastport, Maine

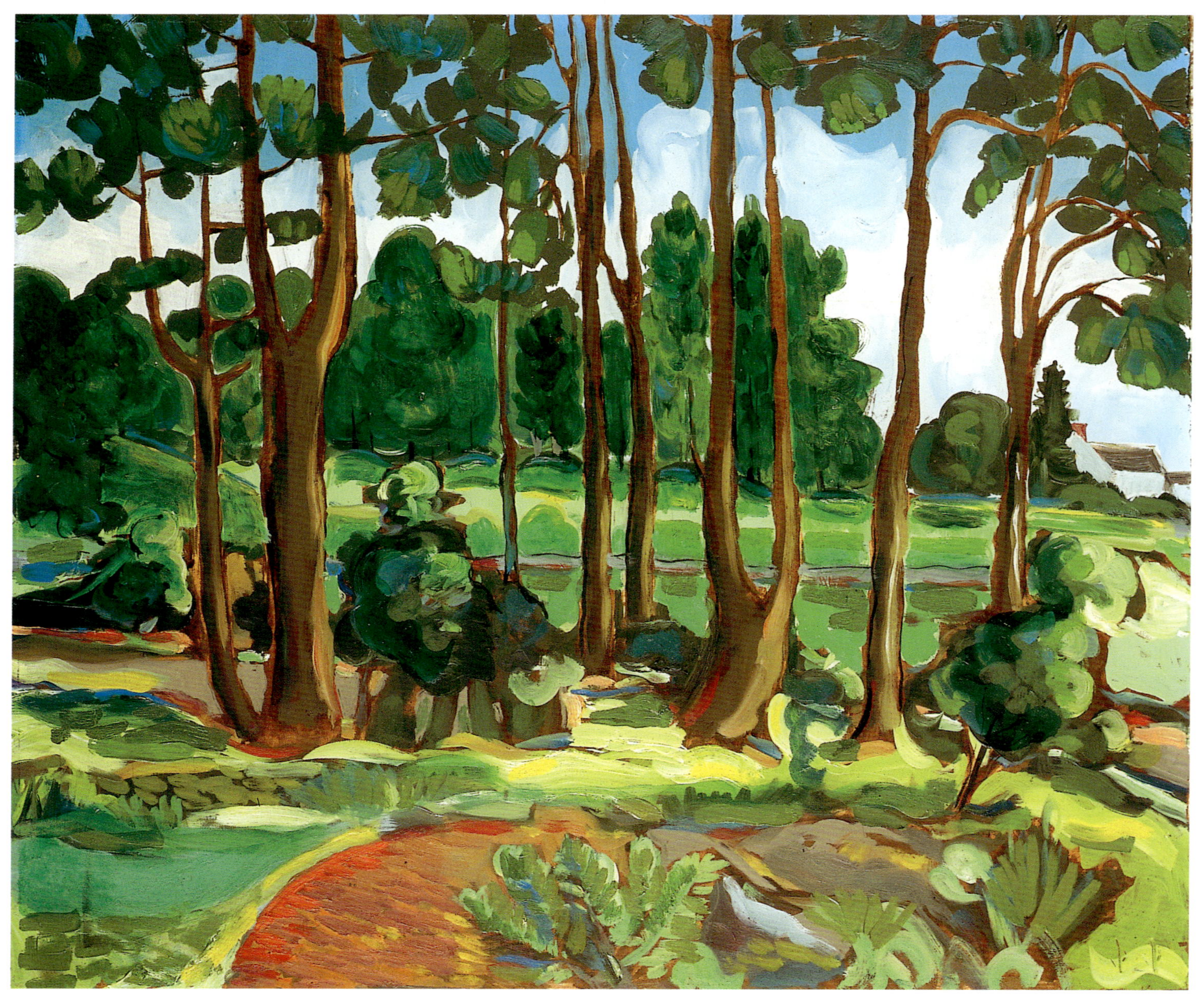

David Driskell, *The Yard at Falmouth,* c. 1963, oil on masonite, 19 1/2 x 23 in., collection of the artist

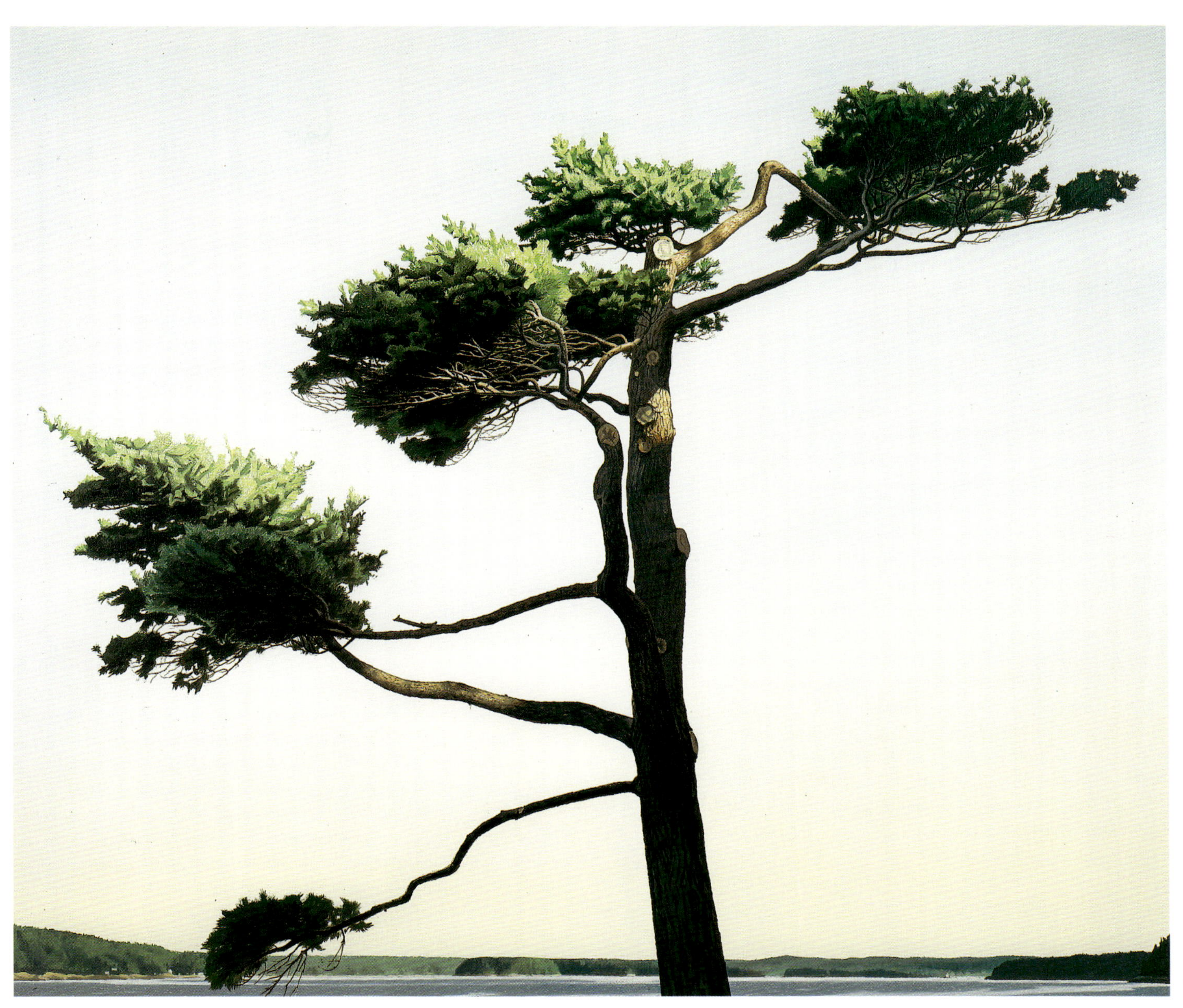

Sam Cady, *Cropped Pine, Somes Sound, Morning,* 1996, oil on canvas, 46 x 56 in.
Collection of Gordon and Sylvia Whitman, Weston, Massachusetts

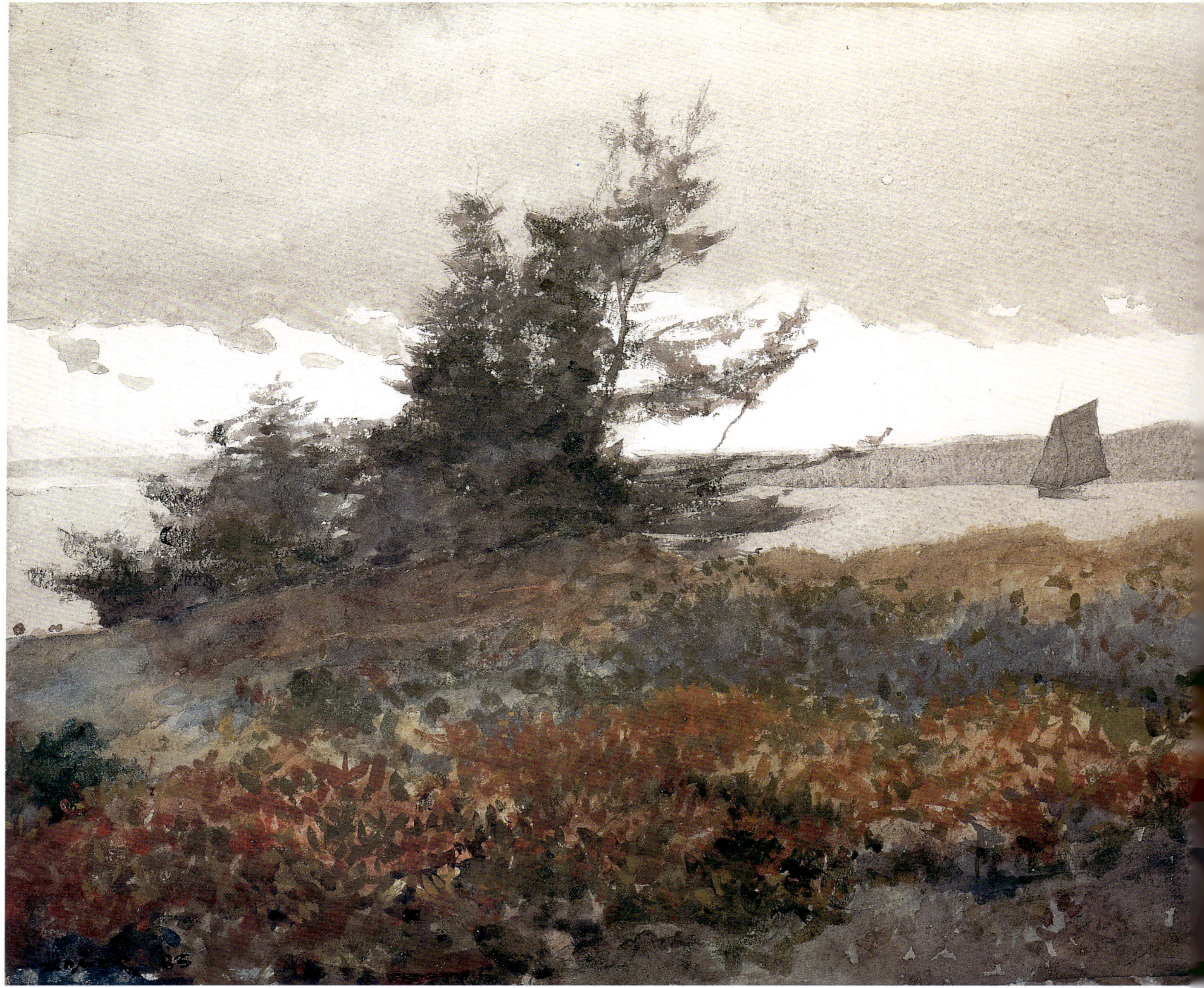

Winslow Homer
Prout's Neck Looking Toward Old Orchard, 1883
Watercolor and graphite on wove paper, 14 x 20 in.
Addison Gallery of American Art, Phillips Academy, Andover, Massachusetts.
Gift of anonymous donor. 1930.14.

Along the Southern Coast

When Winslow Homer (1836–1910) moved to Maine for good in the 1880s, he settled at Prout's Neck, a rocky promontory south of Portland. The painter roamed very little from that favored spot, finding just about everything he needed in the way of landscape motifs to satisfy him for the rest of his painting life.

The same thing happened to Charles Woodbury (1864–1940) in Ogunquit. As a young Boston art teacher, he came to Maine in 1888. "Perkins Cove was nothing but a cluster of fishermen's dwellings," Woodbury recalled in a 1937 interview. "The only place to stay was the old Ogunquit House in the village. They told me it had been a great season. Four strangers had been there." By the time Woodbury died, Ogunquit had become a bustling art colony, and he had painted his fill of bathers and fishermen.

A later Ogunquit regular, Nebraskan John Falter (1910–1982) was known for the many covers he created for the *Saturday Evening Post*. He once said that what he sought to accomplish in his painting was "to put down on canvas a piece of America, a stage set, a framework for the imagination to travel around in." His painting of Ogunquit in the wake of a nor'easter captures that quality of cleansed air that follows a storm.

Gertrude Fiske (1869–1962), a blue-blooded Bostonian, painted with Woodbury and served as a director of the Ogunquit Art Association, founded in 1928. Fiske discovered poetry in a graveyard at Cape Neddick, the headstones tilting in sun and shadow. "In Maine," wrote poet Elizabeth Coatsworth, "the dead sooner or later feel the hug of rootlets / and shadowy branches closing out the sun."

Rachel Carson, the great ecologist who spent her later years on the coast of Maine, once noted that wildlife refuges resist the trend of encroaching civilization, preserving and restoring "the conditions that wild things need in order to live." The refuge that bears her name in Wells not only provides shelter for migrating birds and other animals, but also offers material for painters. Patricia Hardy (b. 1940) from North Berwick was drawn to the zigzag course of water flowing through the marshes.

From the early days, the water views along the southern coast attracted visitors. Summer colonies sprang up on the beaches and coves. The first cottages were developed at Lord's Point in Kennebunk in the 1870s. The unknown artist who painted a view of the spot in 1885 captured the ambiance of the place: simple seaside residences, a woman with a parasol being rowed across the water, a sailboat rounding the point.

Edward Hopper (1882–1967) made stops in Portland, Rockland and Monhegan Island while exploring the Maine coast. At Portland Head Light, he painted the towering lighthouse and the lightkeeper's house. George Luks (1867–1933) stayed at nearby Cape Elizabeth. A member of the Eight—a group of New York artists who sought to represent the vitality of everyday life—Luks practiced a bold brushwork that led one critic to refer to him as "a swashbuckler in paint." Trained in illustration, Rob Sullivan (b. 1970) offers a more "refined" view of Cape Elizabeth—through a glass of Merlot.

John Bradley Hudson Jr. (1832–1903) found much of the material for his landscapes in the countryside surrounding his native city of Portland. Hudson's 1892 view of Casco Bay encompasses green fields, sailboats, distant islands and a sky full of blowsy clouds—an idyllic day on the coast of Maine.

On one of her sojourns to Cushing's Island in Casco Bay, Alison Rector (b. 1960), a Monroe resident, was struck by a complex stairway view that mixes interior and exterior. The details—red sneakers on the porch, lobster buoys in nearby waters—represent the elements of a Maine summer island idyll.

The greater Portland area offers today's painters a wealth of subject matter. Brett Bigbee (b. 1954), who lives in South Portland, evokes the mood of a classic song in his painting *Moon River.* A kindred romanticism marks a painterly view of the glowing city seen across the harbor waters by Portland-based painter David Little (b. 1952).

With the arrival of immigrants from around the world and an influx of young professionals, Portland has blossomed into a multicultural happening city, attracting painters with its vitality and architecture. Robert Solotaire (b. 1930), who makes his home in the city, captures the flatiron Hay Building (named for pharmacist H. H. Hay and designed by Charles Q. Clapp and John Calvin Stevens) in Congress Square on a bright summer day. Buckfield painter Joel Babb (b. 1947), acclaimed for his vertiginous cityscapes, focuses on the stately mansard-roofed United States Custom House, built in 1868–1871.

The view of the Portland waterfront by Bath-based artist Tina Ingraham (b. 1947) brings to mind views of European fishing villages from another century. The long low façade is an arrangement of light and shadow, with boats tied to the pier. In a like manner, an appealing arrangement of floats in South Freeport caught Stephen Etnier's eye. Etnier (1903–1984), a student of Rockwell Kent, was a master limner of the working harbor, the quiet cove, the still reach of estuary and thoroughfare.

A Waldoboro resident, Robert Eric Moore (b. 1927) is known for his award-winning watercolors of crashing waves, winter woods and other Maine motifs. While exploring the coast near Hermit Island off Bath, he found the patch of chicory that glows in the shadowed foreground of his handsome view.

James Elliott (1919–2002) grew up in Augusta and Southwest Harbor, later teaching at the School of Fine and Applied Art in Portland and directing the Portland School of Art (now the Maine College of Art). His love of the Maine coast comes through in his painting of herring fishermen on Orr's Island.

Ann Lofquist (b. 1964) draws much of her material from the region around her home in Bath. She is expert at capturing particular atmospheric conditions and specific times of day, as well as the particulars of the place she paints. Likewise does Lucy Barber (b. 1951) bring out the special qualities of a particular scene, including a view of the dam near the Fort Andross mill complex in Brunswick where she lives. She is inspired, she says, "by light, spirit of place and color."

York painter Beverly Hallam (b. 1923) continues to be one of Maine's most inventive artists, currently exploring the genre of computer art. A pioneer in the use of acrylic, Hallam turned to this medium for her cubist rendering of the famous Brunswick-Topsham Bridge. She added collage elements—including snippets from *Architectural Digest*—to represent the bridge's dynamic shape, as it spans the bent bow of the Androscoggin River.

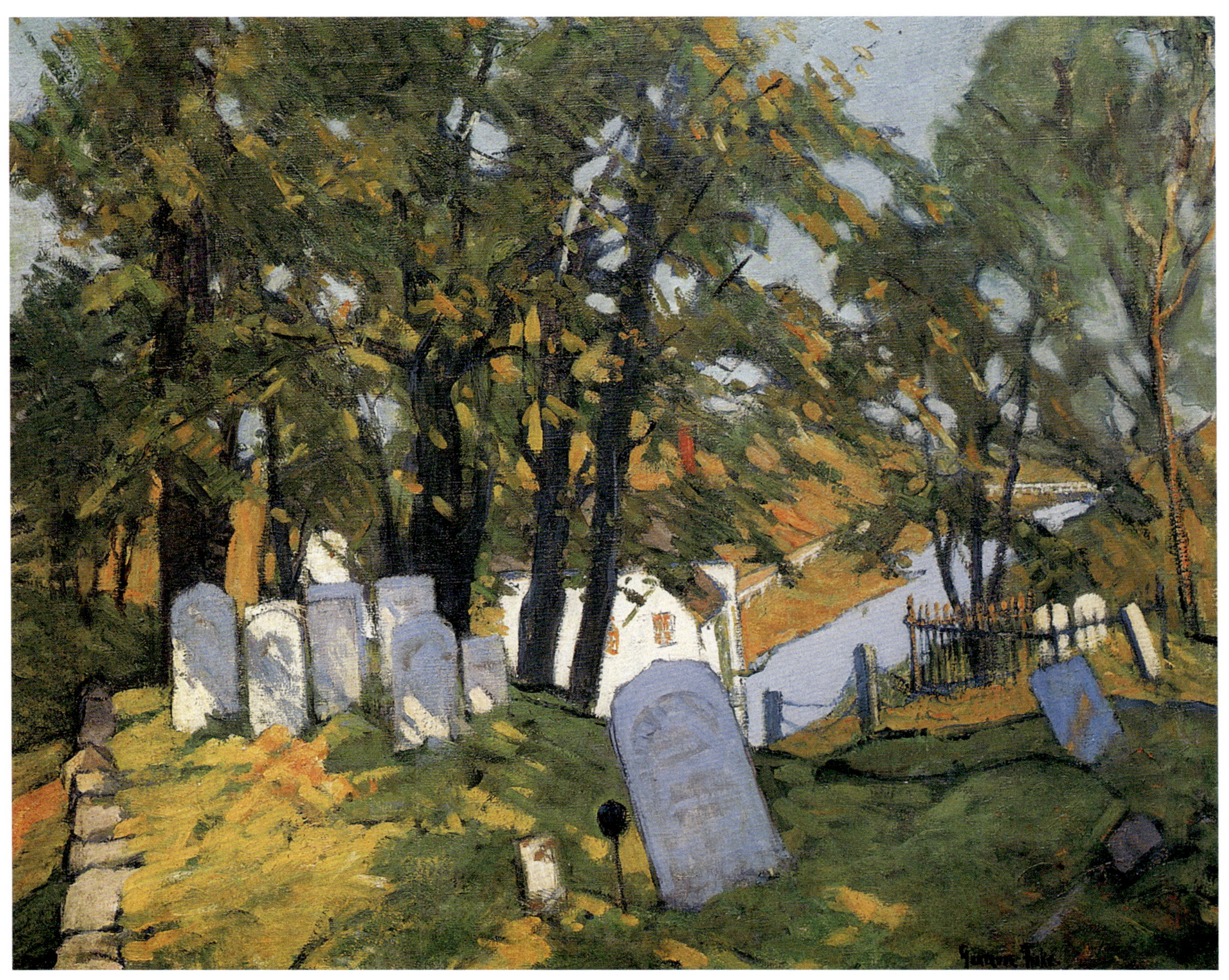

Gertrude Fiske, *Graveyard, Cape Neddick,* n.d., oil on canvas, 24 x 30 in., courtesy Veilleux Gallery

Beyond the breakers, there is a sanctuary of immense proportions, a refuge from daily thoughts and preoccupations. I feel my biological limitations here, my closeness to the sea creatures from whom all land life evolved. The ocean is a place, its own land, with its own seasons and patterns of life. When I am in the water, I am reminded of our need for a sea ethic, a new conservation paradigm that embraces the wilderness beyond the shore.

—NANCY OLMSTEAD, FROM *MAINE VOICES,* 2004

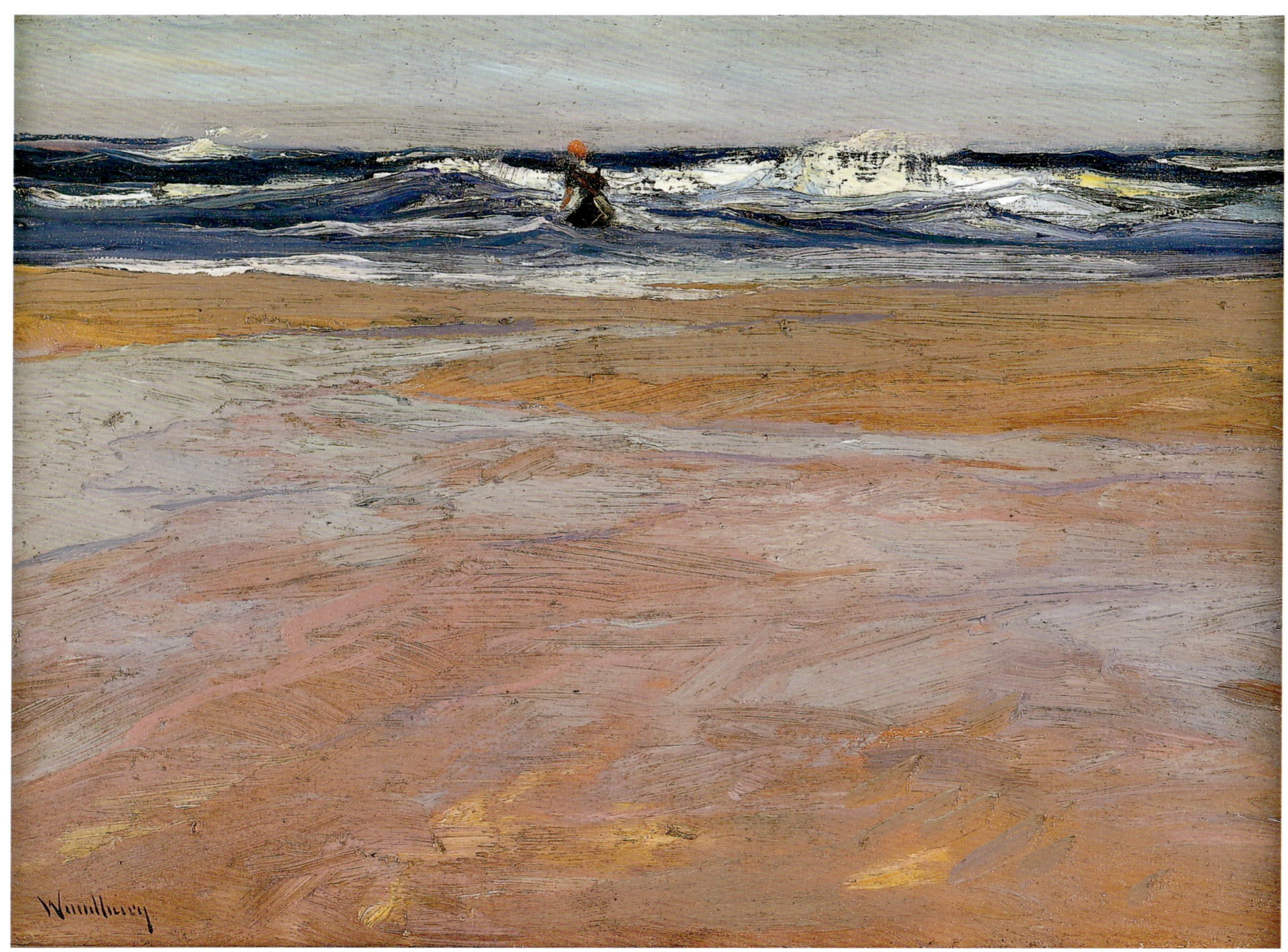

Charles Woodbury, *Low Tide, Ogunquit,* n.d., oil on canvasboard, 10 x 14 in., collection of Remak Ramsay

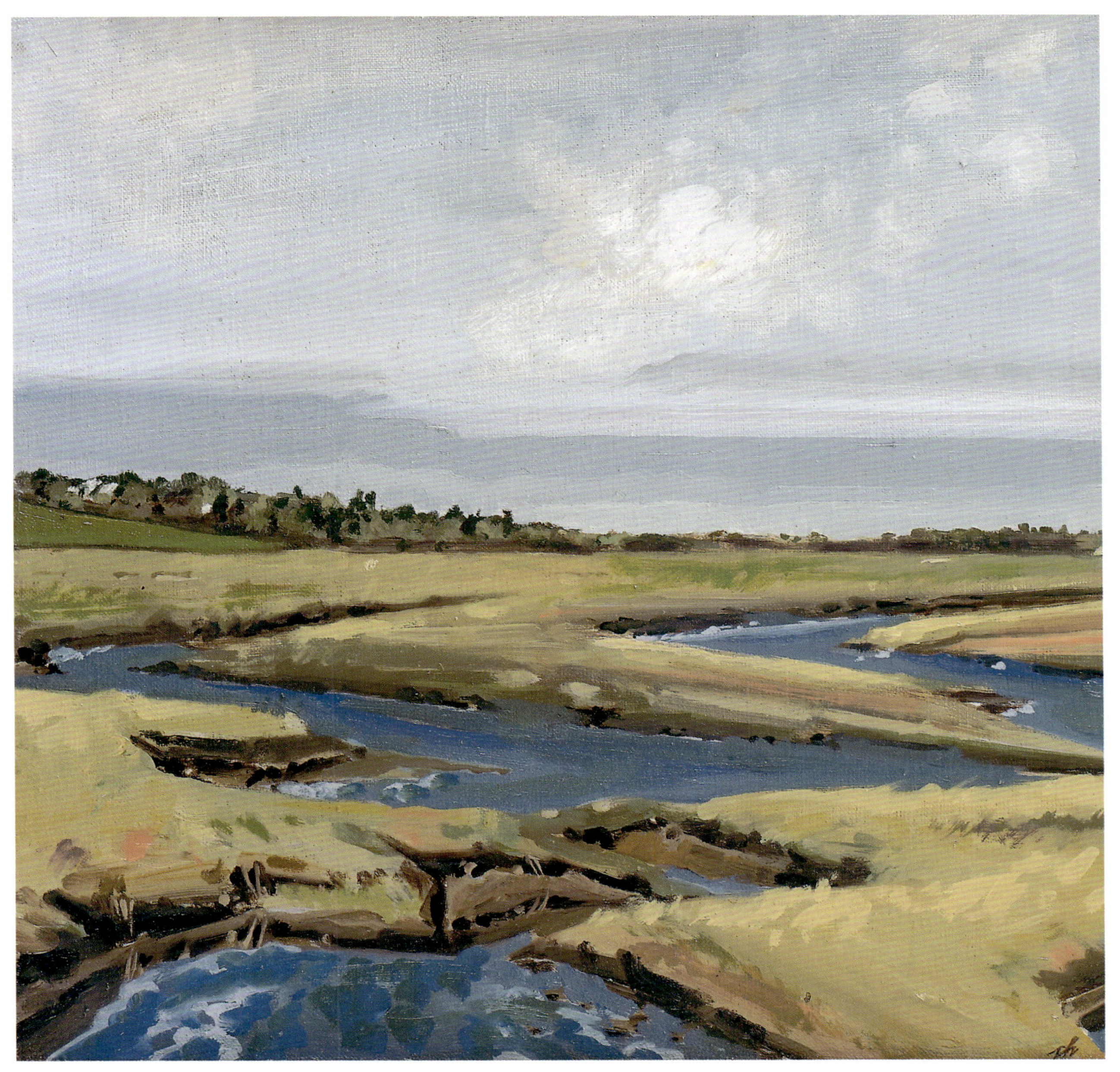

Patricia Hardy, *Fall Marsh,* 1987, oil on canvas, 17 x 15 in.
Bates College Museum of Art, Museum purchase, BCMA 1989.4.1

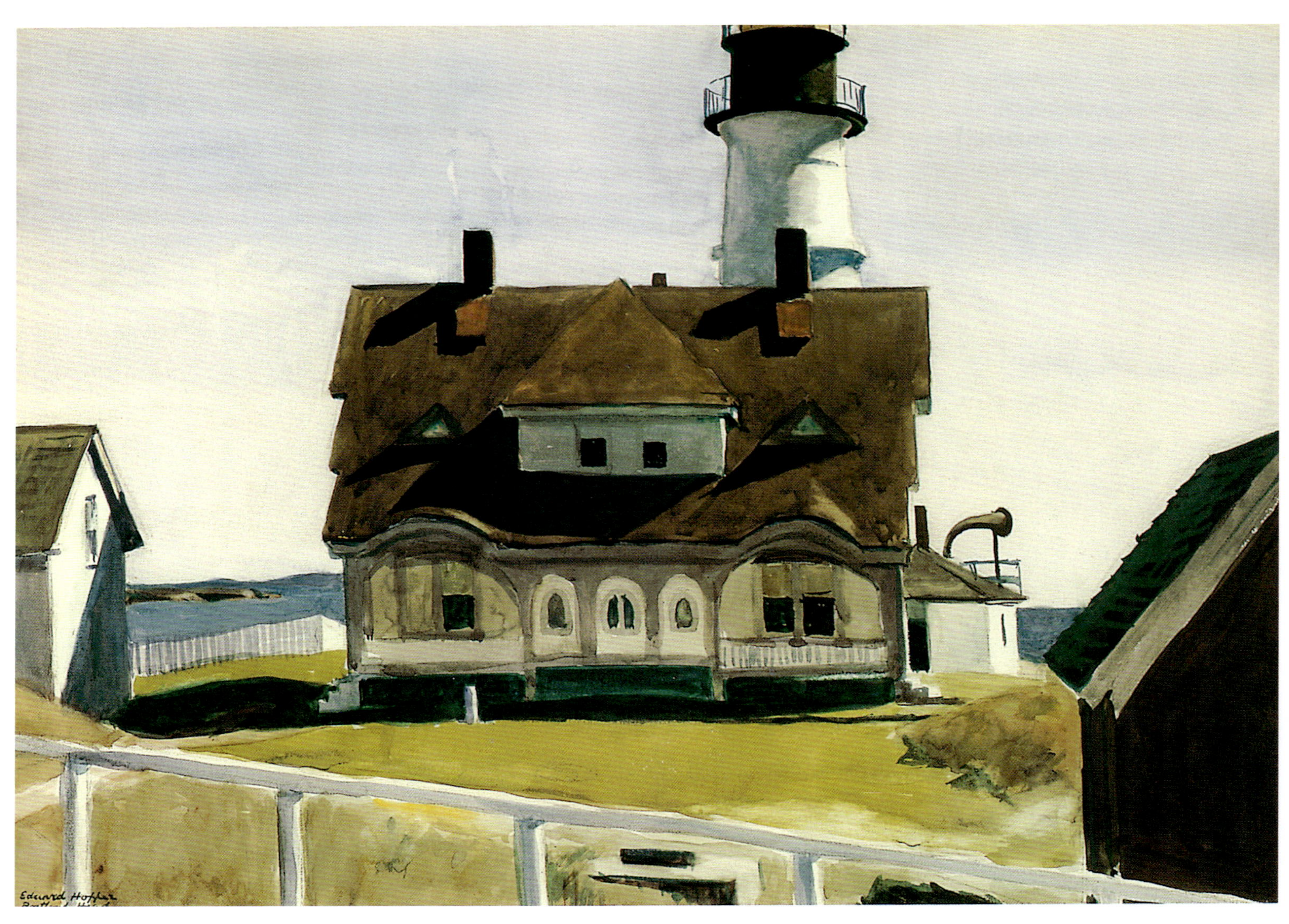

Edward Hopper, *Captain Strout's House, Portland Head,* 1927, watercolor on paper, 14 x 20 in.
Wadsworth Atheneum Museum of Art, Hartford, Connecticut
The Ella Gallup Sumner and Mary Catlin Sumner Collection Fund

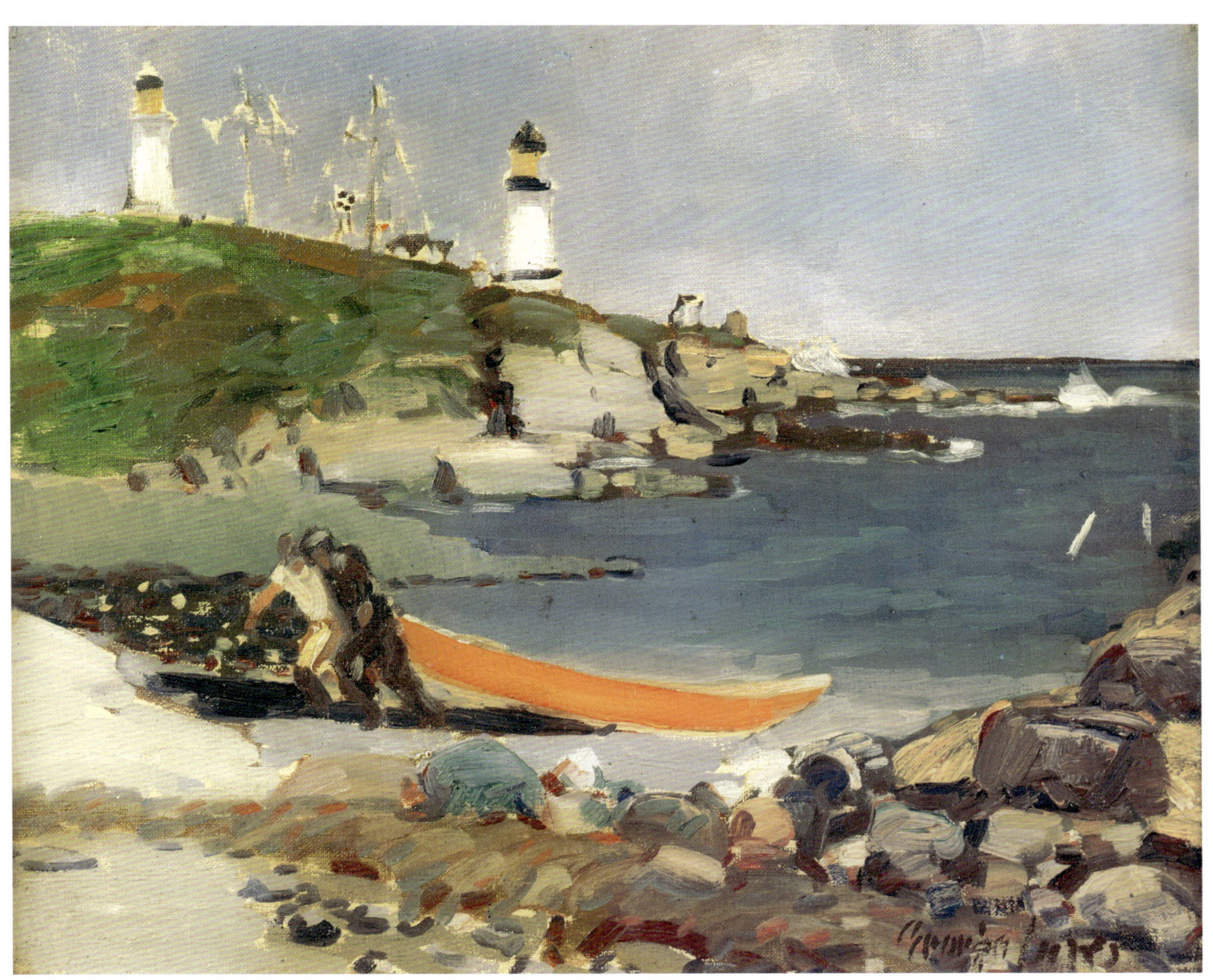

George Luks, *Hannaford's Cove,* 1922, oil on canvas, 16 x 20 in., courtesy Owen Gallery, New York

They are, of course, fragile communities built on the sand of biblical warning. These places are no more than sand berms, the product of "once-a-century" storms. Behind them are salt marshes, with miles of meandering creeks and life-filled muds, giving nurture to the sea's life beyond. Here the studious or adventuresome summer kid has an alternative to the frenzy of skin, sand and sun at the beach—a view into the stuff of natural history along these shores.

—GEORGE PUTZ, *THE MAINE COAST,* 1985

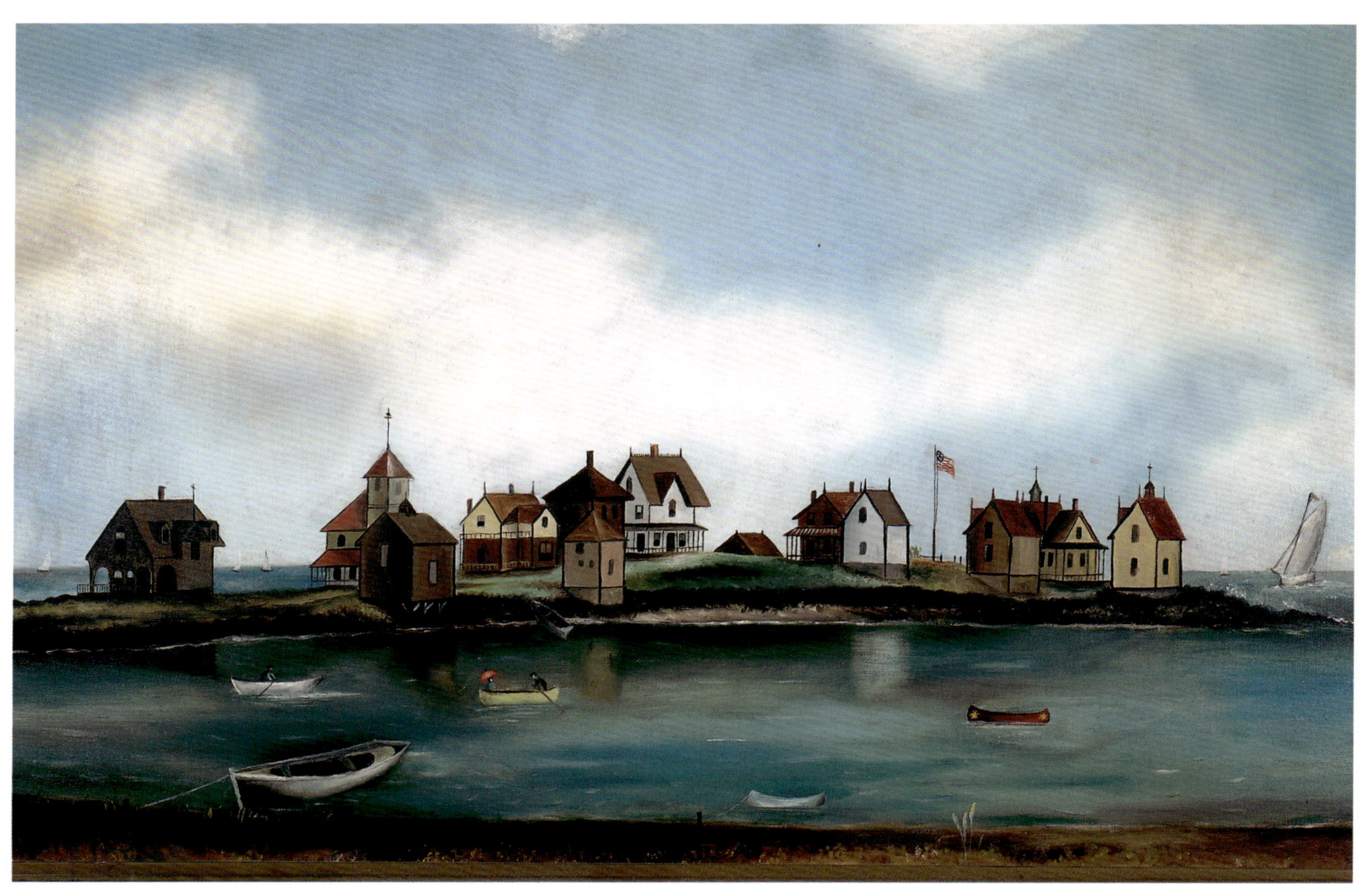

Unknown, *Lord's Point, Kennebunk Beach, Maine,* c. 1885, oil on canvas, 24 x 36 in.
Collection of the Maine Historical Society, Gift of Earle G. Shettleworth Jr.

—where hillside oaks and beeches
Overlook the long blue reaches,
Silver coves, and pebbled beaches,
And green isles of Casco Bay.

—JOHN GREENLEAF WHITTIER

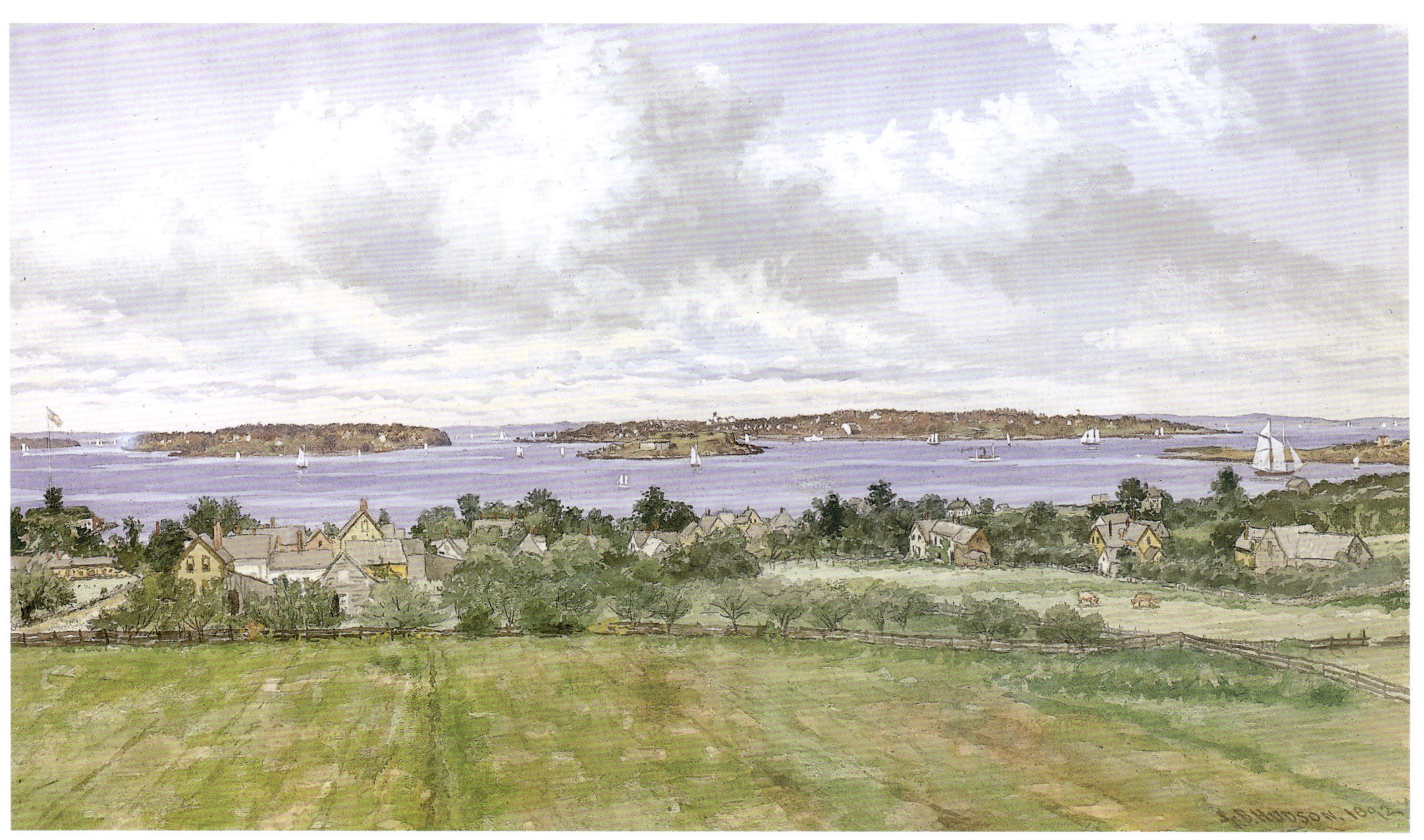

John Bradley Hudson, *A Panoramic View of the Islands of Casco Bay, from the House of Daniel Pillsbury Cobb, South Portland,* n.d.
Watercolor on paper, 15 1/2 x 27 1/2 in., private collection; photograph courtesy Barridoff Galleries, Portland, Maine

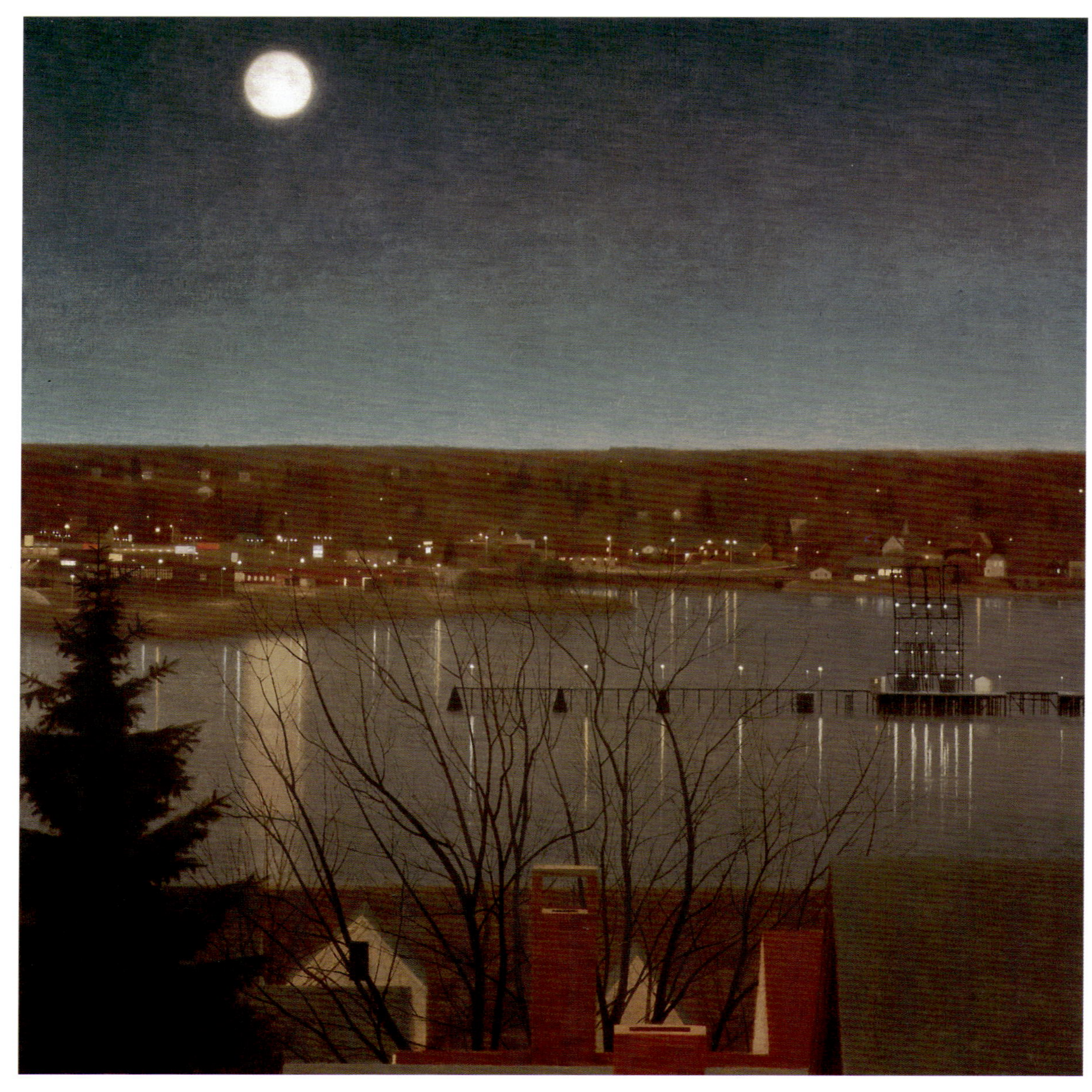

Brett Bigbee, *Moon River,* 1989–90, oil on canvas, 24 x 24 in., photo: Alexandre Gallery, New York

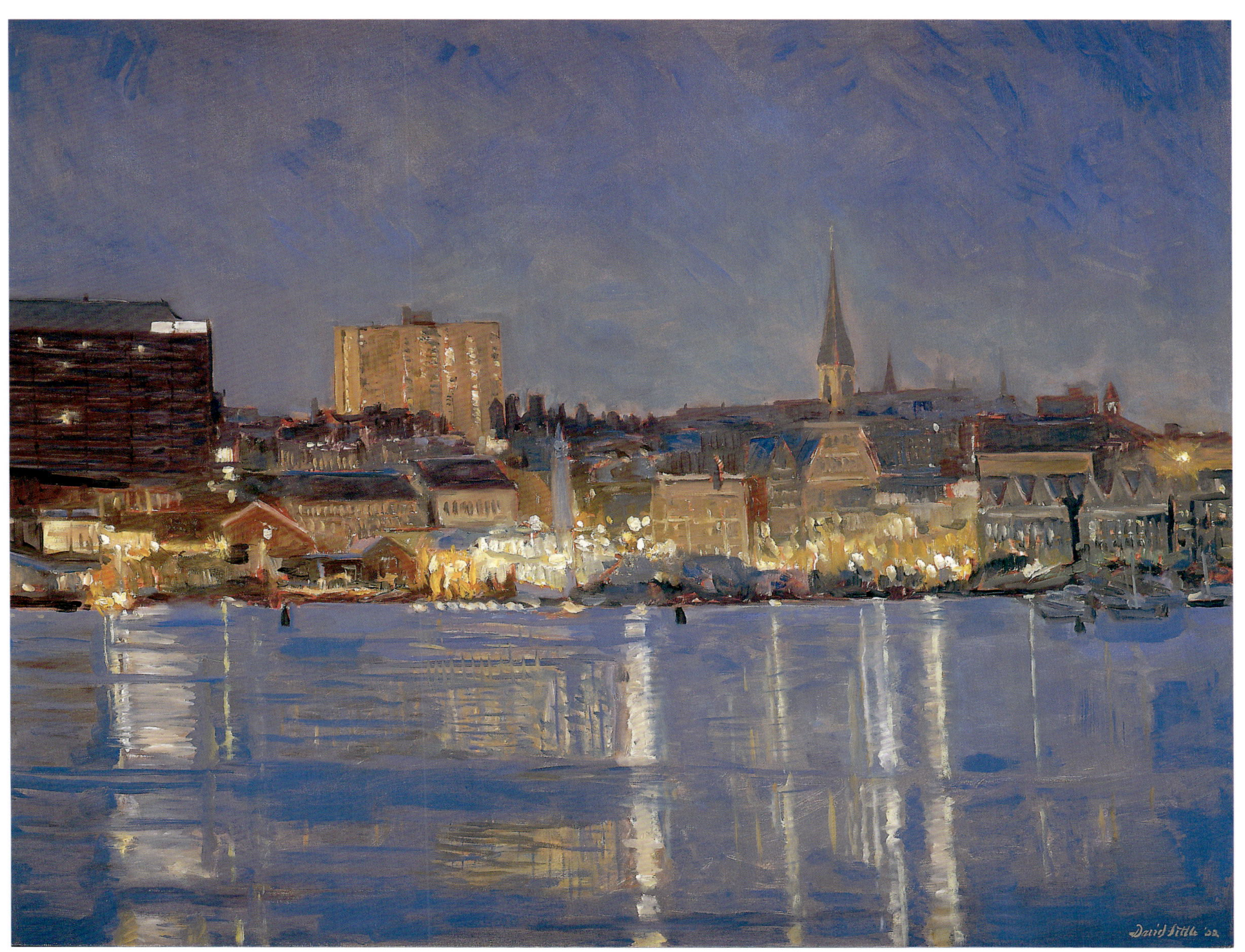

David Little, *Twilight, Portland Skyline,* 2002, oil on canvas, 36 x 48 in., courtesy Thos. Moser Cabinetmakers, Freeport, Maine

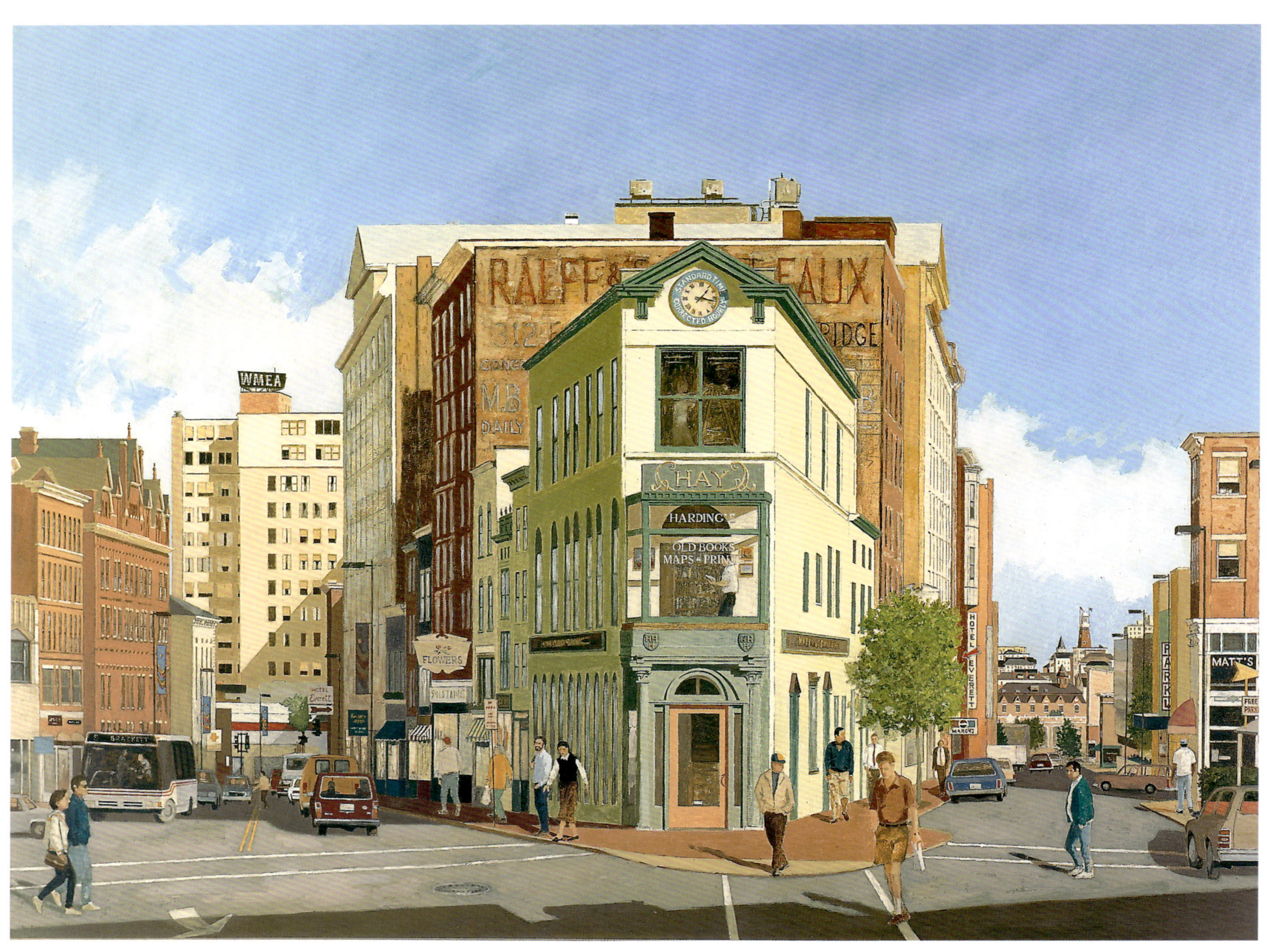

 Robert Solotaire, *Congress Square,* 1995, oil on paper, 38 x 27 1/2 in., collection of Philip Cox of Inn on Carleton, Portland, Maine

Portland is certainly the prettiest little city out of doors. Every man, woman, and child has an inalienable freehold in pure air, generous sunshine, and the most exquisite sea-scapes.

—SAMUEL ADAMS DRAKE, *THE PINE TREE COAST,* 1891

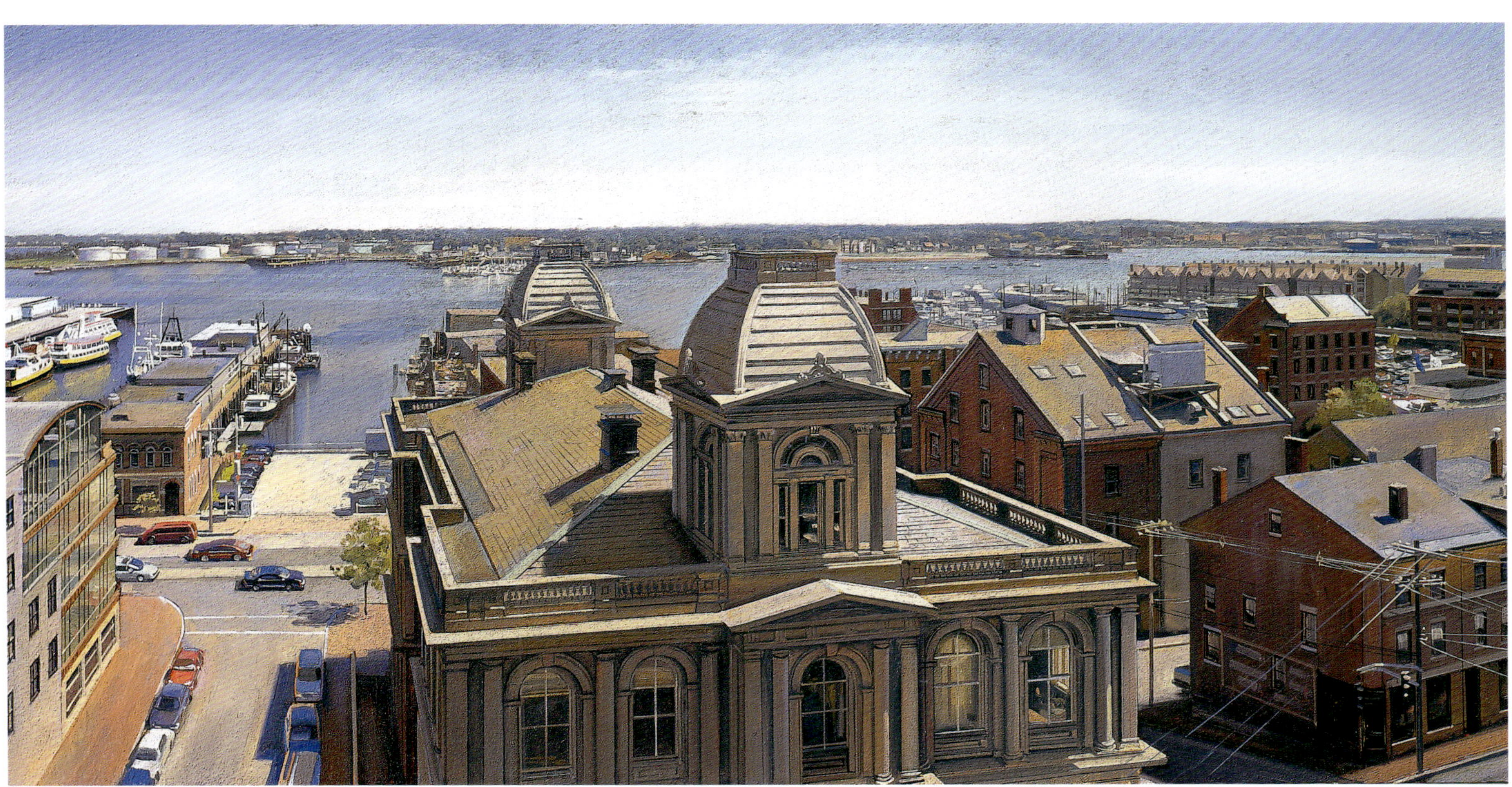

Joel M. Babb, *Customs House, Portland,* 2002, oil on linen, 15 x 30 in., collection of Dan and Sara Boxer, Cape Elizabeth, Maine

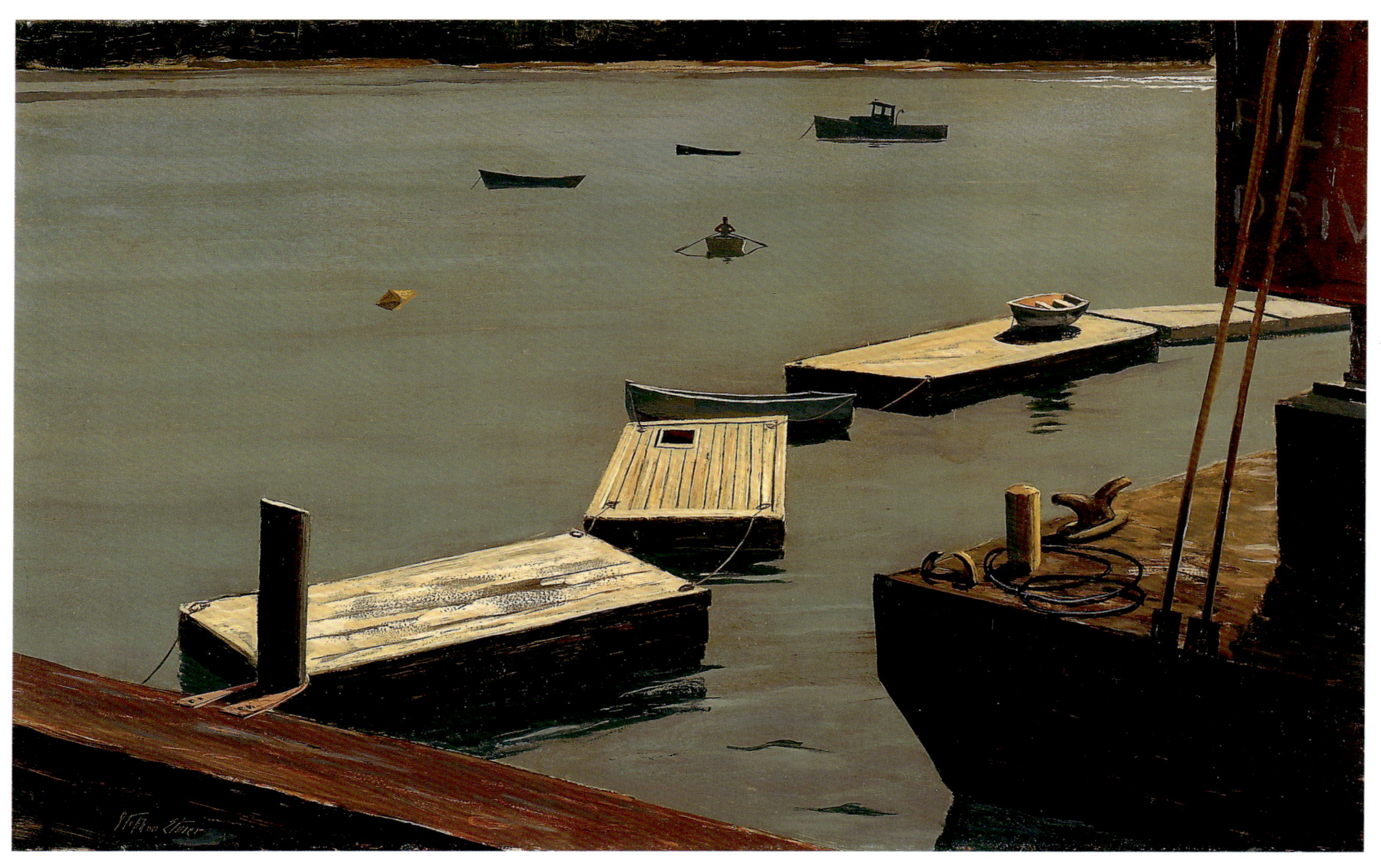

Stephen Etnier, *Scows, South Freeport, Maine*, c. 1970, oil on masonite, 22 1/4 x 36 1/4 in.
Portland Museum of Art, Maine. Gift of Marion P. Dana, 1983.69

Did you know . . . that here in Maine we get more sun than most places in the northern hemisphere; and that it shines with the same intensity that it does in Florence, Italy? "Sunny Italy," as it has long been known, has produced some of the greatest artists of the ages, partly because of the light that enhances their work. Maine has the same sun.

—JOHN COLE, *IN MAINE,* 1974

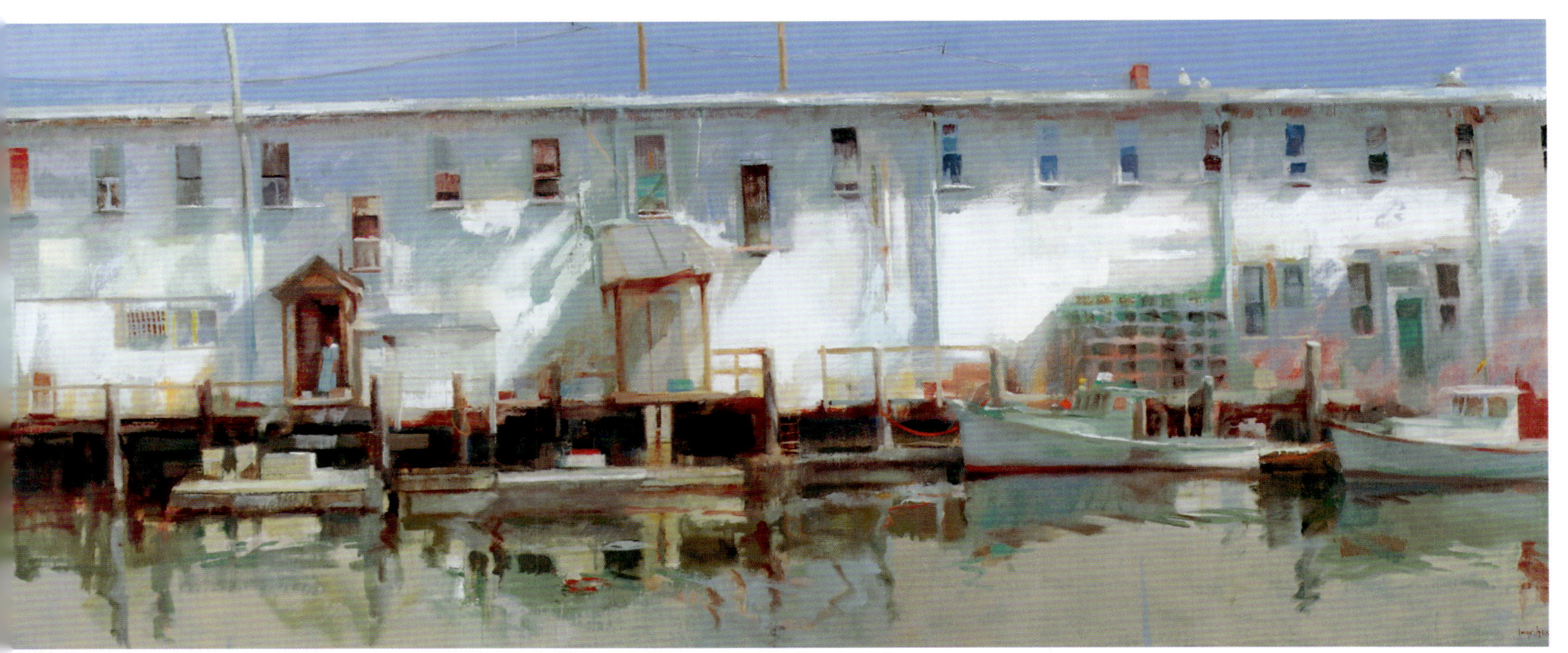

Tina Ingraham, *Harbor Fish Market, Portland Pier,* 2005, oil on linen, 32 x 76 in.
Collection of Betsey and Peter Wiley, Portland, Maine

In those extraordinary days of the Watergate scandal, just following the so-called "Saturday Night Massacre," just-fired investigator Archibald Cox was asked by the press what his plans were, now that his services had been dismissed. He replied, "I'm going back to the coast of Maine!"

—GEORGE PUTZ, *THE MAINE COAST,* 1985

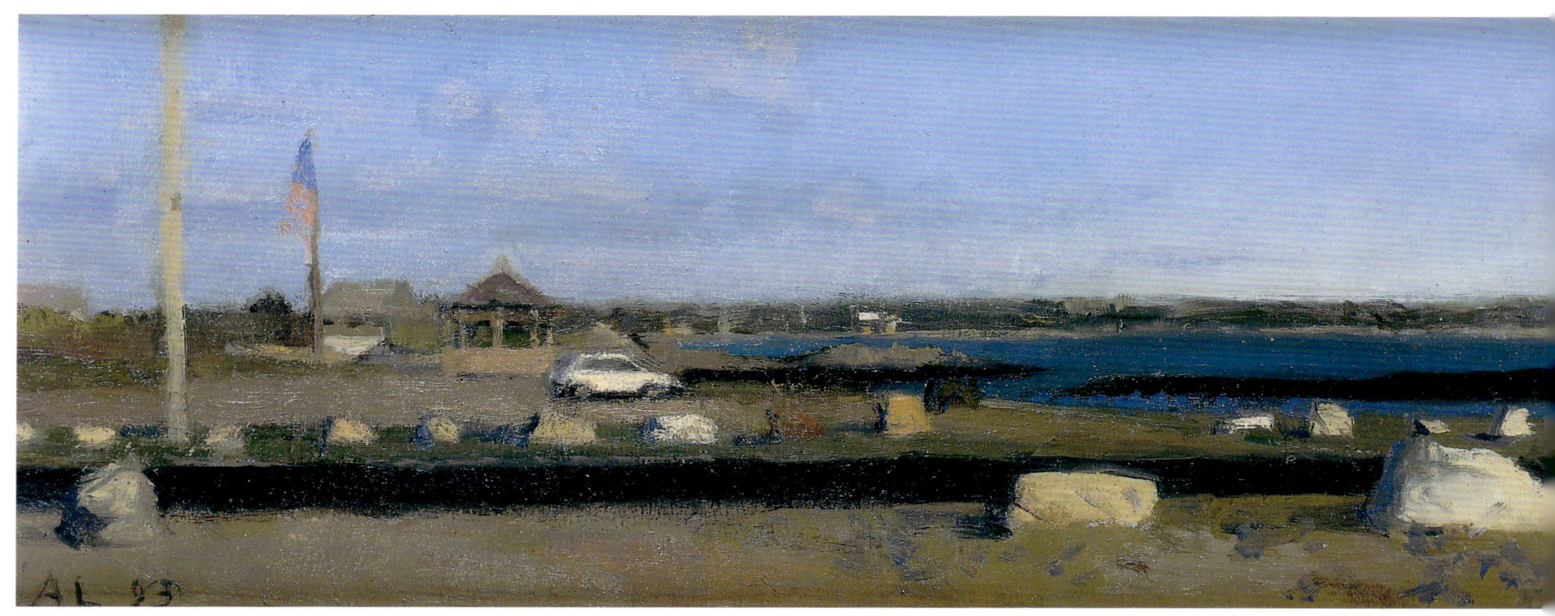

Ann Lofquist, *Evening, South Harpswell,* 1993, oil on panel, 3 1/2 x 12 in., collection of Remak Ramsay

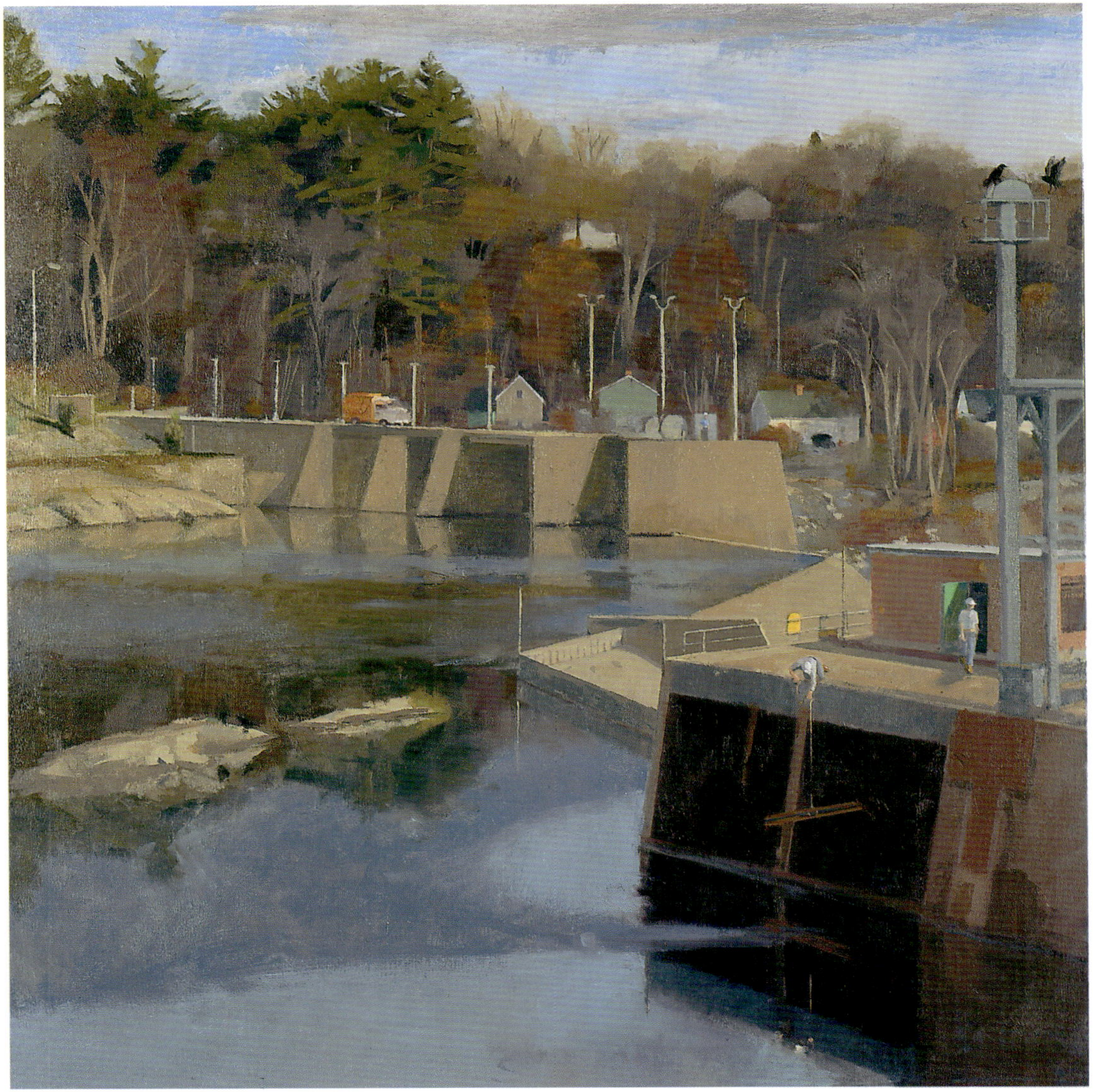

Lucy Barber, *Untitled (Androscoggin River)*, 2004, oil on canvas, 48 x 48 in., collection of the artist

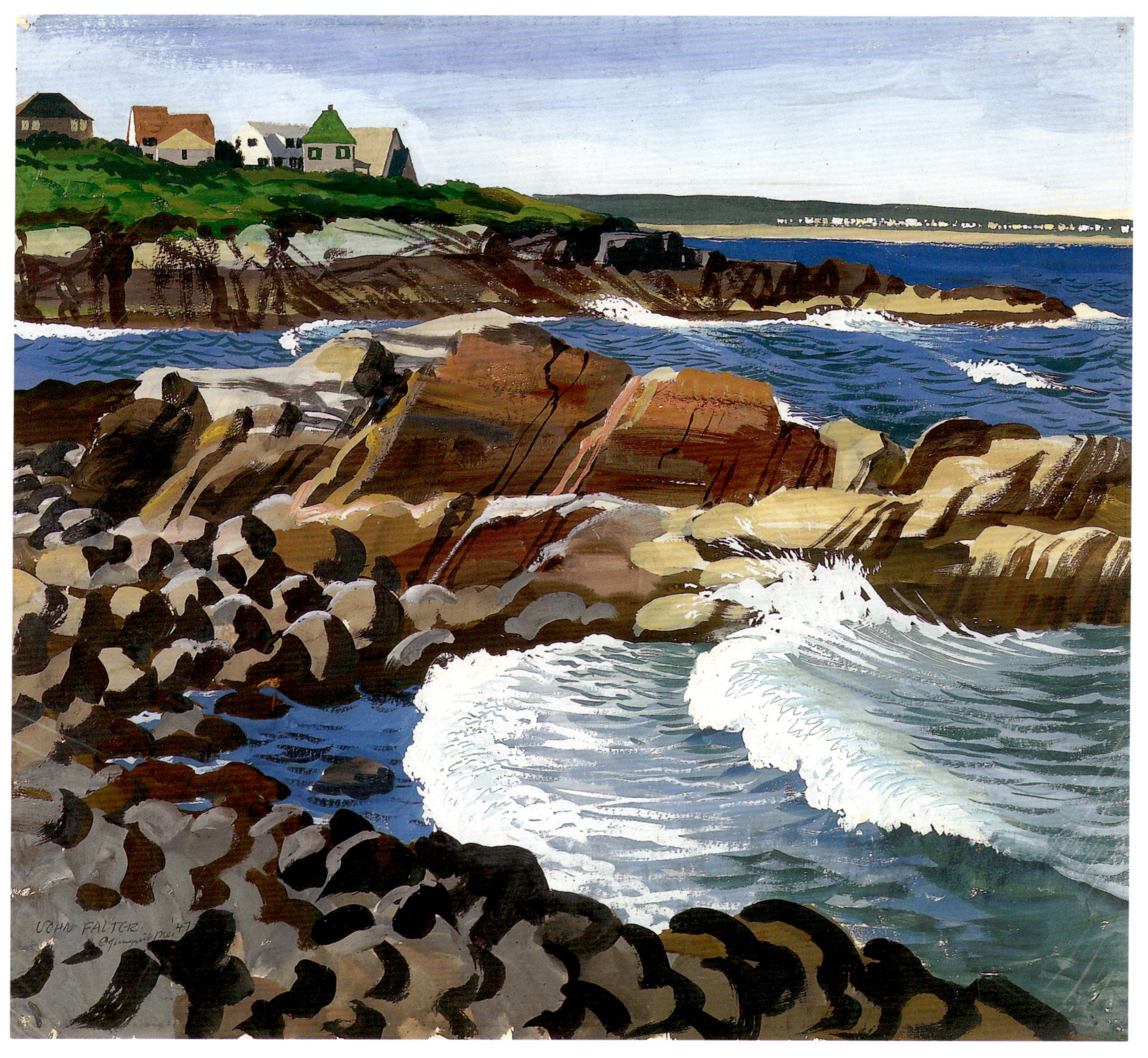

John Falter, *After a Nor'easter, Ogunquit,* n.d., gouache, 20 x 22 1/4 in.
Collection of Nancy McFadden Copp; photograph courtesy Barridoff Galleries, Portland, Maine

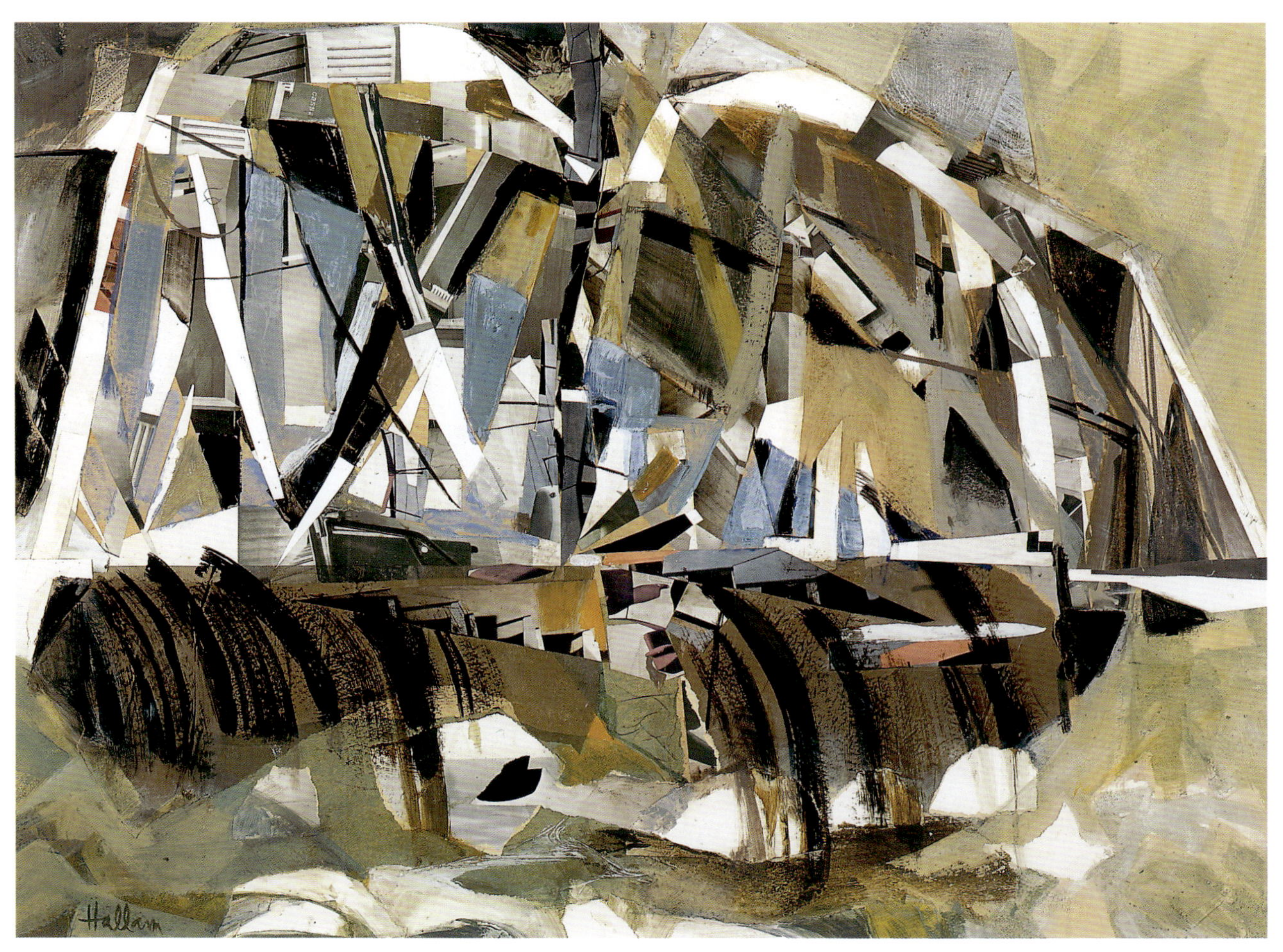

Beverly Hallam, *Brunswick-Topsham Bridge,* 1959, acrylic and collage on paper, 22 x 30 in.
Collection of Dana and Terry Hilt; photograph courtesy Barridoff Galleries, Portland, Maine

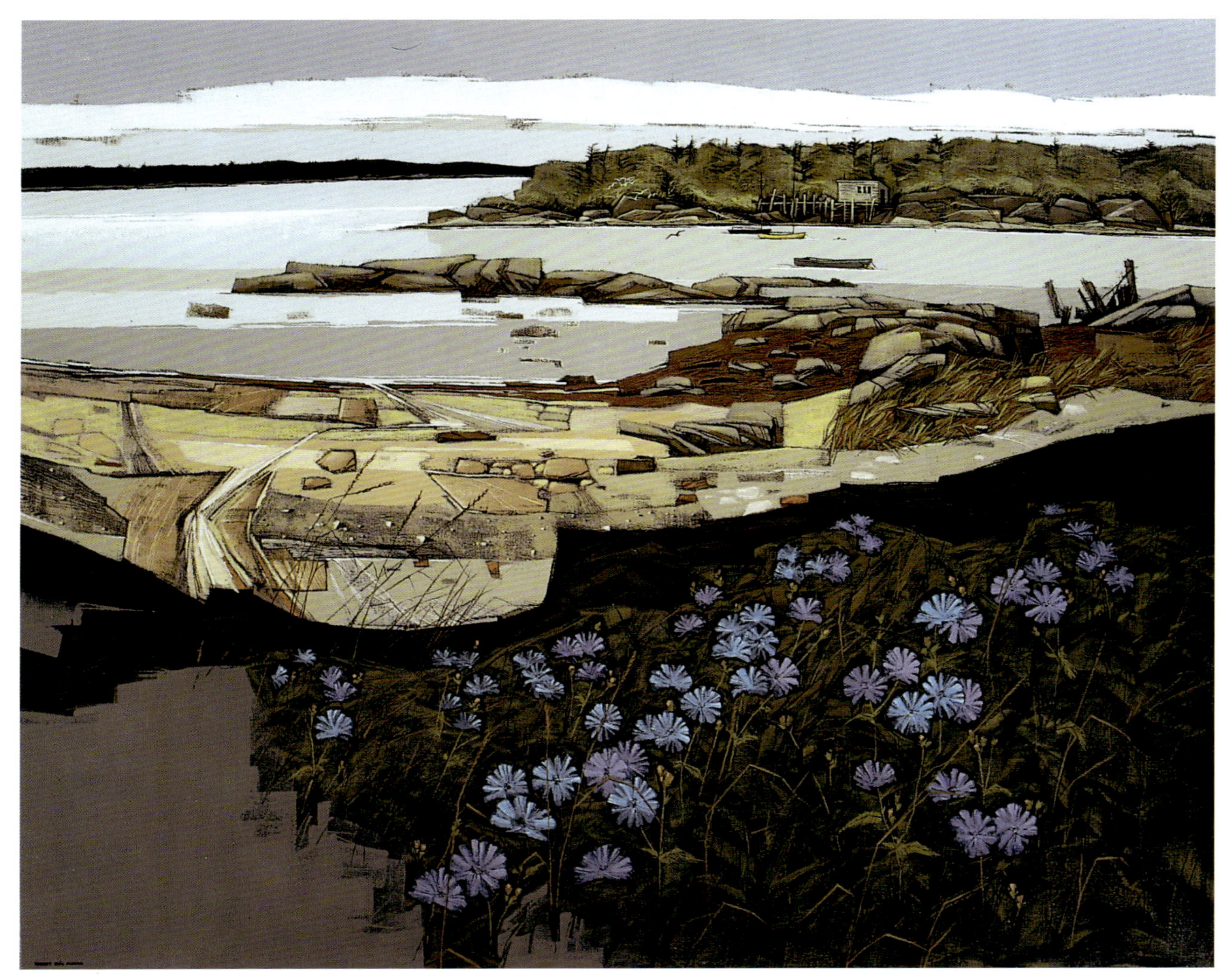

Robert Eric Moore, *Chicory,* 2000, acrylic, 48 x 60 in., private collection

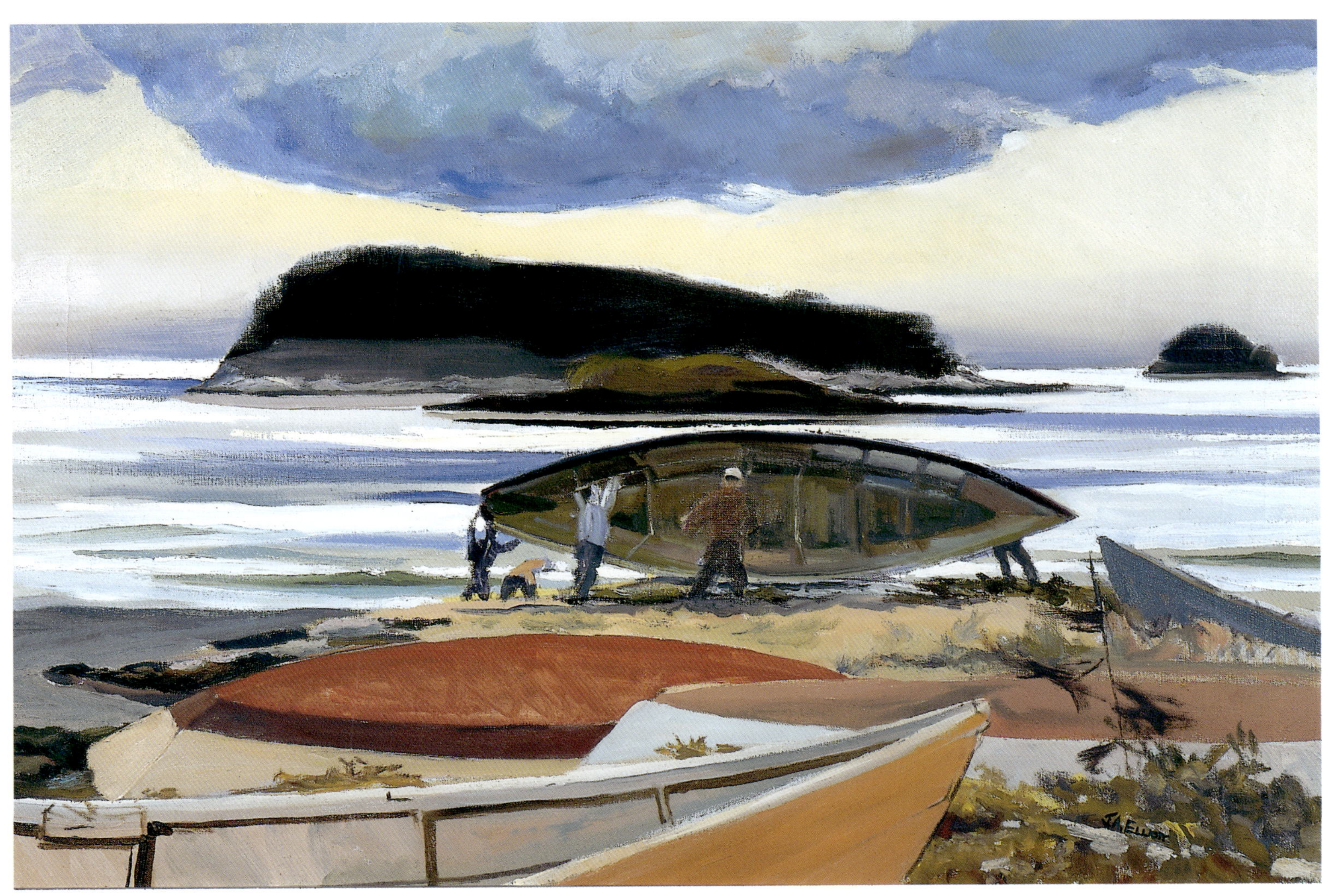

James Elliott, *Shore Duty—Herring Fishermen*, 1961–62, oil on canvas, 19 1/4 x 29 1/2 in.
James A. Elliott estate, courtesy The Clown, Portland, Maine

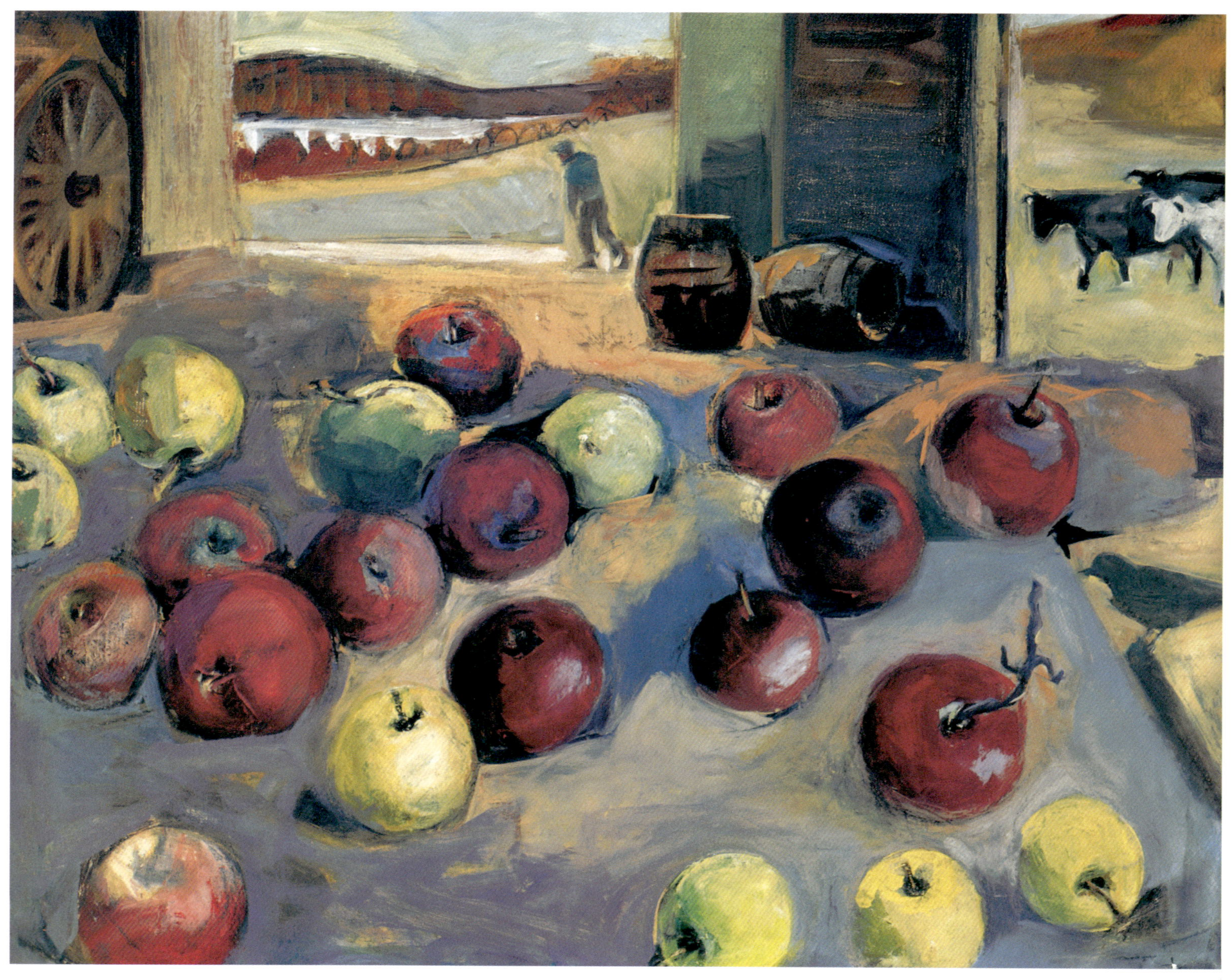

Carl Sprinchorn, *Apples on a Barn Floor,* 1950, oil on canvas, 28 x 34 in., courtesy Veilleux Gallery

A Glimpse of the Interior

When one speaks of the interior of Maine, a wide range of images arises in the mind's eye, both urban and rural. On the one hand, there's Lewiston, Maine's second largest city. In Robert Solotaire's remarkable panorama, the city's mills, stretching across the skyline, are reflected in the Androscoggin River. On the other hand, there are simple ice-fishing houses, like the ones on a lake in Piscataquis County painted by Alan Bray (b. 1946). Bray, originally from Waterville and now living in Sangerville, heightens the surreal quality of this makeshift community, tied together by the desire to be outdoors and catch togue and trout.

Born in Lisbon Falls in Androscoggin County, Delbert Dana Coombs (1850–1938) studied landscape painting in Portland with Harrison Bird Brown and worked for a time in Boston before settling in Maine. Fond of the White Mountains, Coombs also painted closer to home, specializing in pastoral scenes. The view of humble Mount David near Lewiston features a grazing cow, a subject for which Coombs was well known.

John Moore (b. 1941) has always been fascinated with the complexity of urban views and with those places—industrial neighborhoods, factory towns—that are so ordinary as to go virtually unnoticed except by real estate investors. On teaching stints at the Skowhegan School of Painting and Sculpture, Moore has painted such "workingscapes," including houses huddled below a bridge spanning the Kennebec River in Augusta. His passion for the unpretentious landscape is also apparent in a view of Monroe.

The Maine woods have never attracted the hordes of painters that the coast has. Part of it relates to accessibility: whole swaths of northern Maine are truly out of the way compared to the seashore. That said, a number of painters have turned to the interior, which offers seemingly inexhaustible material.

Born in Lovell, Maine, artist Eastman Johnson (1824–1906) painted an impressive series of canvases documenting the gypsy-like maple-syrup camps in Fryeburg, near the border with New Hampshire. For an artist who often focused

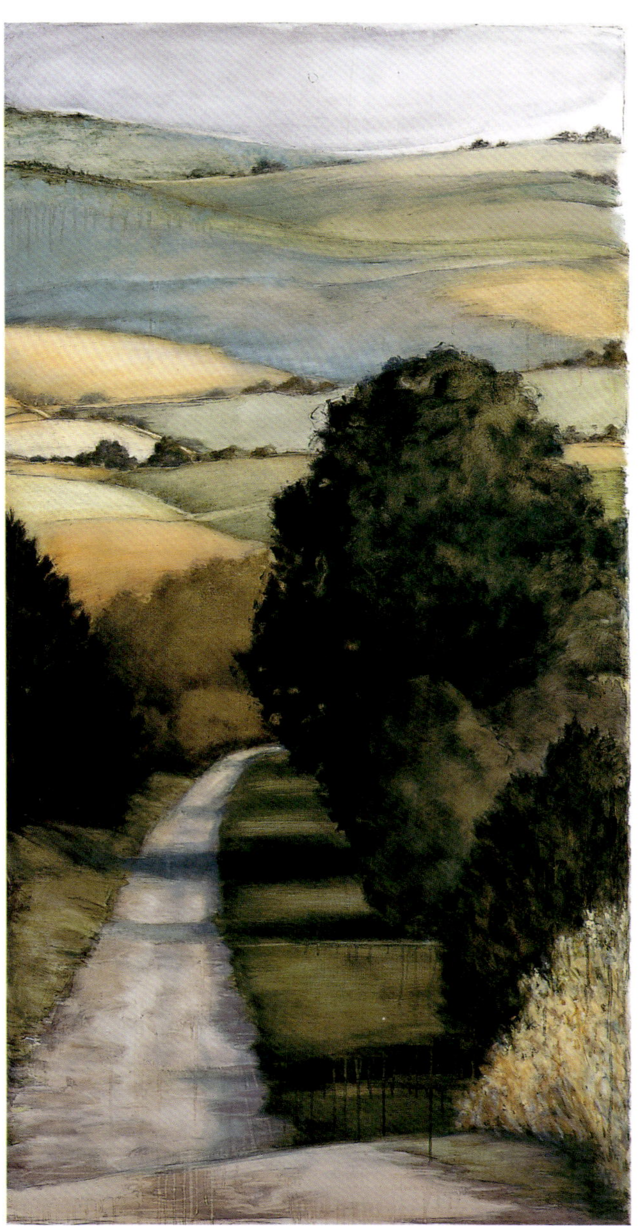

Marguerite Robichaux, *Heading Up North,* 2004
Oil on linen, 66 x 36 in., collection of the artist

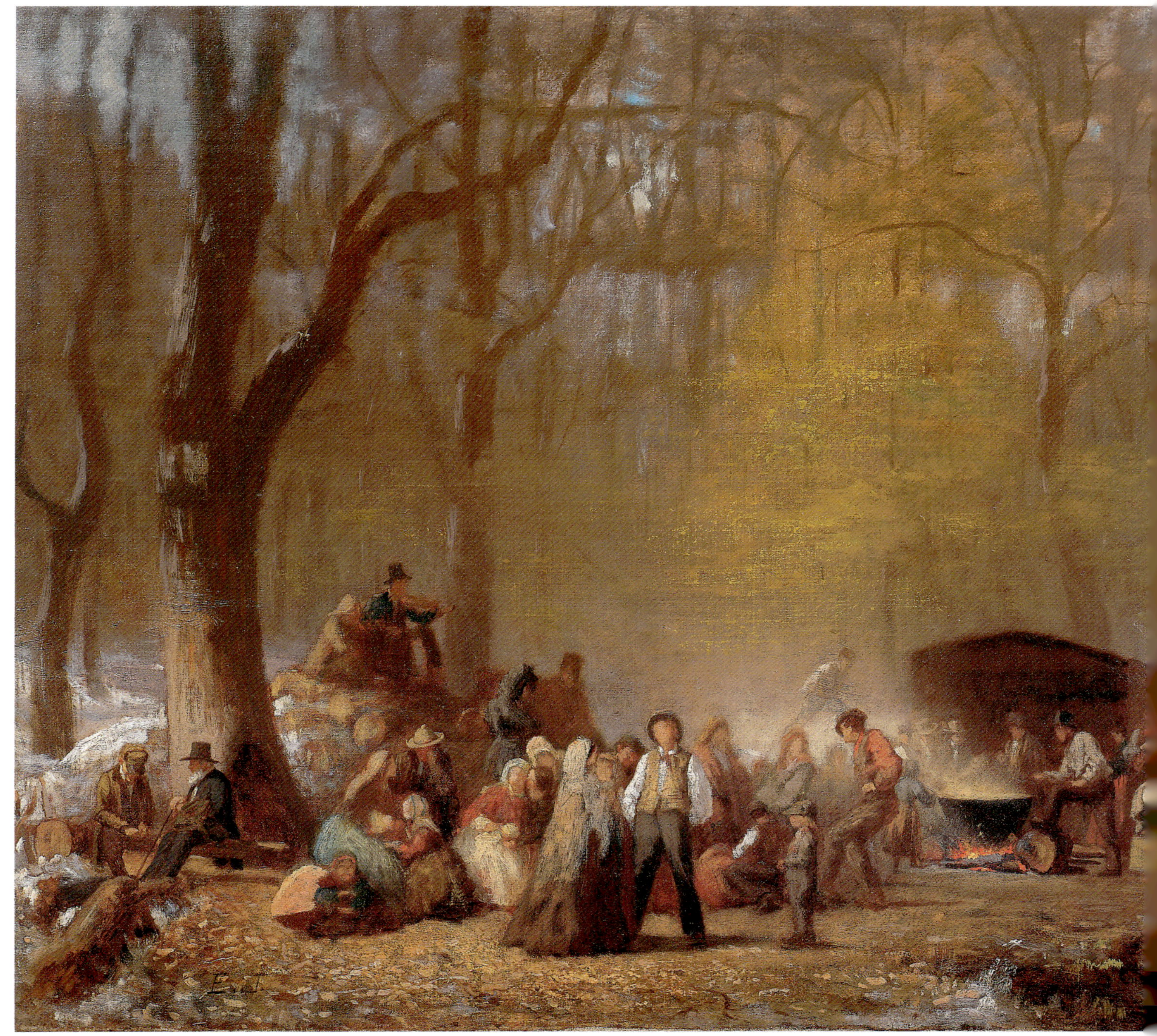

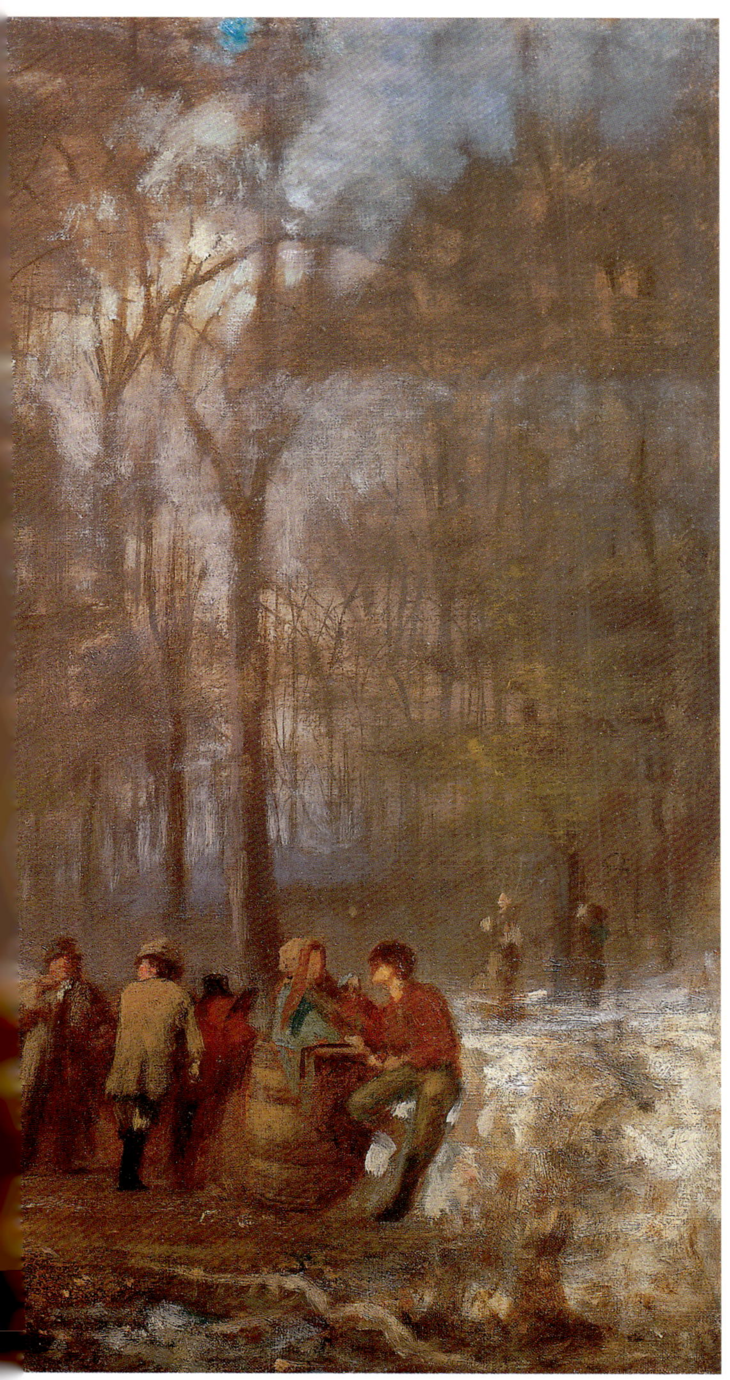

on distinctive American activities, from farming to picking cranberries on Nantucket, a gathering in the Maine woods to transform sap into sugar proved irresistible. One wonders if these paintings, dating from 1861 to 1865, weren't a response to the Civil War, offering scenes of communal celebration far from the bloody battlefields.

Scenic nineteenth-century views of Lake Sebago and Mount Kineo on Moosehead Lake by Charles Codman and John Joseph Enneking (1841–1916), respectively, epitomize the painted panoramic vistas that attracted early "rusticators" to inland Maine. Figures in the foreground of both canvases serve to underscore the grandeur of the settings.

Enneking, who summered in North Newry, was the "first man" Vivian Milner Akers (1886–1966) ever saw painting the landscape "in colors as Maine really looks." With tutoring from the older artist, Akers—who spent much of his life in nearby Norway, Maine—painted throughout the Oxford Hills region. He also gained fame as a photographer, woodcarver and portraitist (Chief Justice Earl Warren was among his most famous sitters).

Marguerite Robichaux (b. 1950), who lives year-round in Stratton, traverses the majestic Bigelow Range in search of subject matter. "The terrain of gentle hills, forests and mountains, long vistas, the sky, the quality of light and the abundance of water are gifts to a painter," Robichaux states. Her landscapes often bring to mind an observation Louise Dickinson Rich made in *We Took to the Woods* (1942): "There is not a leaf or a stone or a bend of road or a sun-glinting stretch of lake or river anywhere here that is not to me a lost lane-end into heaven."

Handsome Vienna Mountain just west of the Belgrade Lakes region in the Kennebec Highlands captured J. Thomas R. Higgins' eye on a winter outing. A dedicated plein air painter from Readfield, Higgins (b. 1943) deploys a swift brush to capture place, season and light. "I paint nature," he states, "because I am committed to search for beauty and have yet to find anything that can compare."

Eastman Johnson
Sugaring Off at the Camp, Fryeburg, Maine, 1864–66
Oil on canvas, 19 $^{3}/_{4}$ x 34 in.
Curtis Galleries, Minneapolis, Minnesota

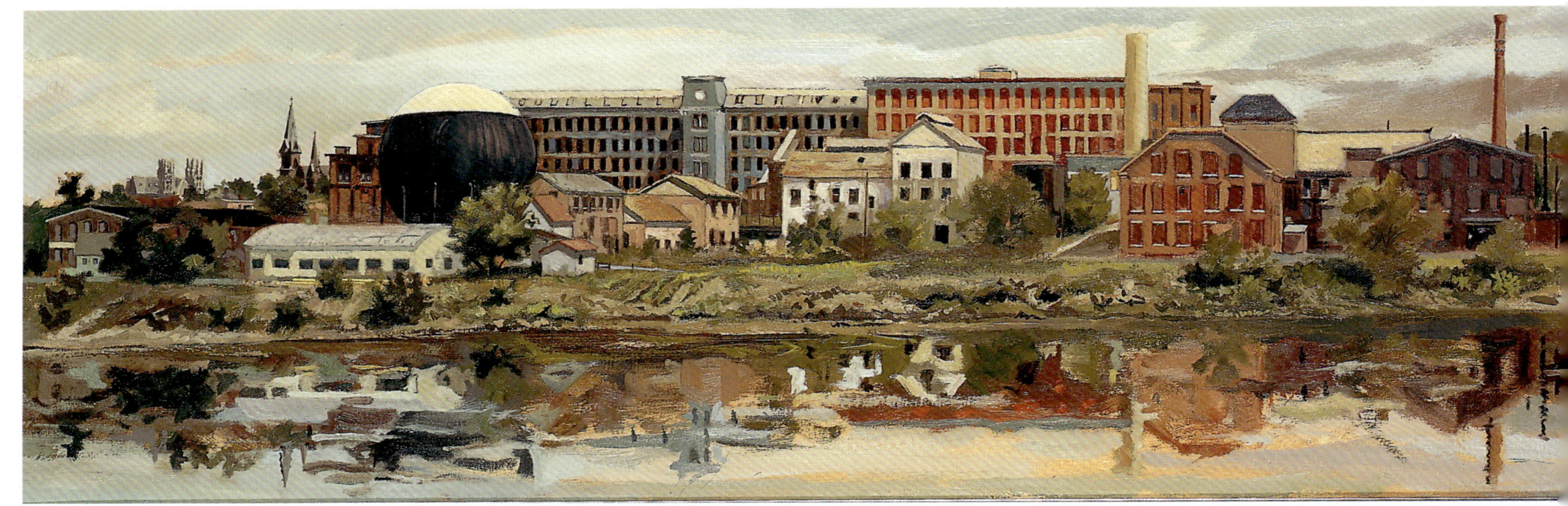

Bangor has a long and distinguished legacy of painters, none so colorful and dynamic as native son Waldo Peirce (1884–1970). A bon vivant who lived in Paris in the 1920s, Peirce accompanied his friend Ernest Hemingway to Spain to witness the annual running of the bulls in Pamplona. Among his most memorable paintings are scenes of Maine life, including a lively depiction of children cavorting under the elms at the Pond Street School in Bangor, which Peirce attended as a child.

Since moving to Bangor from Iowa in 1999, Jeff Loxterkamp (b. 1960) has been drawn to, in his words, "the strange visual juxtapositions" encountered in his travels around the state. His view of the Brewer shipyards focuses on the commercial freighter *Wanderbird,* which was restored and transformed into a cruise ship to ply the Penobscot River and the Maine coast. The Bangor Auditorium is visible in the distance.

Driving north from Bangor, one starts to look for Mount Katahdin, its eminence prominent from many miles away, depending on the weather. In a mountain-top view, painter George Hallowell (1871–1926) focused on one of Katahdin's most distinctive features, the Knife Edge—a treacherous stretch of trail that only the bravest hikers traverse. Hallowell's Maine landscapes often present a captivating blend of realism and romanticism.

There is clarity in the landscapes of Richard Estes (b. 1932) that can take one's breath away. Dividing his time between New York City and Mount Desert Island, in recent years the acclaimed photo-realist has spent more time painting views of his adopted state. When he set out to paint Mount Katahdin, Estes sought the spot on Millinocket Lake where Frederic Church painted his view of the mountain in 1895.

Swedish-born Carl Sprinchorn (1887–1971) made his first trip to Maine in 1909. In *Apples on a Barn Floor,* painted

Robert Solotaire, *Riverfront, Lewiston*, 1968, oil on canvas, 12 x 44 in., private collection

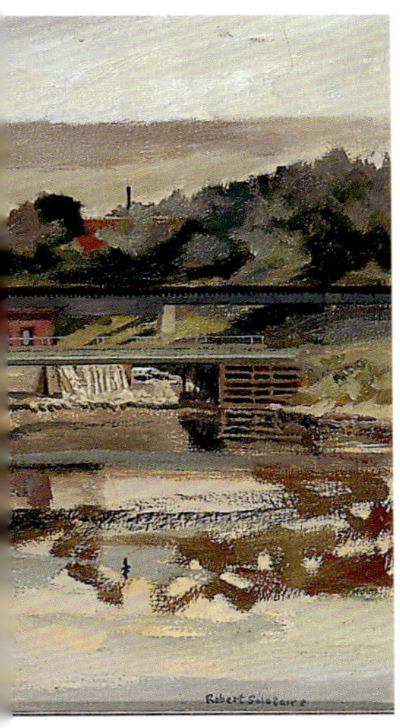

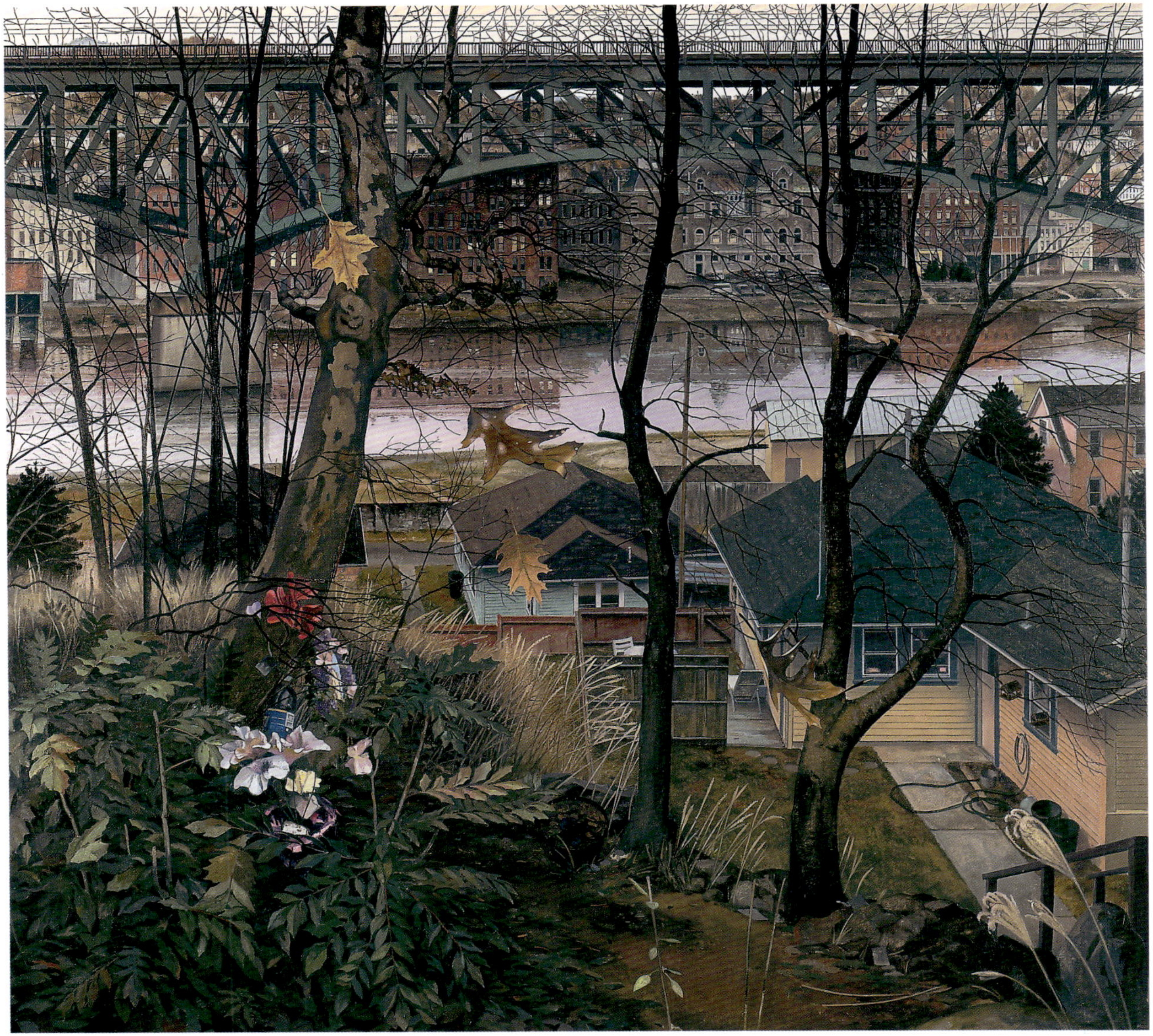

John Moore, *Bridge,* 2000, oil on canvas, 64 x 72 in., private collection, New York

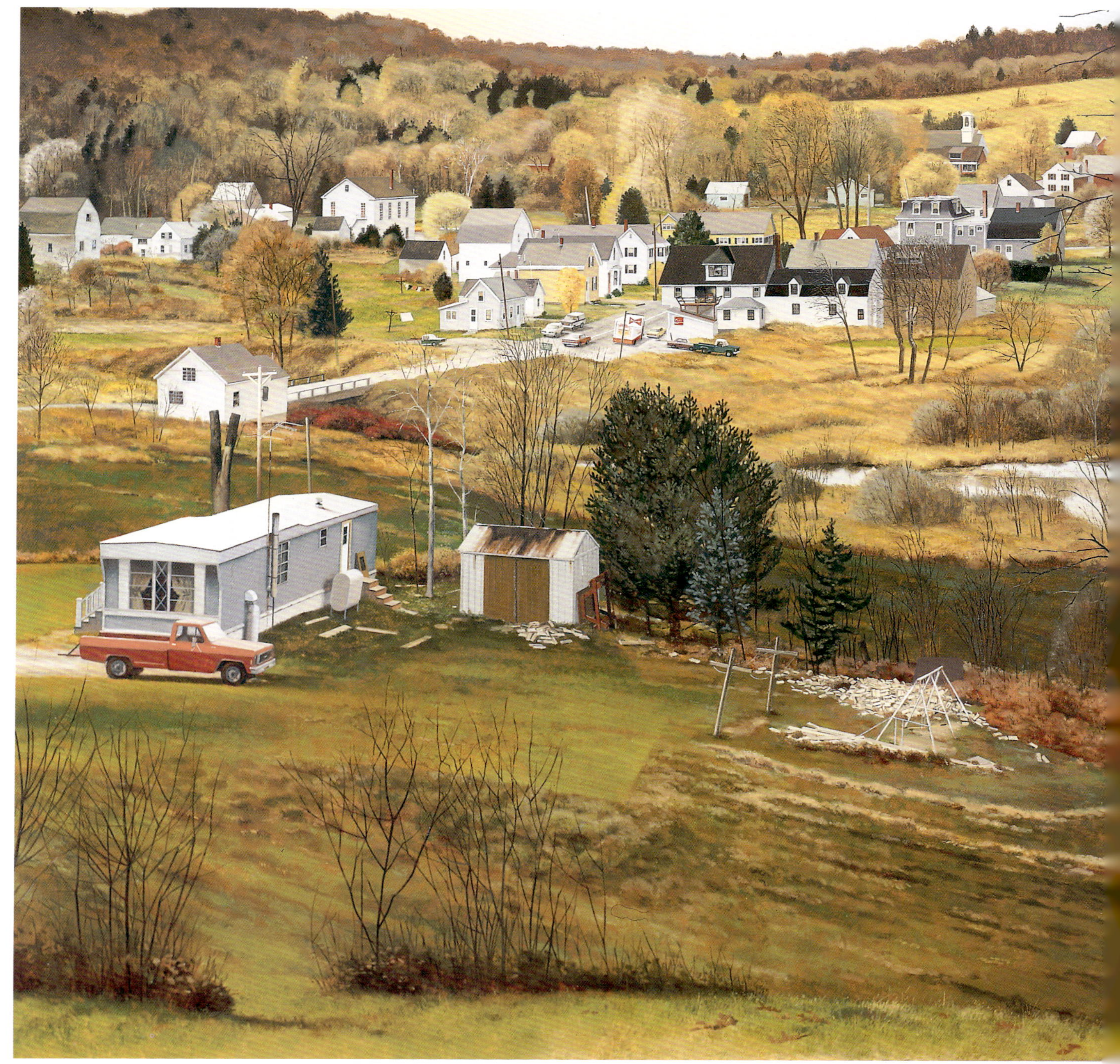

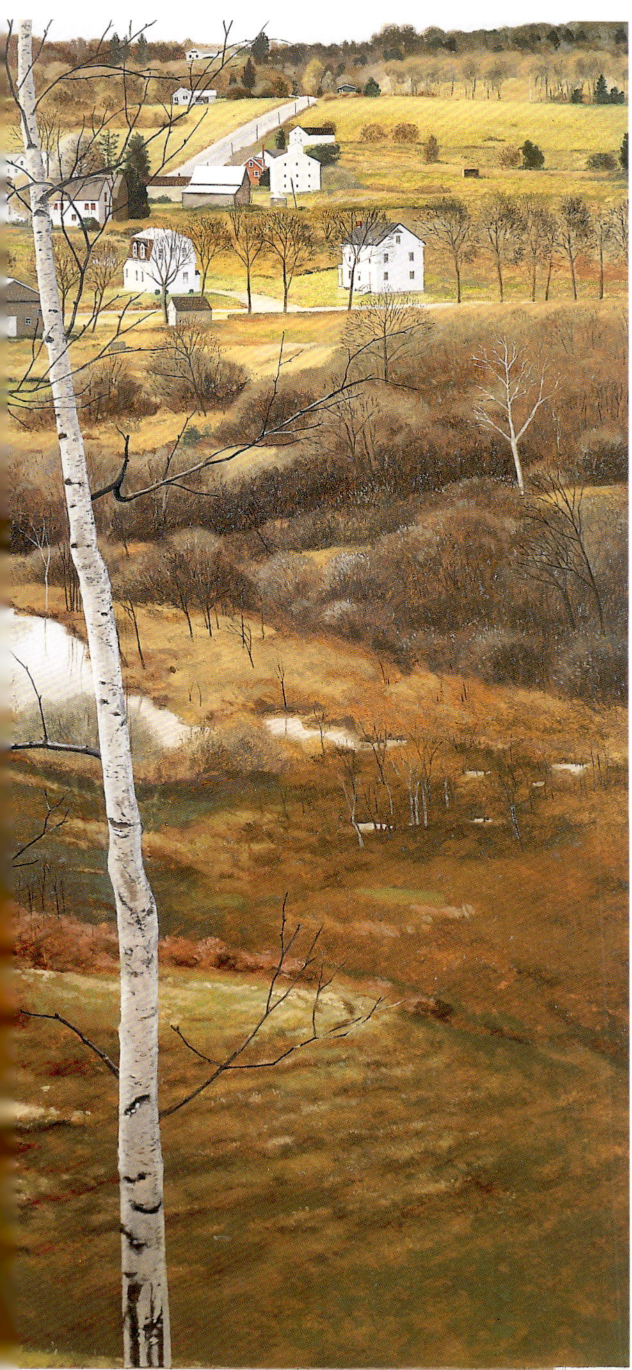

while boarding at the Crommett Farm in Shin Pond, Sprinchorn sought, he once explained, "to round out a sort of composite, or Apotheosis, of a farm, not only what is in front but behind it, of sensations experienced as I stand painting the twenty-two apples, conscious of the outdoors, the late, orangey afternoon sun, birds, men, animals and topography."

In Edward Nadeau's painting of the Airline Road—aka Route 9, one of Maine's most dangerous thoroughfares, running from Bangor to the Canadian border at Calais—a logging truck has turned over, spilling its load of raw timber. Born and raised in northern Maine, Nadeau (b. 1958), who now resides in Orono, based the painting on the death of Eddie Ouellette, a young man who one winter night went off the road and paid the ultimate price. The opening lines from Baron Wormser's poem "Somerset County" come to mind:

The log-crammed trucks smash the yielding air,
Whine like leviathan gnats.
Last week a trucker died at the wheel
On the way home from the mill.
He fell asleep. Or did he wake before?
The wreck looked like a freighter run aground.

Antonia Munroe (b. 1952) first visited Aroostook County, the "rooftop" of Maine, in 1991 and fell in love with the landscape "of huge fields and dramatic skies." The still life painter, who lives in Camden, found that "a solitary barn surrounded by an expanse of golden wheat," which she came across on the road between Presque Isle and Caribou, made the same imprint in her mind's eye as an "apple sitting on a white linen tablecloth."

Munroe's view recalls writer Martin Dibner's description of Aroostook's "sprawling" landscape, "with fifty-mile sunsets and a man's shadow at noon twenty feet long." Dibner made that admiring observation in a book about seacoast Maine.

John Moore, *Monroe,* 1985, oil on canvas, 90 x 144 in.
Private collection, New York

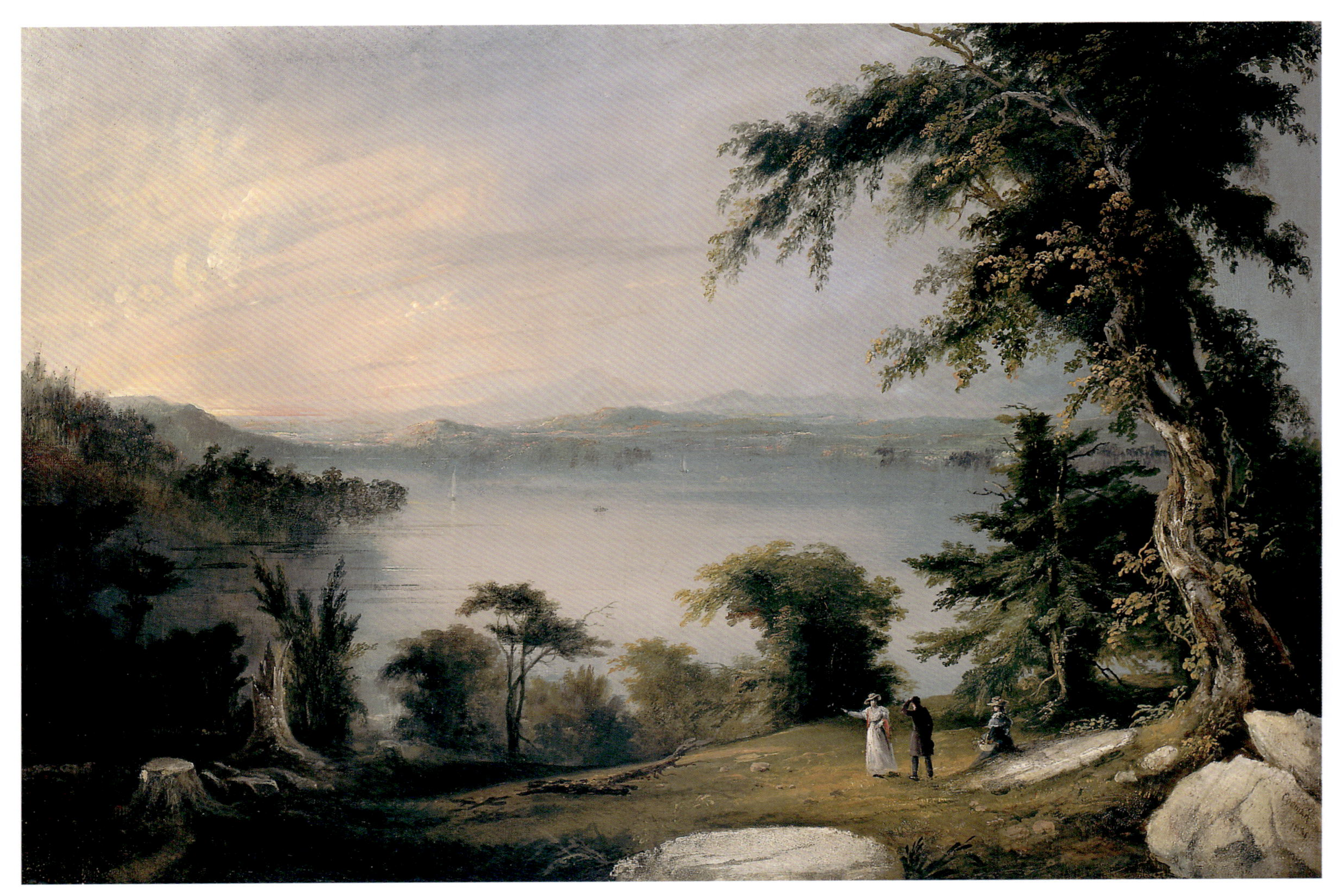

Charles Codman, *Lake Sebago,* 1831, oil on canvas, 23 1/4 x 35 1/4 in., private collection, © 2002 NAM DOL

There are so many, many Maines that it would take lifetimes to learn them all by heart, as children say, which is more than knowing them with the mind and memory. There is the land itself: the hills rising ridge upon ridge in slow majesty to the west, and the loon-haunted lakes—Moosehead, the Rangeleys, Sebago, Cupsuptic—strewn like fragments of splintered crystal on the thick green carpet of the forest.

—LOUISE DICKINSON RICH, *STATE O' MAINE,* 1964

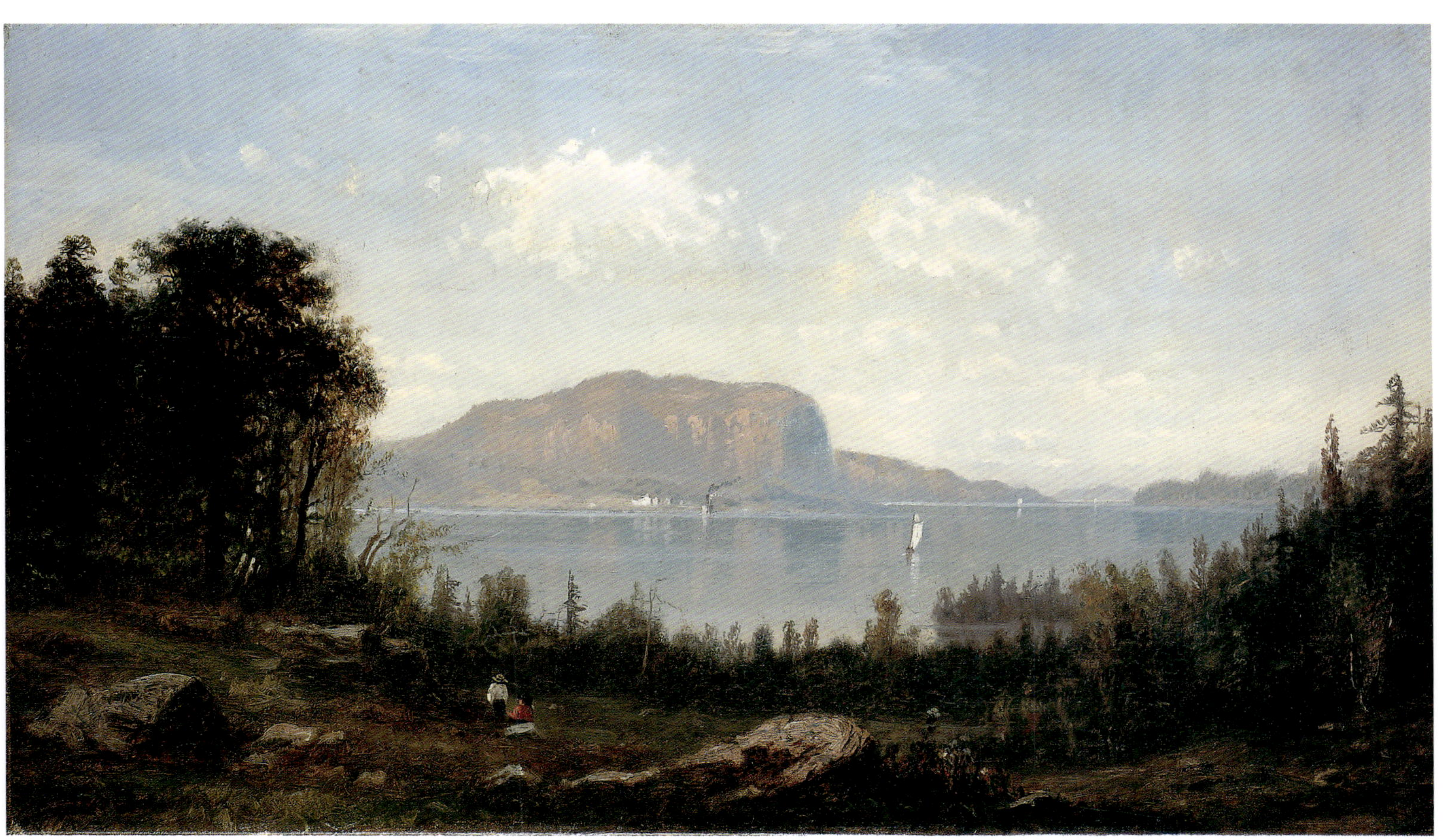

John Joseph Enneking, *Mount Kineo, Moosehead Lake, Maine,* 1871, oil on canvas, 16 15/16 x 30 1/8 in.
Collection of the Farnsworth Art Museum, Museum purchase, 1963 (63.1277)

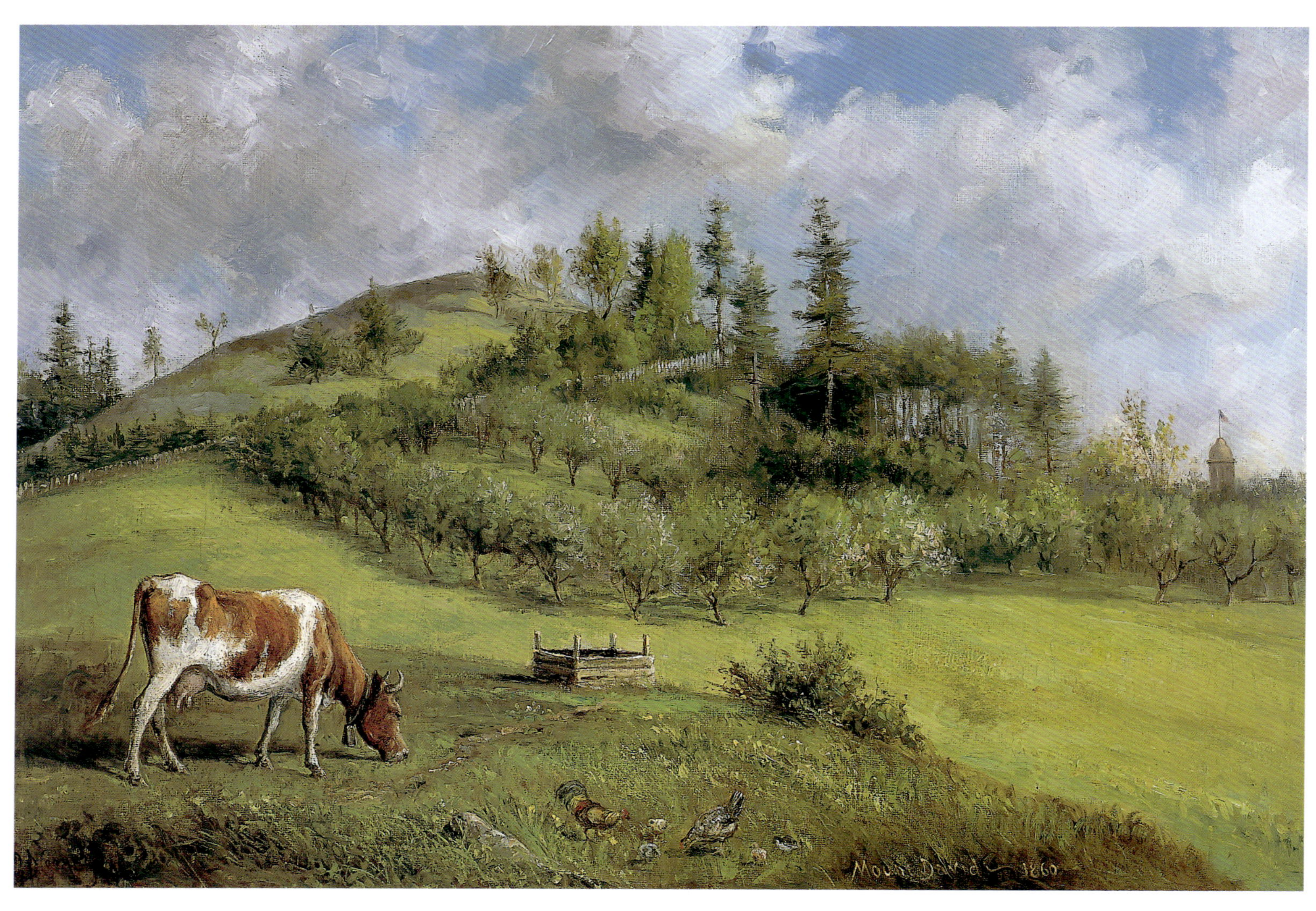

Delbert Dana Coombs, *Mount David 1860,* 1901, oil on canvas, 16 x 24 in.
Bates College Museum of Art, Gift of John and Evelyn White, BCMA 1996.33.1

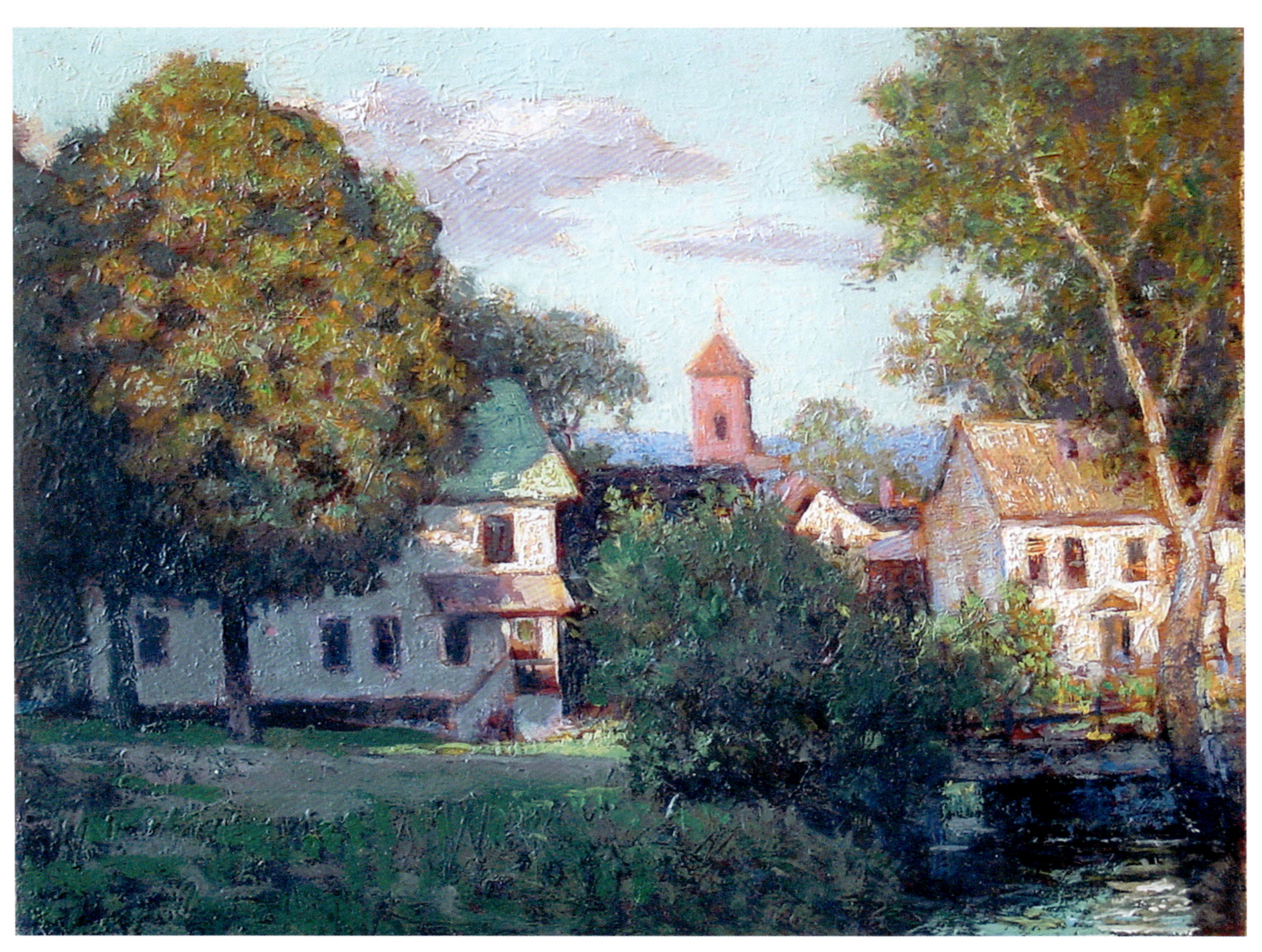

Vivian Milner Akers, *Coat's House, Late Afternoon, Norway, Maine,* 1944
Oil on wood panel, 6 1/2 by 8 1/2 in.; photograph courtesy Gleason Fine Art

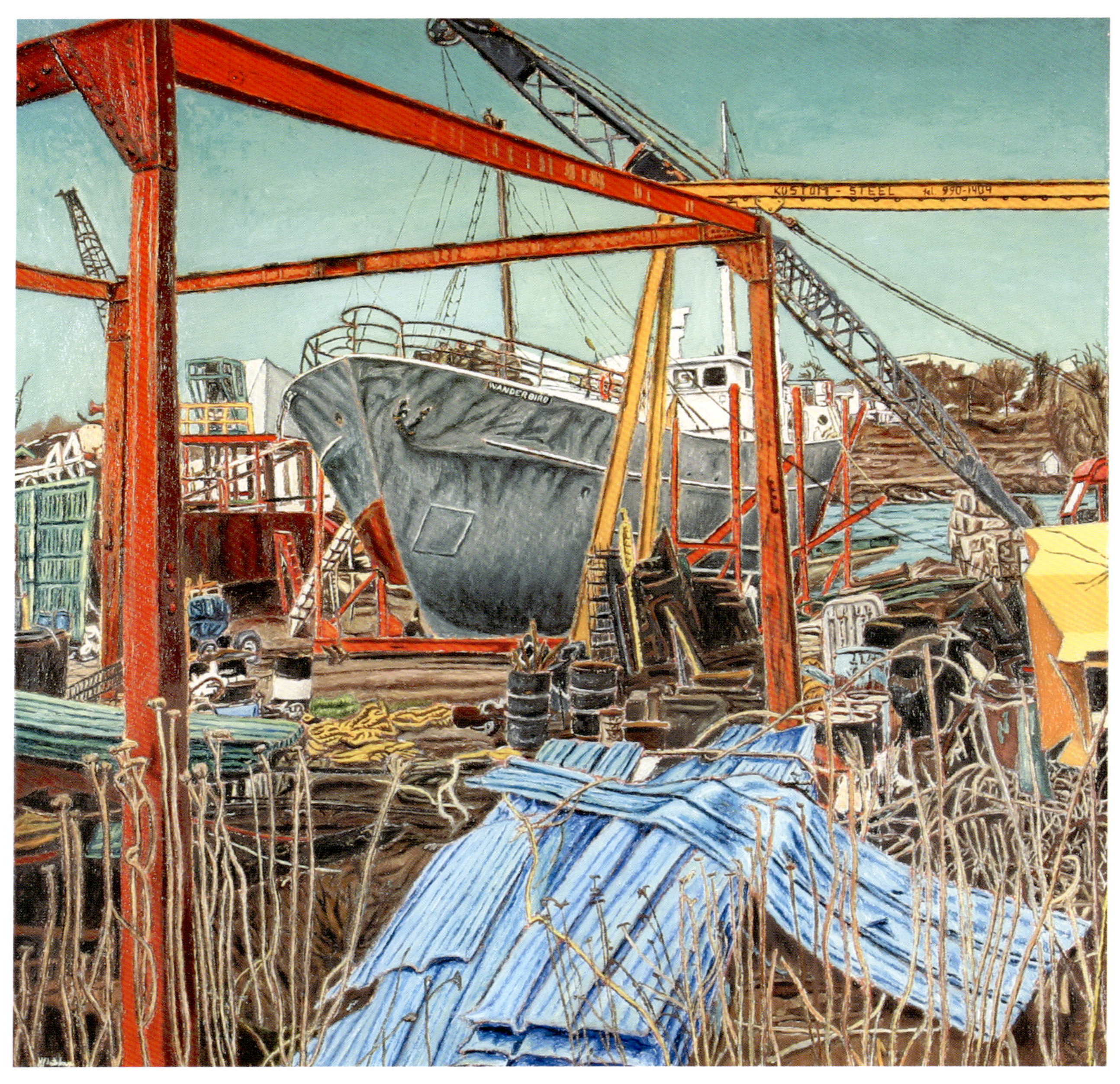

Jeff Loxterkamp, *Wanderbird,* 2005, oil on canvas, 41 x 40 in.
Collection of the artist, courtesy Susan Maasch Fine Art/Clark House Gallery

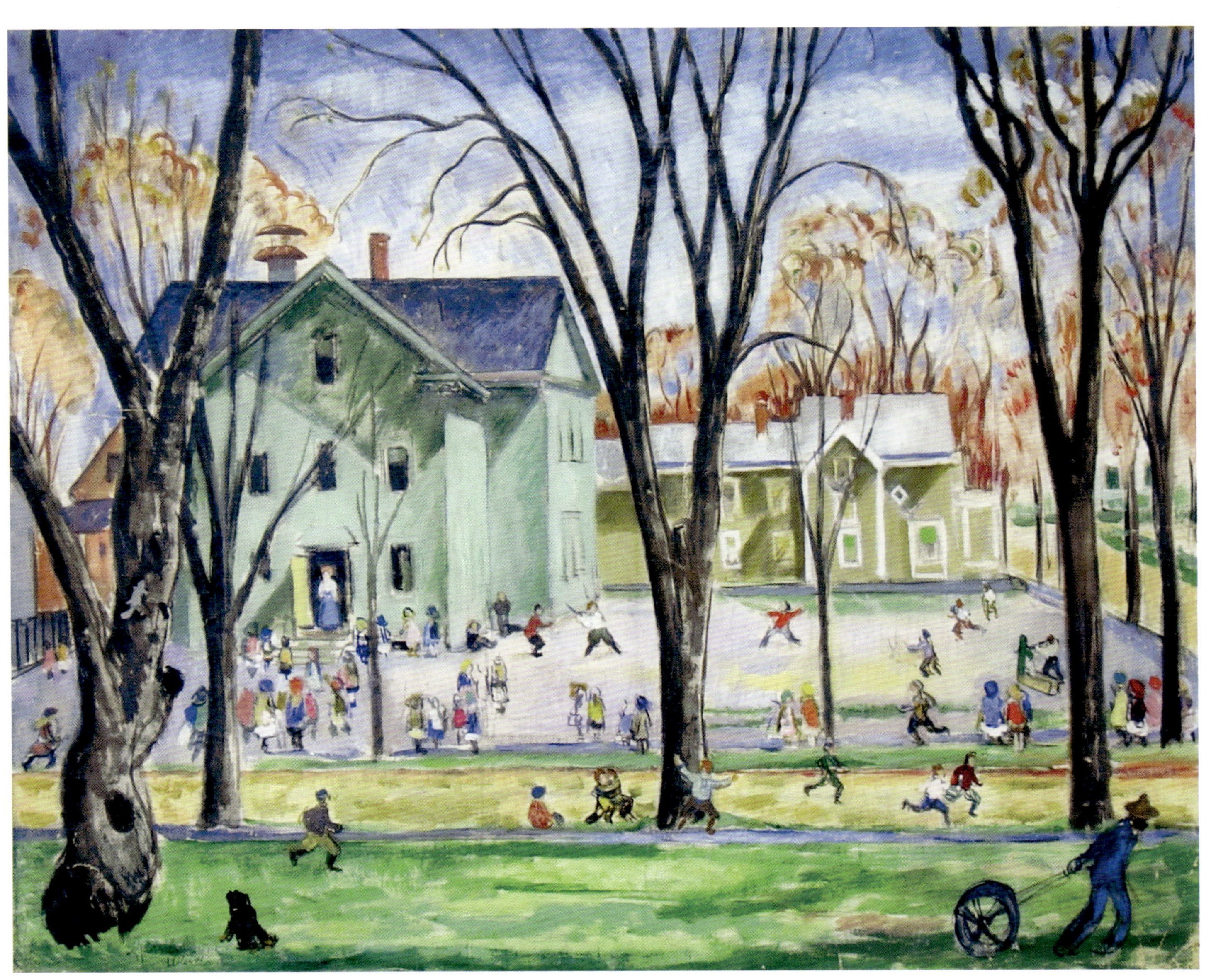

Waldo Peirce, *My First School,* 1934, oil on canvas, 28 x 36 in.
Collection of the University of Maine Museum of Art. Gift of the artist

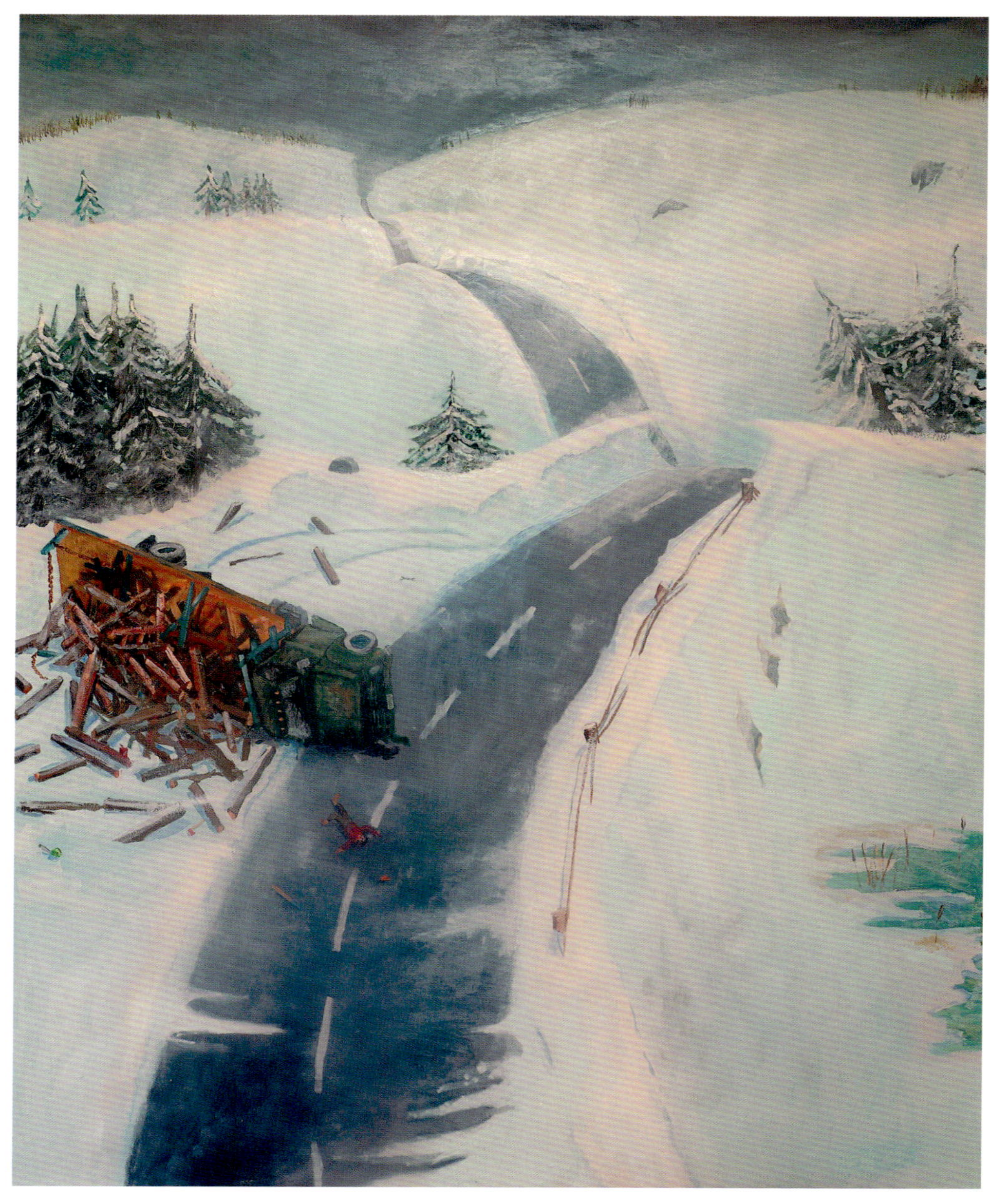

Edward Nadeau, *The Airline,* 1985, oil on canvas, 70 x 59 in., collection of the artist

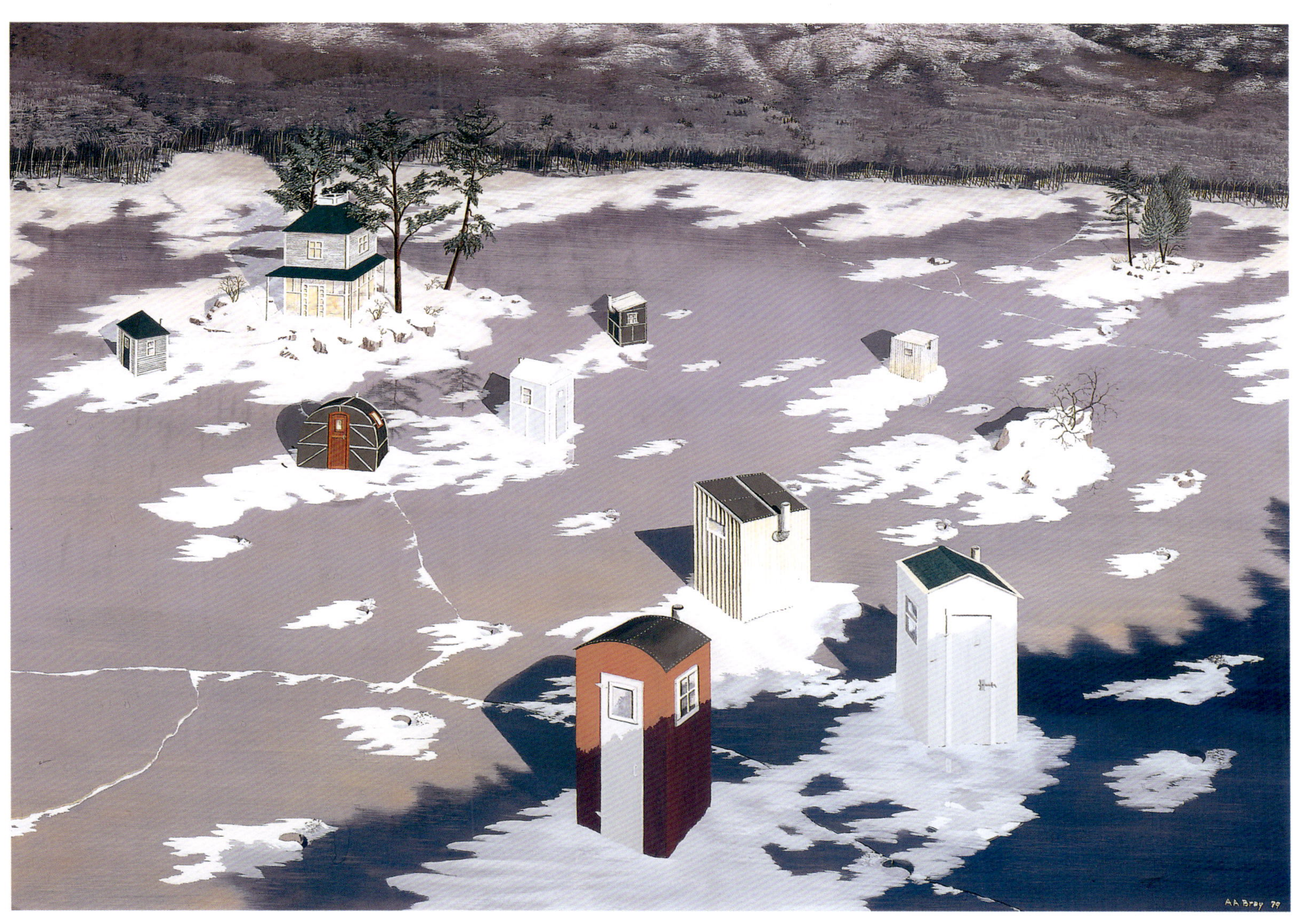

Alan Bray, *Fish Houses,* 1979, casein on panel, 24 x 32 in.
Private collection; photograph courtesy Barridoff Galleries, Portland, Maine

I know people who have a kind of snow phobia; they panic when they learn of approaching storms; they complain when the first flake falls; they sigh every time they must pick up a shovel to clear a path. For them, I feel real sorrow. They are missing the most of Maine's winters. If they are so preoccupied with snow's inconvenience, they never notice its beauty. Yet that beauty is incredible, more of a transformation than spring's first fragile green, more powerful than the lush crest of summer, more striking than autumn's frosty colors.

—JOHN COLE, *IN MAINE,* 1974

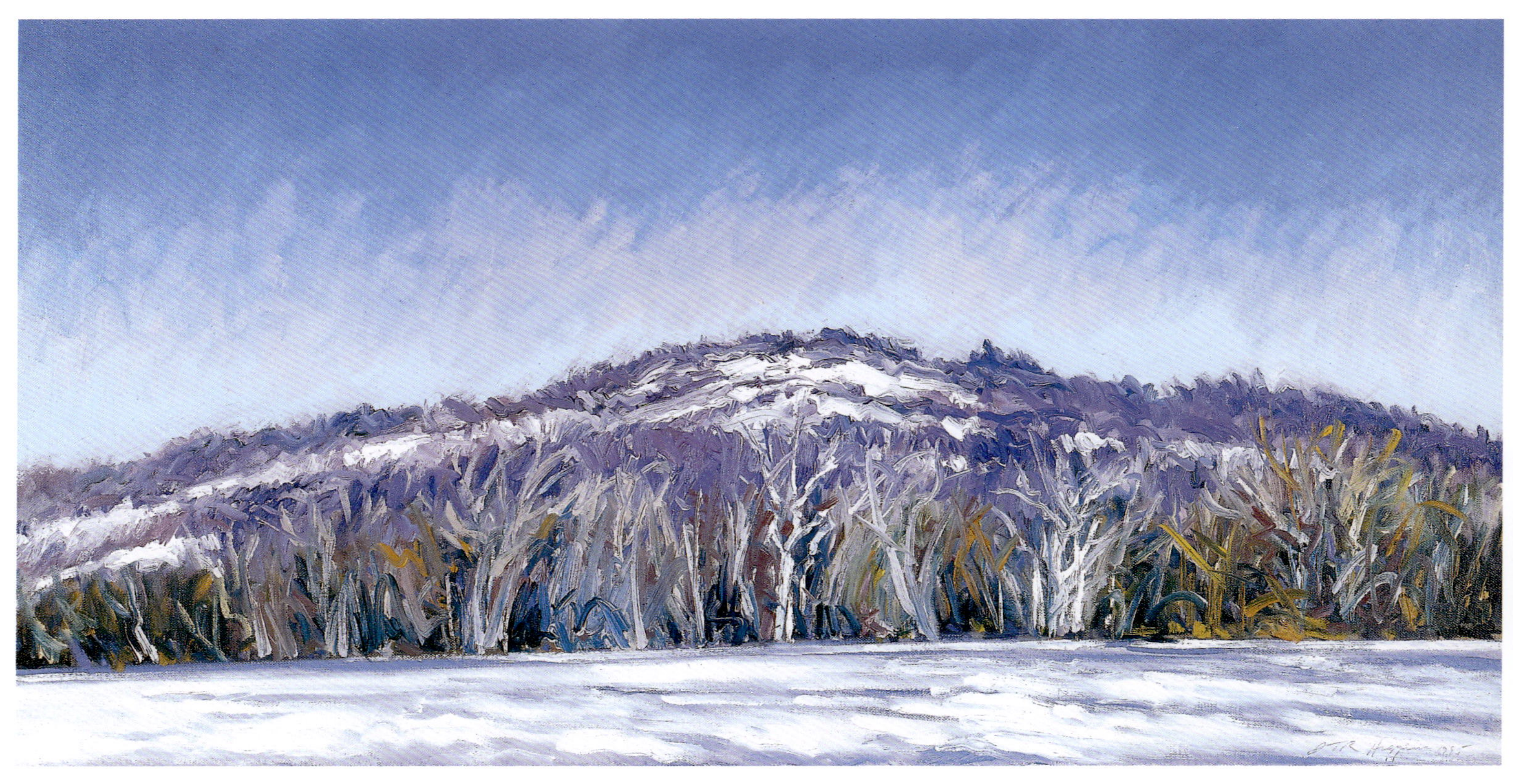

J. Thomas R. Higgins, *Vienna Mountain in Snow,* 1995, oil on linen, 20 x 40 in., collection of the artist

Farms, it seems to me, are the closest analogue to the Creation we have. All our mythologies tell us that God or the gods made an ordered universe from incomprehensible chaos. Equipped with less than divine powers, we make smaller ordered universes out of the vast, teeming complexity of nature. . . . A farm is in nature and of nature but contrary to nature; it is our small gear that meshes with the greater one of creation. We have some influence, though hardly complete control, over the part of creation we have staked out as our own; but if we hold up our end of the bargain, if we stick by the land and keep our little wheel rolling, God (or the gods) will keep the big one turning, too.

—Robert Kimber, "A Slipping-Down Farm"

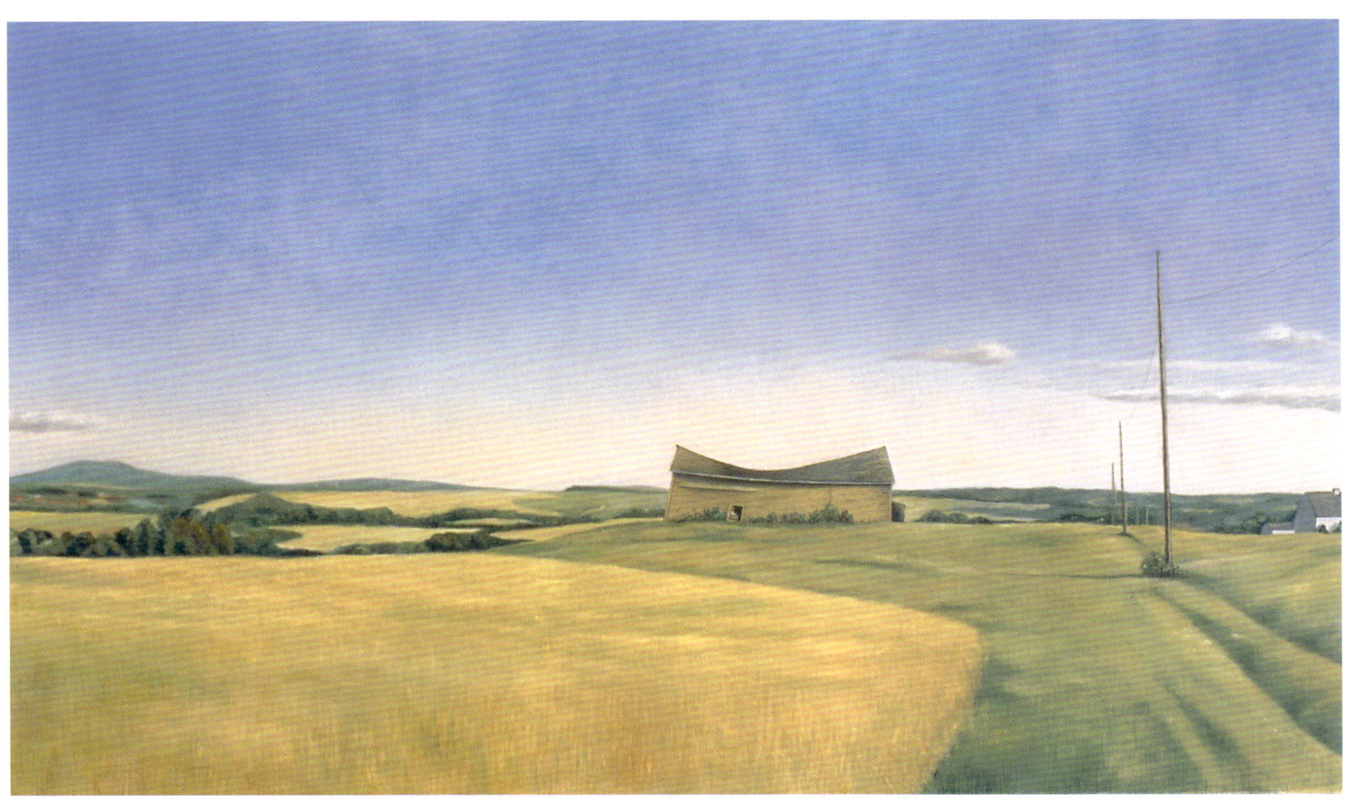

Antonia Munroe, *View from the Caribou Road,* 2002, oil on linen, 28 x 48 in.; photograph courtesy Caldbeck Gallery

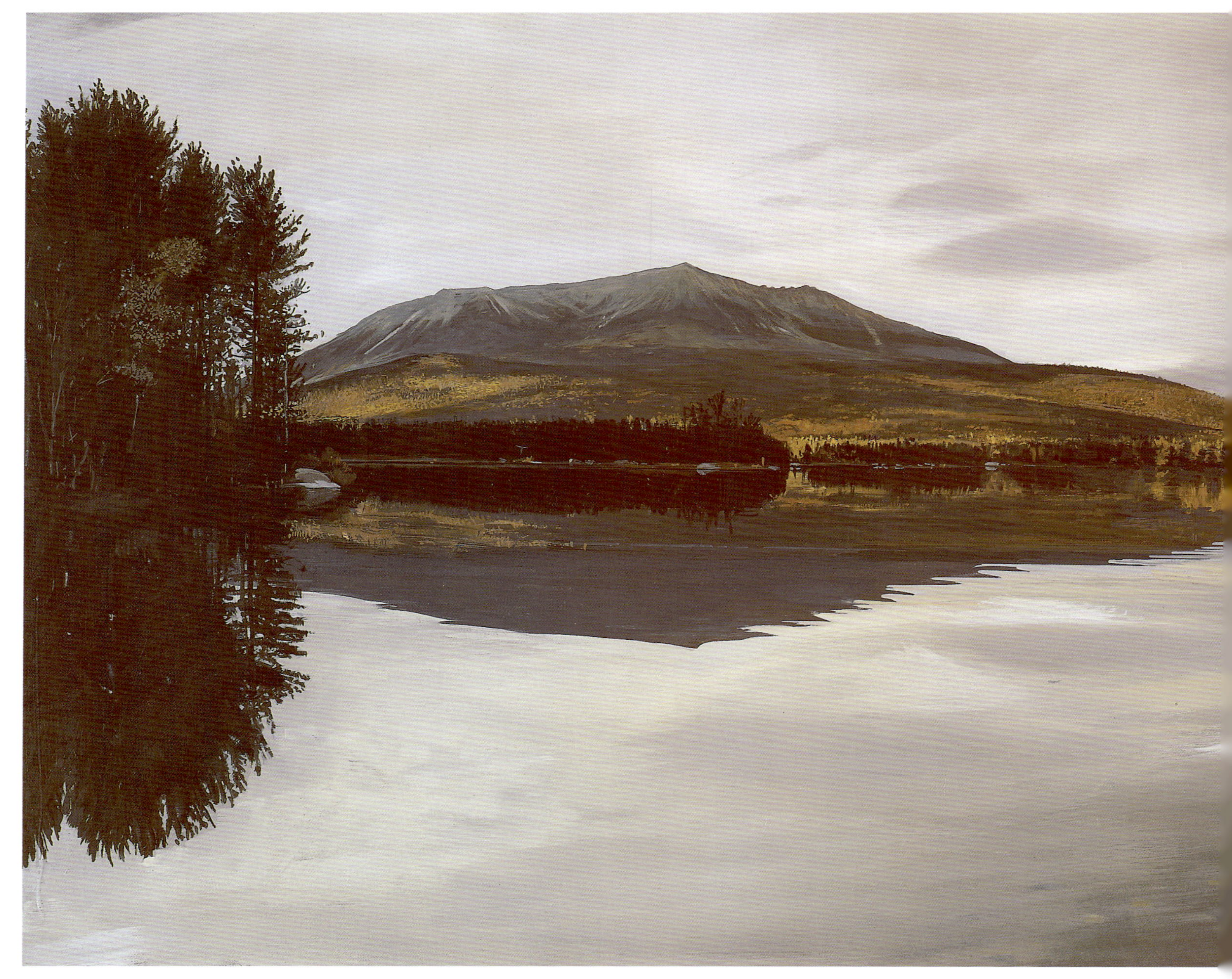

 Richard Estes, *Mount Katahdin—Maine,* 2001, oil on canvas, 22 x 36 in., © Richard Estes, courtesy Marlborough Gallery, New York

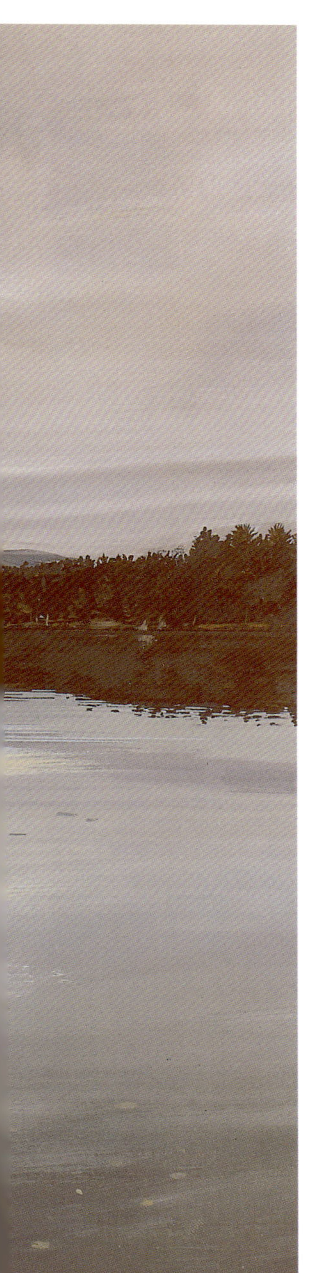

A phrase that park director Buzz Caverly uses a lot is "the magnets of Katahdin." Referring to the power the mountain holds over its devotees, drawing them back to it again and again. I know what he's talking about, but for me the magnets are not just of Katahdin but of Katahdinauguoh, *which Thoreau says is what the Indians called the whole territory around Katahdin. Governor Baxter must have felt this, too. He clearly perceived everything from Katahdin north to Webster Stream and Grand Lakes Matagamon as one place, a world of mountains, ponds, brooks, and streams that he thought it worth a lifetime of effort and anxiety to assemble and protect as an unbroken whole.*

—Robert Kimber, *"Coming to Rest on Katahdin"*

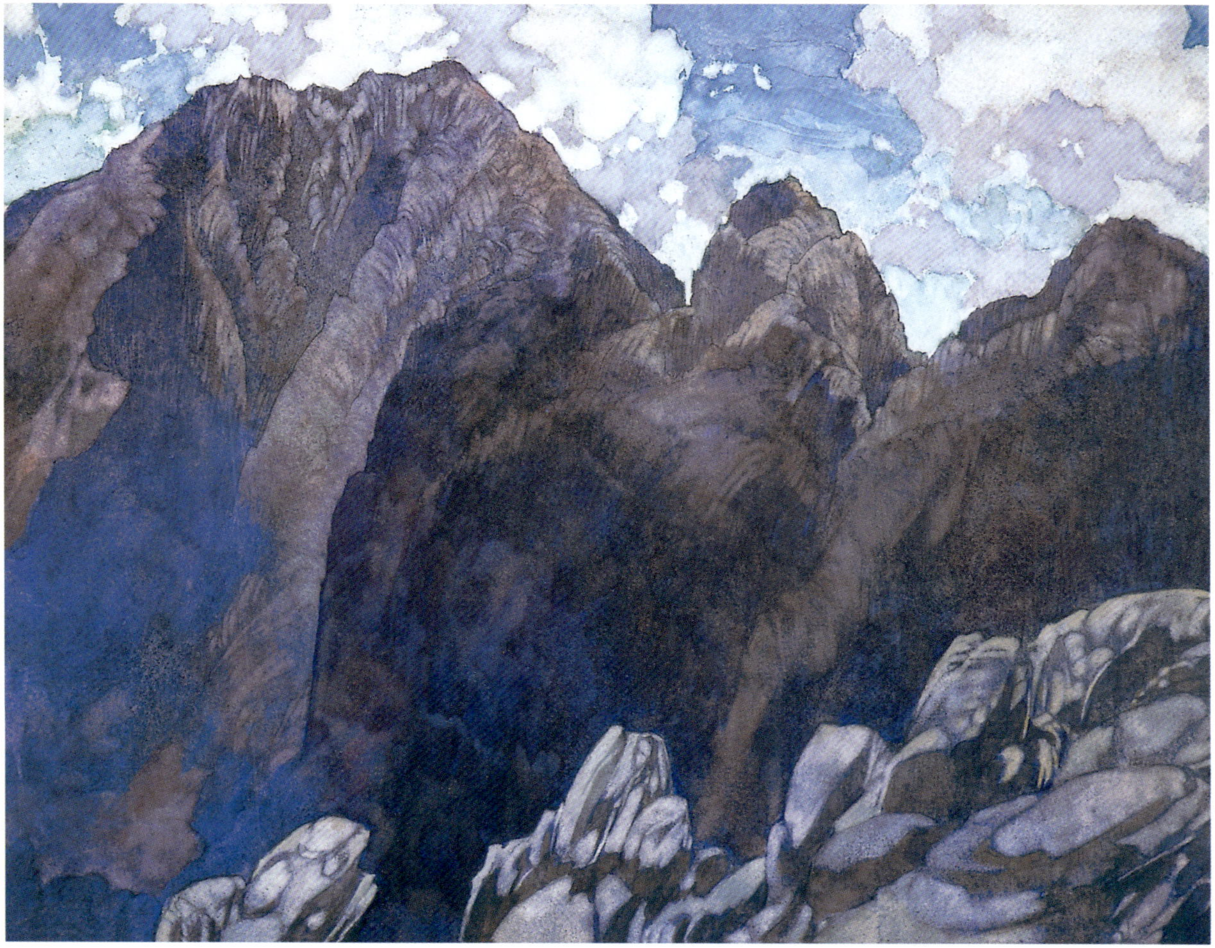

George Hallowell, *Knife Edge at Katahdin,* n.d., watercolor on paper, 10 x 13 in., private collection

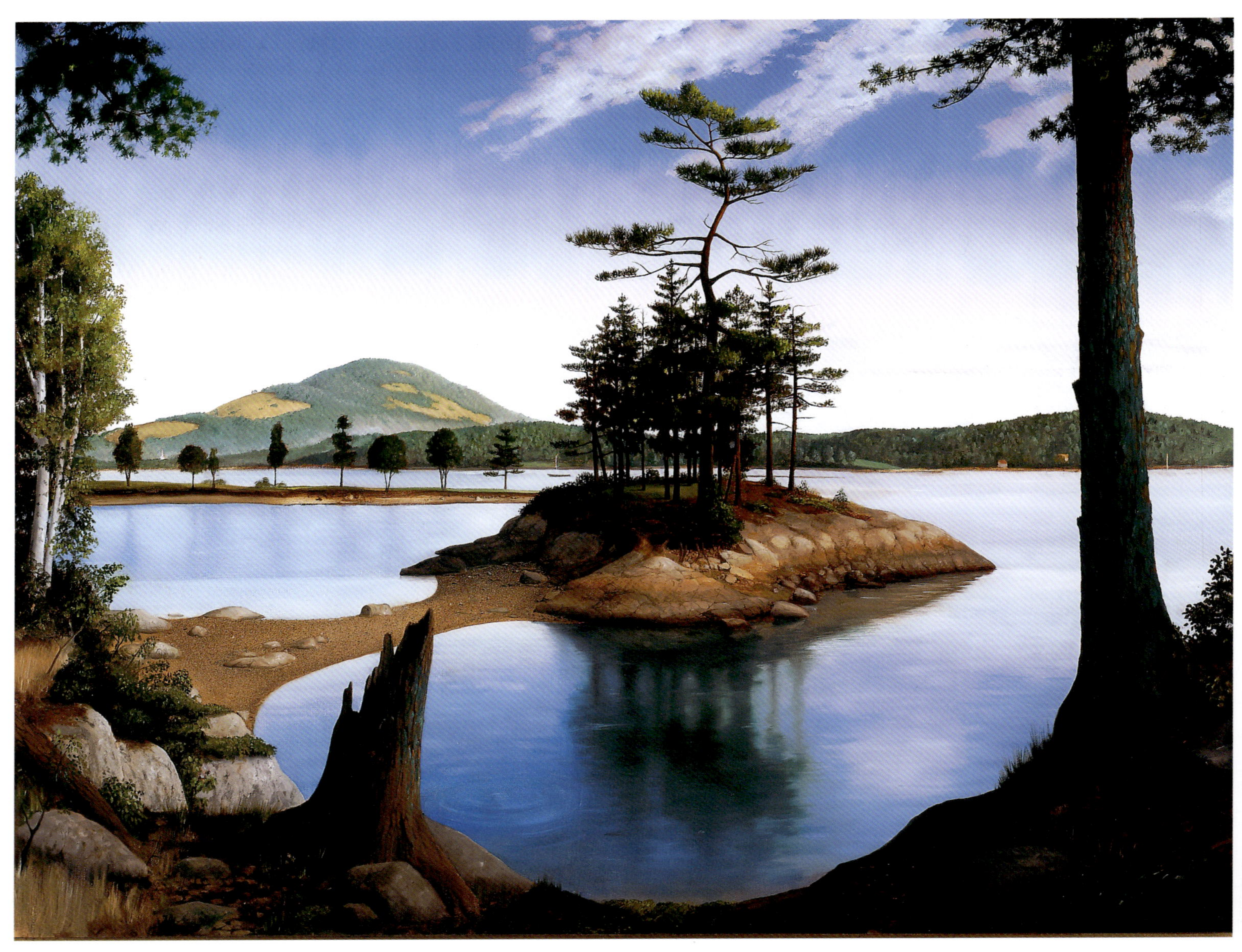

James Aponovich, *View of Blue Hill, Maine,* 2005, oil on canvas, 36 x 48 in.
Photograph courtesy Hackett-Freedman Gallery, San Francisco

A Stretch of Maine Coast

The general impression which the sight of the country left with us is . . . in favor of the province of Maine. One can only augur well of a great province, which combines healthfulness and fertility, whose whole coast is one vast harbor of the sea, which is watered by rivers, lakes, ponds, creeks, and streams in abundance according to the most fortunate distribution.

—Charles Maurice de Talleyrand, 1794

Where Maine's midcoast begins and where it ends depends on where you're standing and with whom you're speaking. The local chamber of commerce may have a different perspective from a sailor cruising the coast or a fisheries manager plotting quadrants.

Robert Henri (1865–1929) was not concerned about questions of demarcation. He was glad to be away from New York City, where he lived and taught, visiting the coast he first fell in love with in 1903. In a study of Boothbay Harbor on an overcast day, Henri practiced the dynamic brushwork he preached to the likes of Rockwell Kent and George Bellows, bringing the landscape to life: fish houses on the rocky shore, a line of dark trees, a blustery sky.

A landscape painter from western New York State who emulated Charles Burchfield's watercolor style, Robert N. Blair (1912–2003) made extended excursions in New England, his watercolors at the ready. The Maine coast was a favorite subject of his over the years. In a painting of sailboats on a swirling sea, a sliver of land with sentinel fir trees is just visible against a weather-filled sky.

In 1966—the year she became an American citizen—

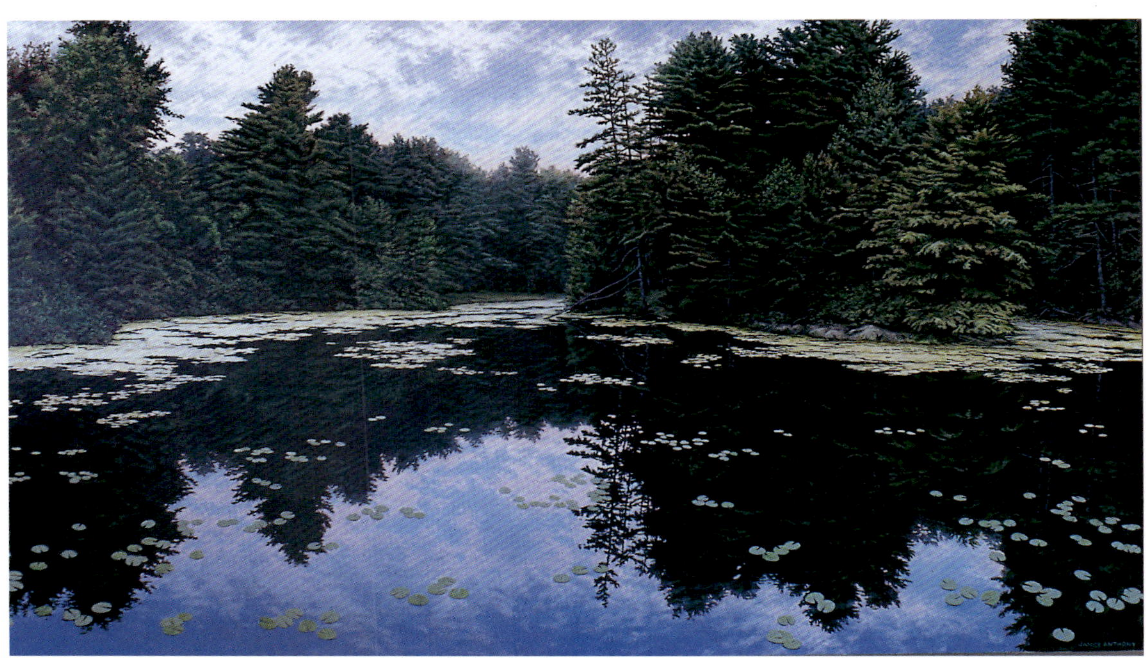

Janice Anthony, *Damariscotta Lake,* 2002, acrylic on linen, 25 x 45 in.
Collection of Mary Lou and Ralph Lancaster

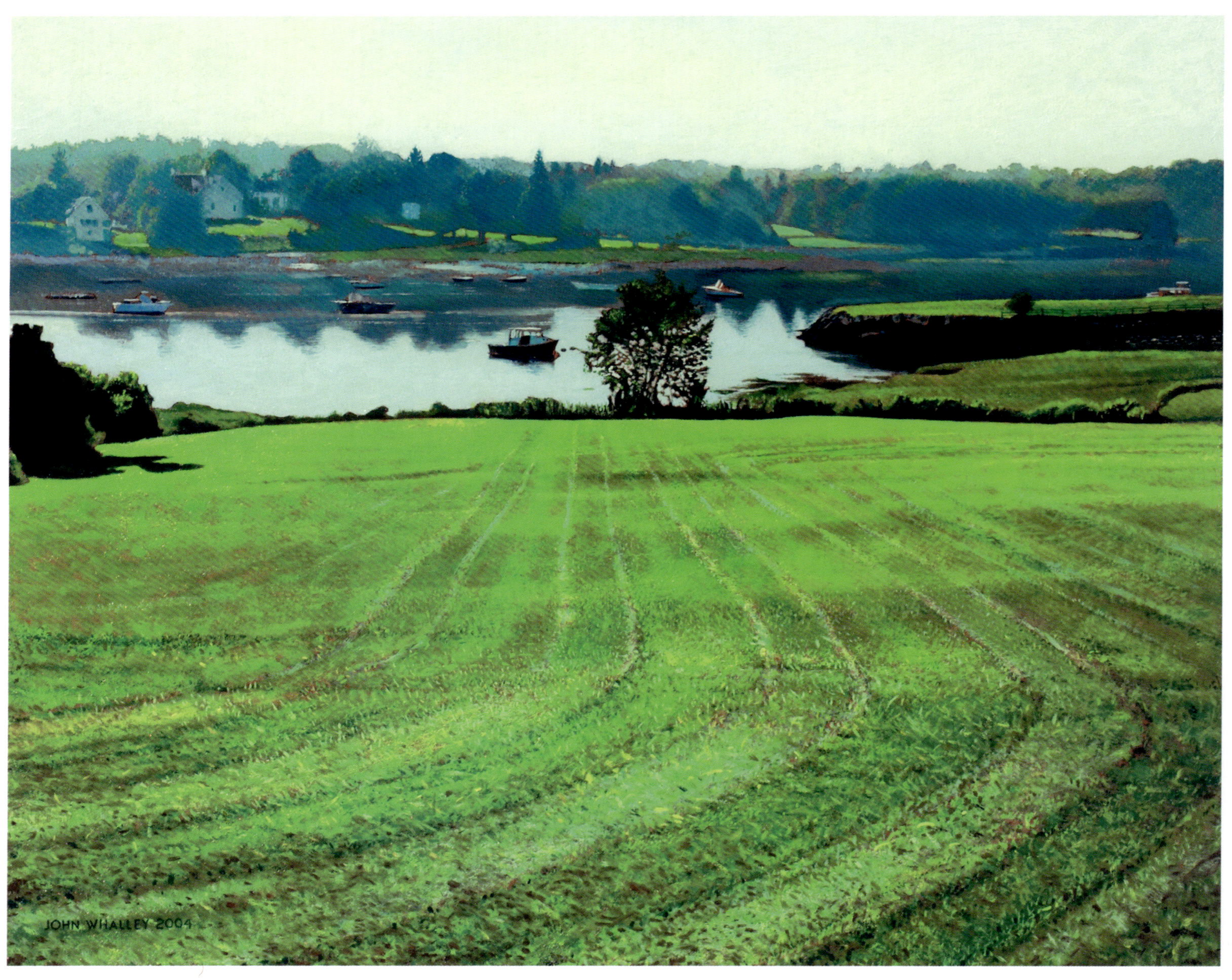

John Whalley, *Damariscotta Harbor,* 2004, oil on panel, 13 7/8 x 17 5/8 in., courtesy Spanierman Gallery, New York

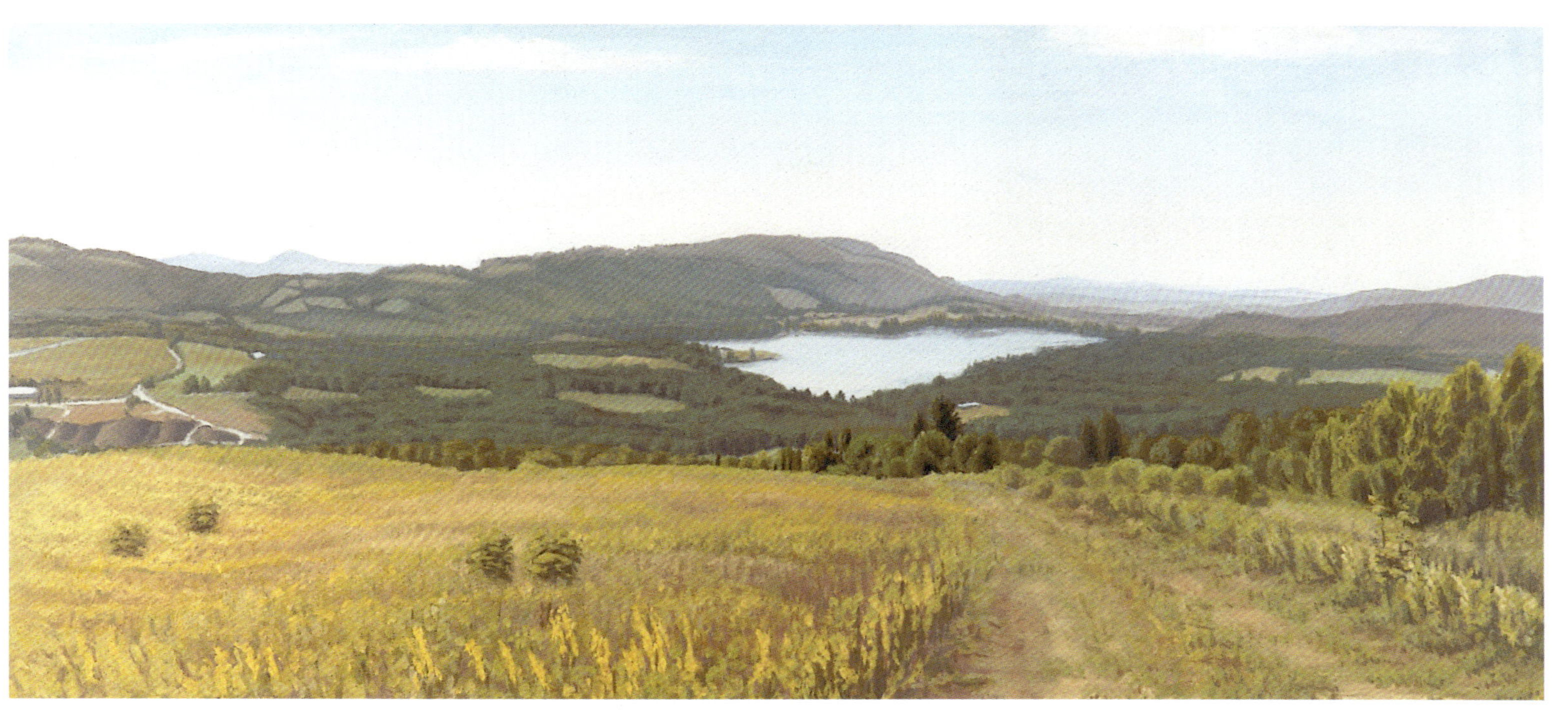

British-born painter Brenda Bettinson (b. 1929) purchased property on Rocky Point on Barter's Island near Boothbay. She eventually built a cottage and later, in 1989, became a year-rounder. Her portrait of an island church is a study of Maine architecture and Maine light (she once described the latter as purer and clearer than any she had seen in her travels).

South Bristol is one of those charming end-of-peninsula towns that attract painters in search of the picturesque. Philip Frey (b. 1967) renders a bold curve in the road with a palette to match: brash and bright. Raised in Ellsworth and now living in Sullivan, Frey is dedicated to painting Maine, be it mighty Mount Katahdin or Cleonice, a restaurant in his hometown.

Janice Anthony (b. 1946) from Jackson is also committed to Maine, seeking out the unsullied corners of the state. In her painting of Damariscotta Lake—the centerpiece of a seventeen-acre state park in Jefferson—she presents a sheltered stretch, where lily pads accent the reflections of thick trees. "I am delighted when I find a place that is perfect in its wholeness, clearly a world apart," Anthony has written.

A resident of Damariscotta, John Whalley (b. 1954) is known for his remarkable realist paintings of diverse objects: crab claw, trowels, chalk line. He is also drawn to the Maine landscape, as witnessed by a view of Damariscotta Harbor, in which tractor tracks in a newly mown field lead the eye to still water, boats and houses shimmering in a midsummer haze.

Marjorie Portnow, *Appleton Ridge, Maine,* c. 1981, oil on board, 12 x 20 in., private collection

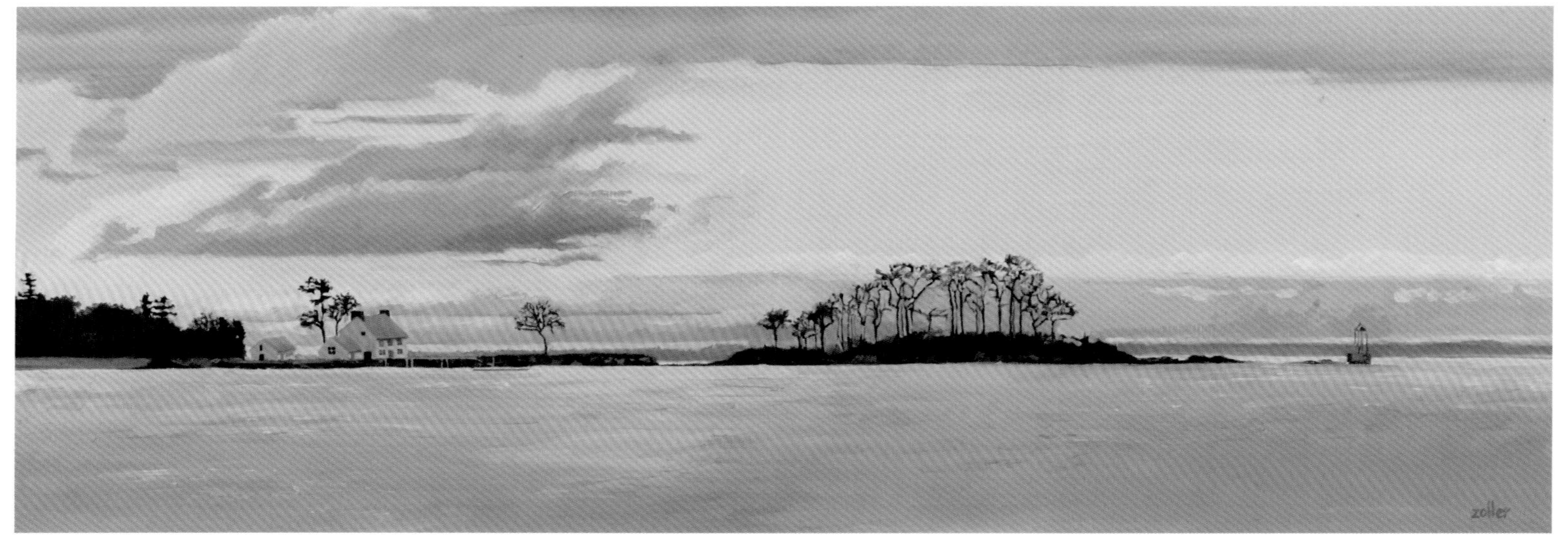

A coastal motif also lured Frederic Kellogg (b. 1942) to his easel. In a painting of Thomaston Harbor, broad floats are pulled up onto land; boathouses face the water along the far shore. Kellogg's childhood summers were spent on Islesboro, where his father served as Episcopal minister and taught him drawing and watercolor. Today the painter divides his time between Washington, D.C., and Thomaston.

Cushing has been Lois Dodd's home away from home for more than fifty extended summer seasons. Every year Dodd (b. 1927) makes the trek from New York City to paint her coastal surroundings. Figures in the landscape, floral motifs (Leslie Land, the esteemed garden writer, is a neighbor) and local quarries are subjects Dodd returns to, bringing a painterly approach to each. "Maine is a simpatico place for artists," she states. "The kind of office hour rush thing just disappears into the background, and you're in another world where people all work independently, or a lot of them do."

On a visit to the coast in 1916, George Bellows; his wife, Emma; their daughter Anne; and fellow painter Leon Kroll barely avoided tragedy when they were caught in a rain squall while rowing across Camden Harbor. Bellows (1882–1925) turned the incident into one of his most dramatic canvases, "an epic of terrific nature," he called it, in which he attempted to express "the fear of it all."

More beneficent conditions prevail in Elise du Pont Zoller's image of Sherman's Point, a distinctive landmark for sailors heading out of Camden. "Maine sky and water have a particular fascination for me," Zoller (b. 1958) notes.

Elise du Pont Zoller, *Leaving Camden,* 2005, oil on board, 10 x 28 in., private collection

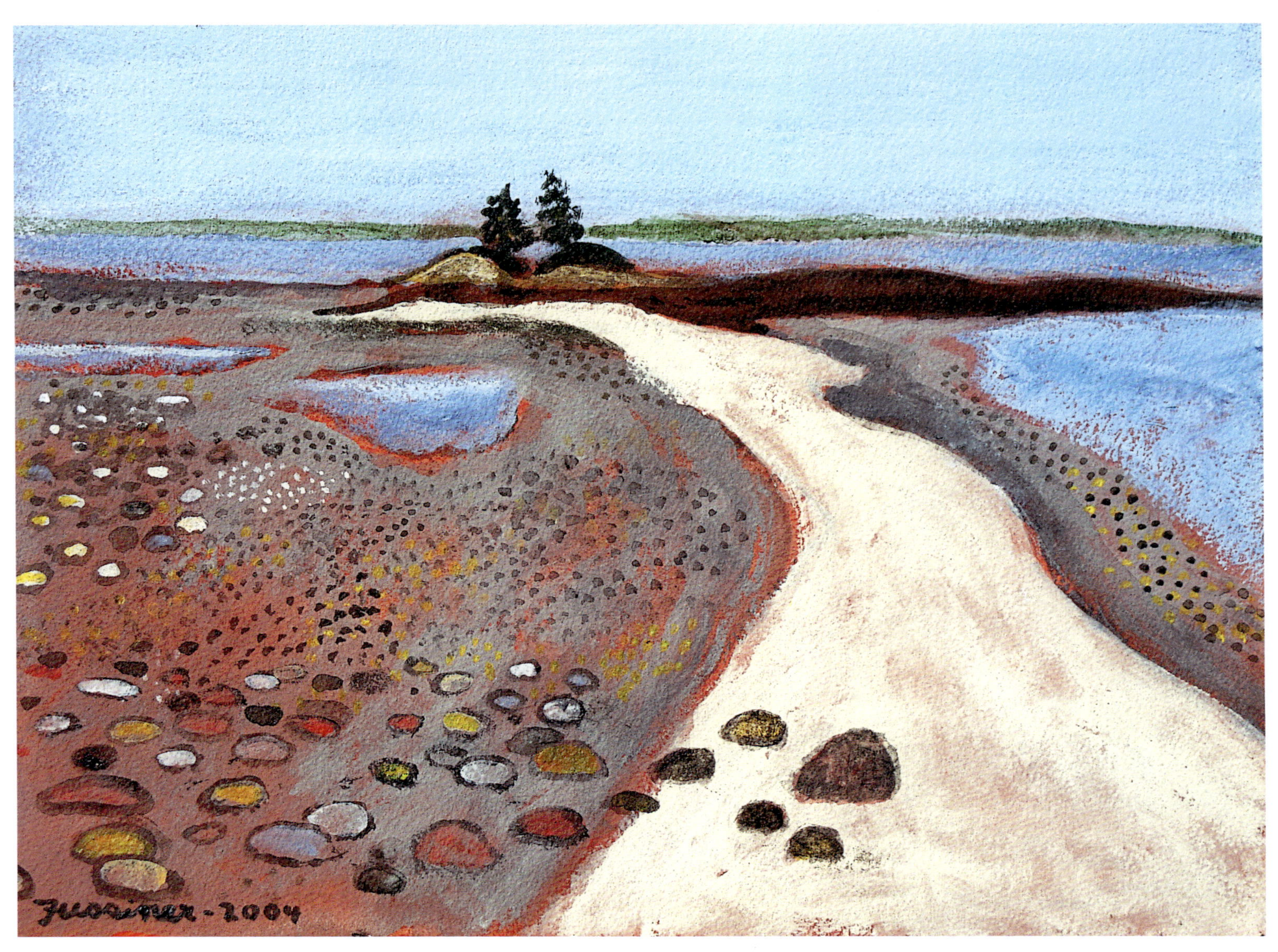

Howard Fussiner, *Flye Point, Brooklin, Maine,* 2004, acrylic on paper, 12 x 16 1/4 in., collection of Dr. and Mrs. Stanley Schwartz

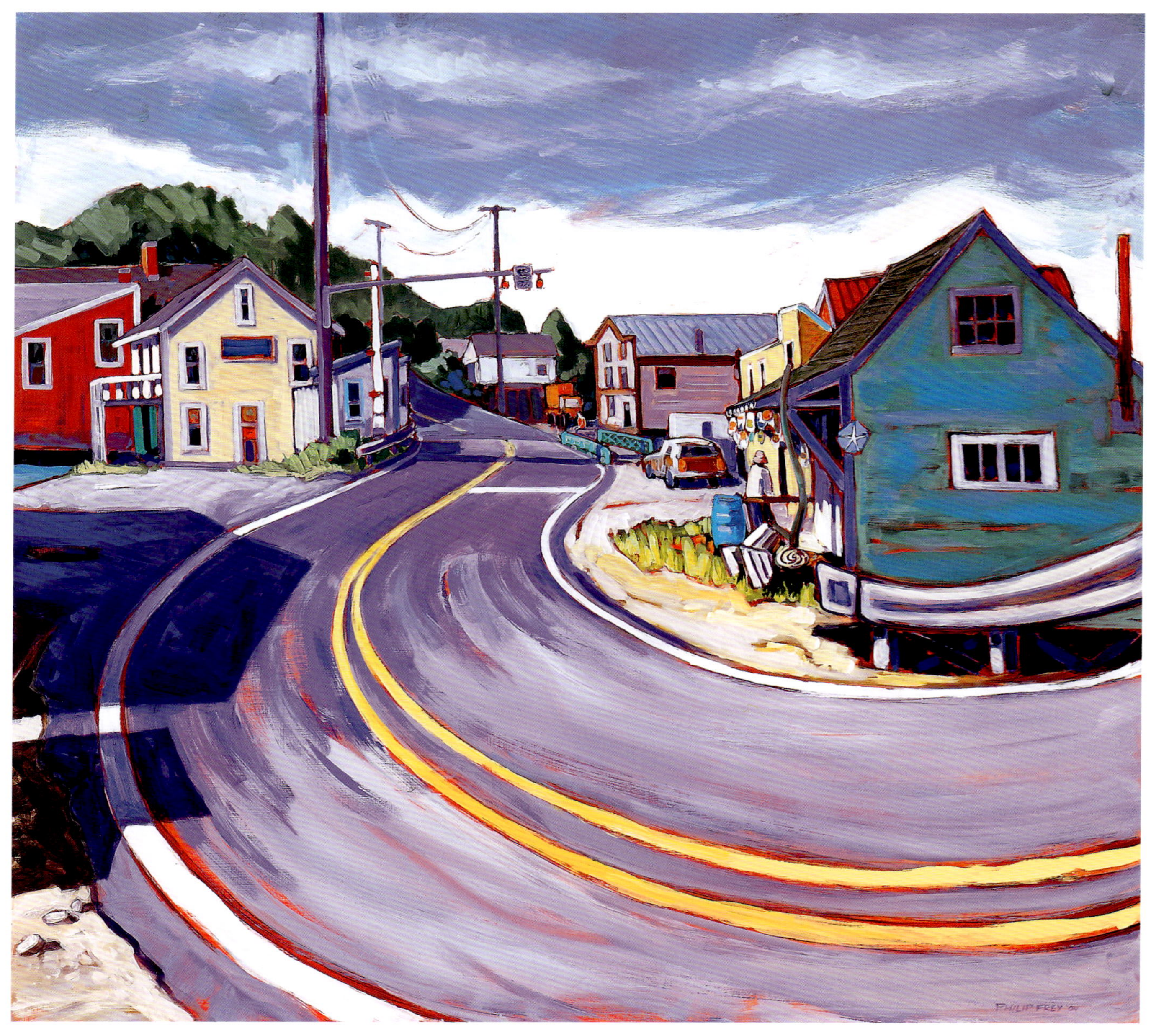

 Philip Frey, *South Bristol Village,* 2005, acrylic on luan panel, 48 x 54 in., collection of the artist

From Westwood, Massachusetts, the painter maintains seasonal ties to the coast.

Another occasional visitor inspired by the Maine coast is Marjorie Portnow (b. 1943). The New York City–based painter has stated her preference for places "with large, panoramic, unobstructed views, without development, houses or people." Portnow found just such an expansive view on Appleton Ridge, slightly inland from Camden.

Founded in 1936, the Camden Snow Bowl is a favorite destination for winter outings (and the site of the U.S. National Toboggan Championships). Richard Saltonstall (b. 1960), who lives year-round in nearby Rockport, provides a fast-and-loose rendering of the resort's carved trails and single ski lift, which mark Ragged Mountain.

A master of the aerial perspective, Yvonne Jacquette (b. 1934) has painted around the world, from the upper floors of the World Trade Center to the skies of Maine (she set down seasonal roots in Searsmont in the 1950s). Her Belfast Harbor nocturne is an engaging arrangement of streets, cars, buildings and boats, rendered in her neo-Pointillist style.

Ships of quite another age fill the harbor in Mary Blood Mellen's moonlit view of Castine. Originally from Sterling, Massachusetts, Mellen (1817–1882) moved to Gloucester in 1840, where she studied with Fitz Henry Lane and served as his assistant (she is known to have finished a number of his paintings). Mellen shared Lane's passion for the New England coast, including historic Castine.

A 2001 transplant to the Maine coast (from southern Indiana), Nancy Morgan-Barnes (b. 1948) has wasted no time exploring all manner of motifs, from a gas station on Deer Isle to a lobstermen's boxing club in Searsport. An impressive feat of civil engineering, the new bridge over the Penobscot River between Prospect and Verona Island (and between Waldo and Hancock counties) caught her eye, its cranes leaning into the sky.

From the bridge's observation tower, there's a clear view of the paper mill in nearby Bucksport. Philadelphian Paul Rickert (b. 1947), whose base in Maine is Brooksville, brings out the beauty of this industrial site, its glowing lights and drifting smoke evidence of a humming complex. "A lot of painters come [to Maine] and they go deep in the woods and paint trees," Rickert once stated. "I like to show man's involvement with his surroundings."

James Aponovich (b. 1948) is drawn to the Italian painters of the early Renaissance, who had "a marvelous sense of discovery," and to early American primitive painters, whose works display "a clarity, a simplicity, a sincerity . . . that is just breathtaking." Qualities of both can be found in his stunning view of Blue Hill.

Blue Hill is one of many towns along the coast that celebrate July 4 with a fireworks display, which can be viewed by sailors anchored along the coast. Francis Hamabe (1917–2002), a longtime resident of East Blue Hill, drew on both his graphic-art skills and his fertile imagination to create a painting of this subject.

For more than forty years, Howard Fussiner (b. 1923) has been spending summers in Stonington, happy to trade his home in New Haven for the refreshing ambience of Deer Isle. He paints the town's Fourth of July parade each year as well as nearby landscapes, including Flye Point in Brooklin—site of an annual folk music festival.

Flye Point affords a fine view of a part of the Maine archipelago. Coastal inhabitants look out over the water, and many of them yearn to embark.

Maine Town

I like this town
that has been starched
and hung out to dry
with its crisp, square houses
and chalk white churches
billowing out in the brisk September wind!

I like this town
that has been scrubbed
and stands clean in the sun—
with its soapsud clouds,
and wrinkled white fences
that need not a bit of ironing.

—Dorothy Boone Kidney, *Reflections on Maine,* 1998

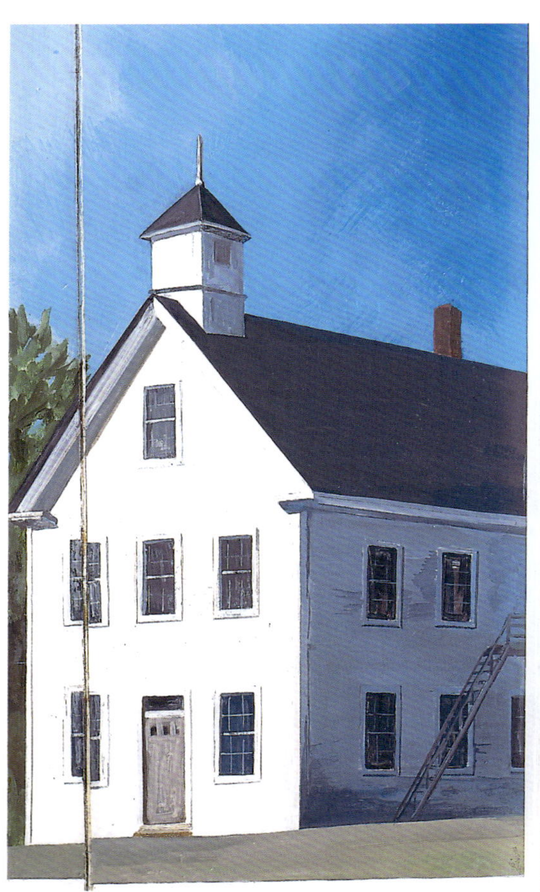

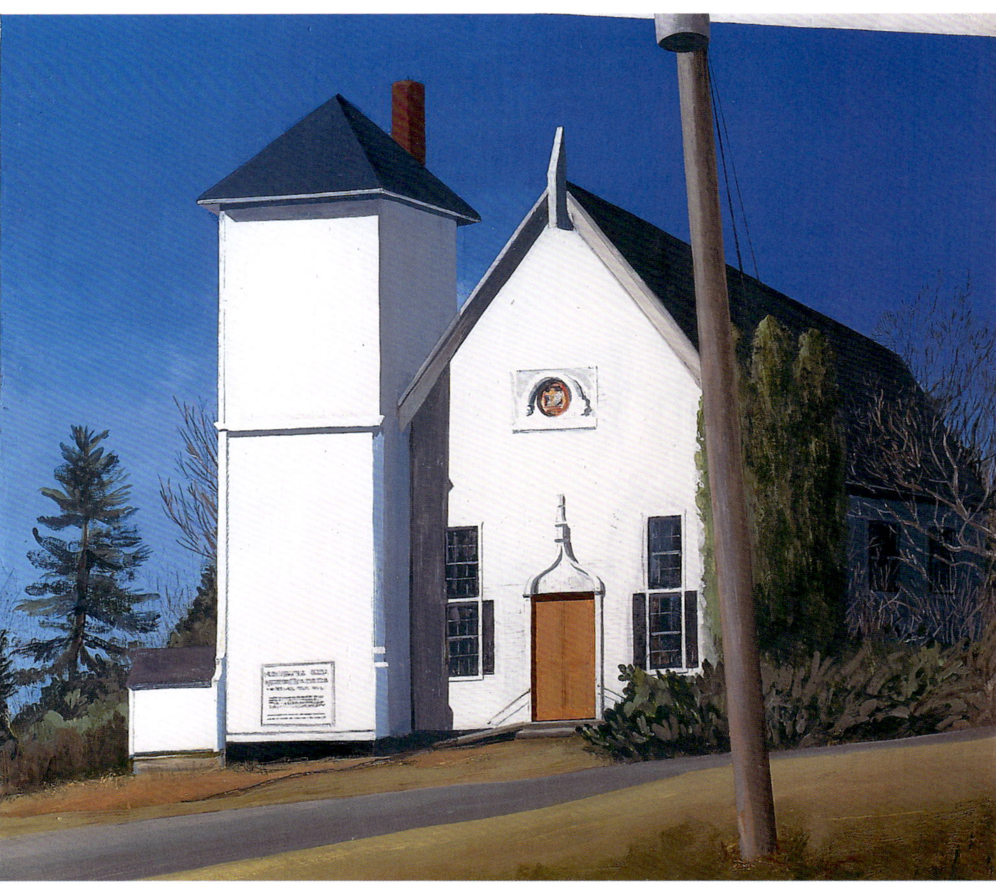

Brenda Bettinson, *Barter's Island Church,* 1995, acrylic on wood, 24 x 42 in.
Private collection; photograph courtesy Mathias Fine Art

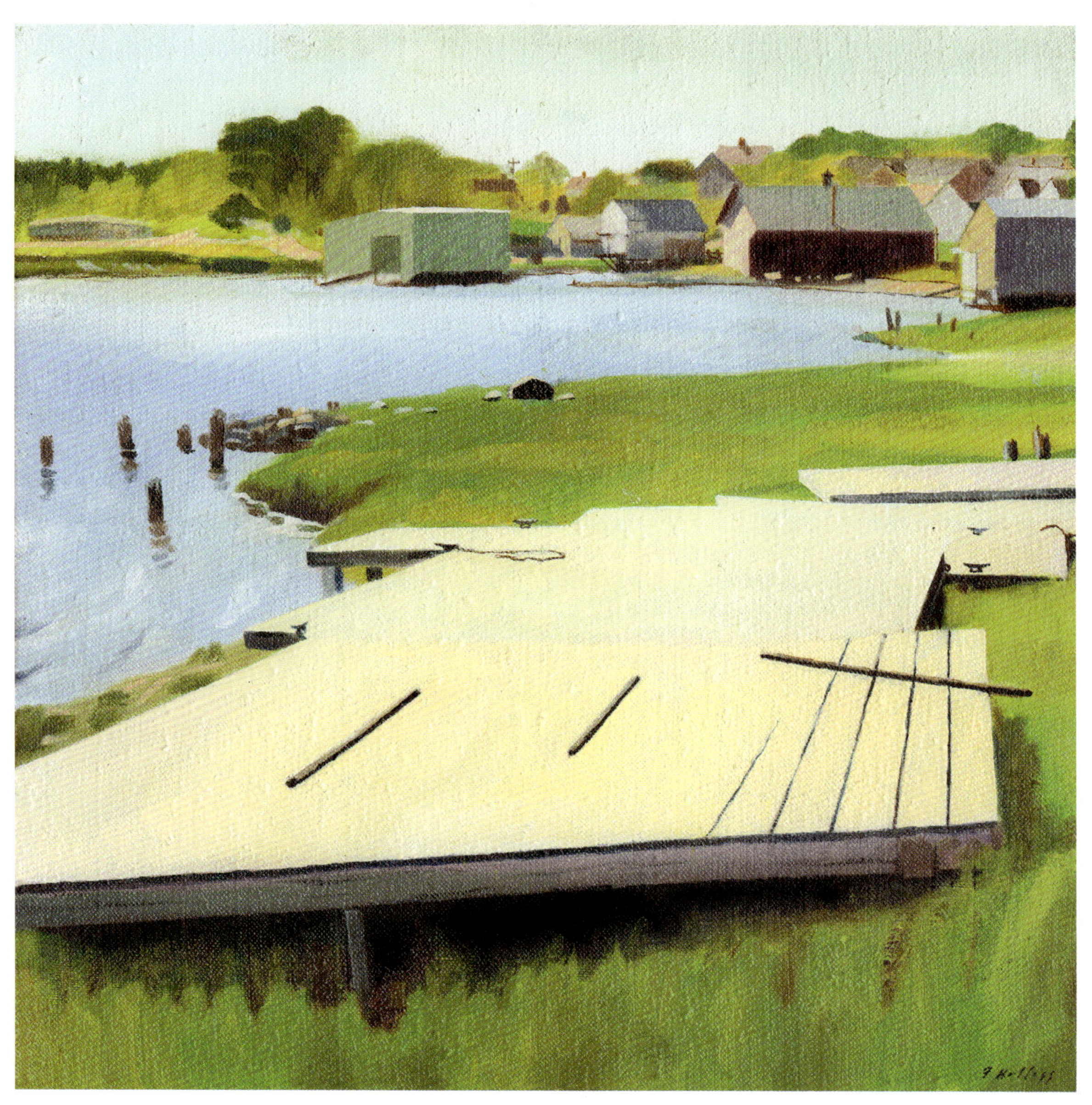

Frederic Kellogg, *Thomaston Harbor,* 2000, oil on linen, 14 x 14 in.
Collection of the artist; photograph courtesy Nan Mulford Gallery

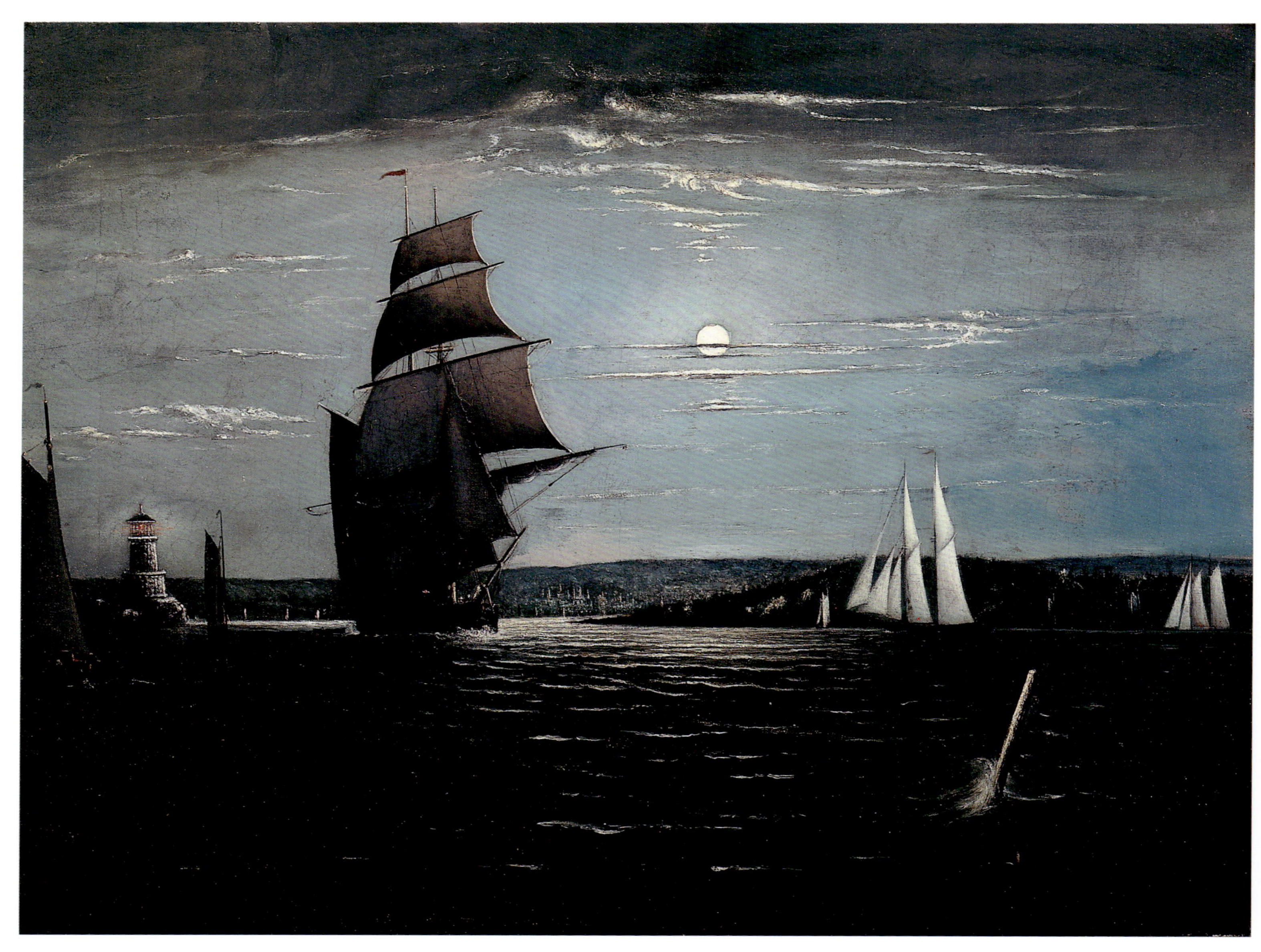

Mary Blood Mellen, *Castine Harbor,* n.d., oil on canvas, 14 x 26 in.
Private collection; photograph courtesy Barridoff Galleries, Portland, Maine

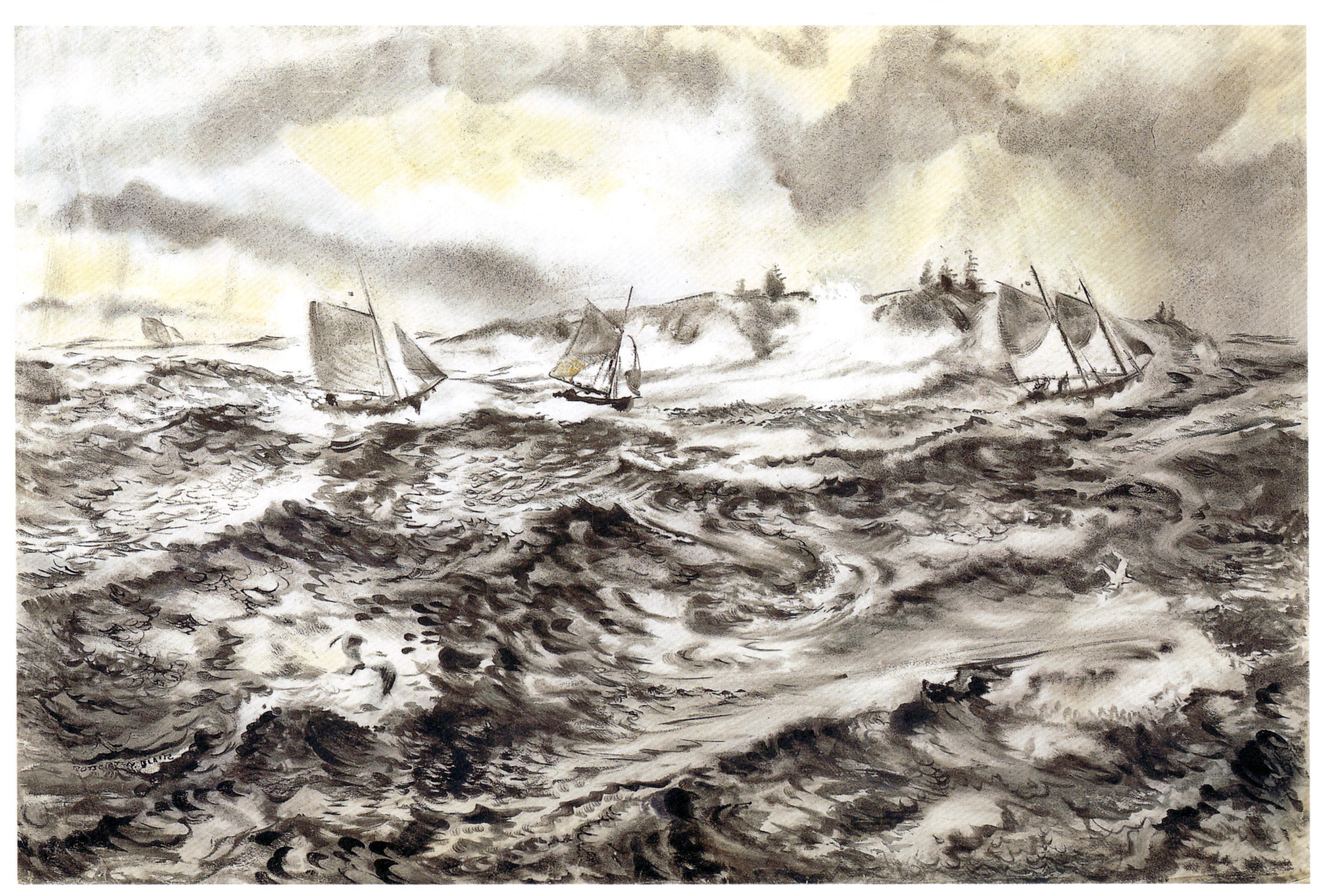

Robert N. Blair, *Silver Sea #2, Ocean Point, Maine,* 1946, watercolor on paper, 25 x 37 3/4 in., Eclectic Art & Objects Gallery

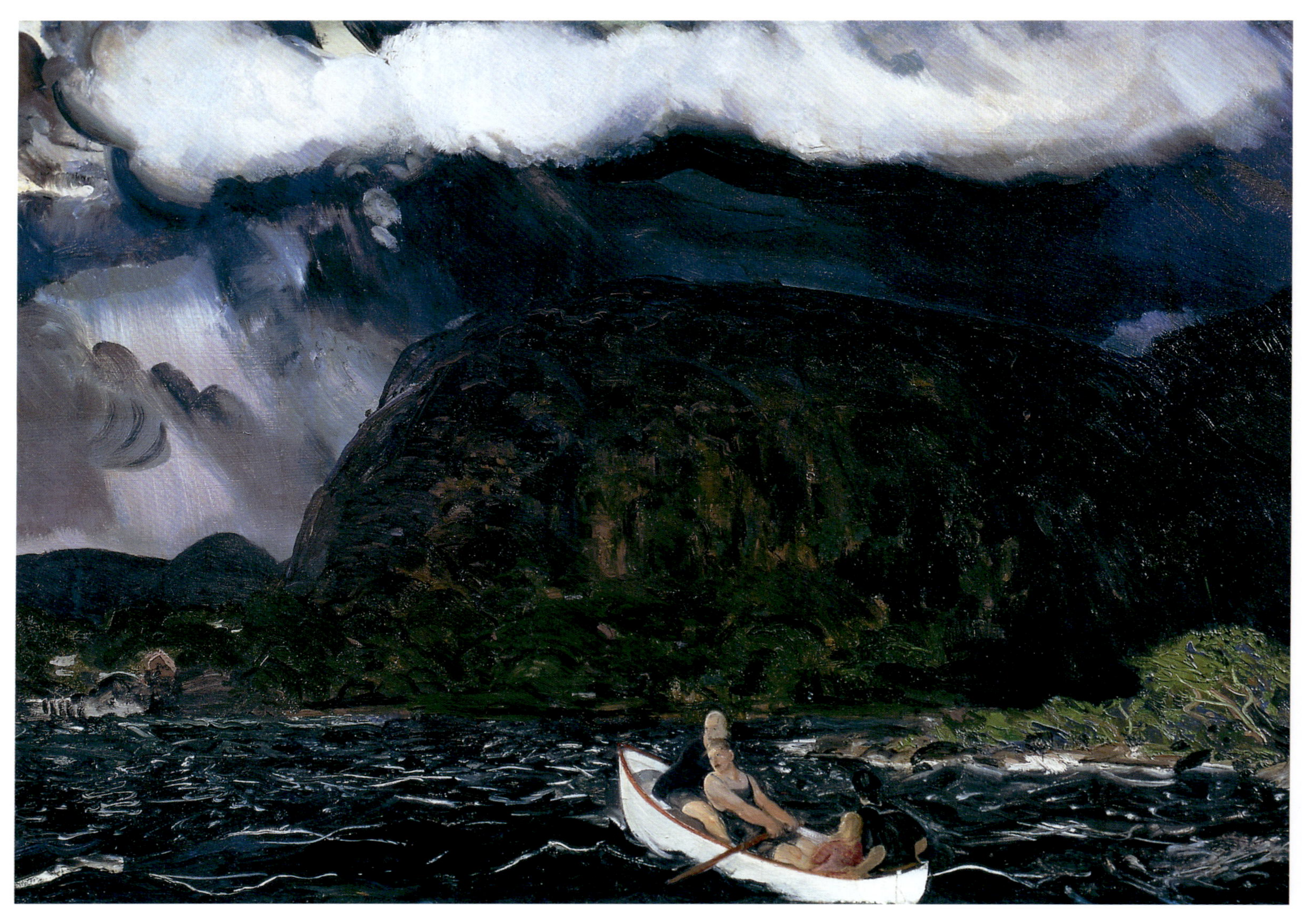

George Bellows, *In a Rowboat,* 1916, oil on canvas, 30 1/2 x 44 1/4 in. collection of the Montclair Art Museum, Montclair, New Jersey
Museum purchase; funds provided by Mr. and Mrs. H. St. John Webb, 1964. 37

The coast of Maine with its granite ledges, twisted spruces, crying sea birds and pounding surfs has something tough and grand and knife-edged about it. Great storms sweep in from the sea—three-day nor'easters, drenching line storms, real old lamb-killers and goose drownders—to be followed by spectacular clearings.

—LOUISE DICKINSON RICH, *STATE O' MAINE,* 1964

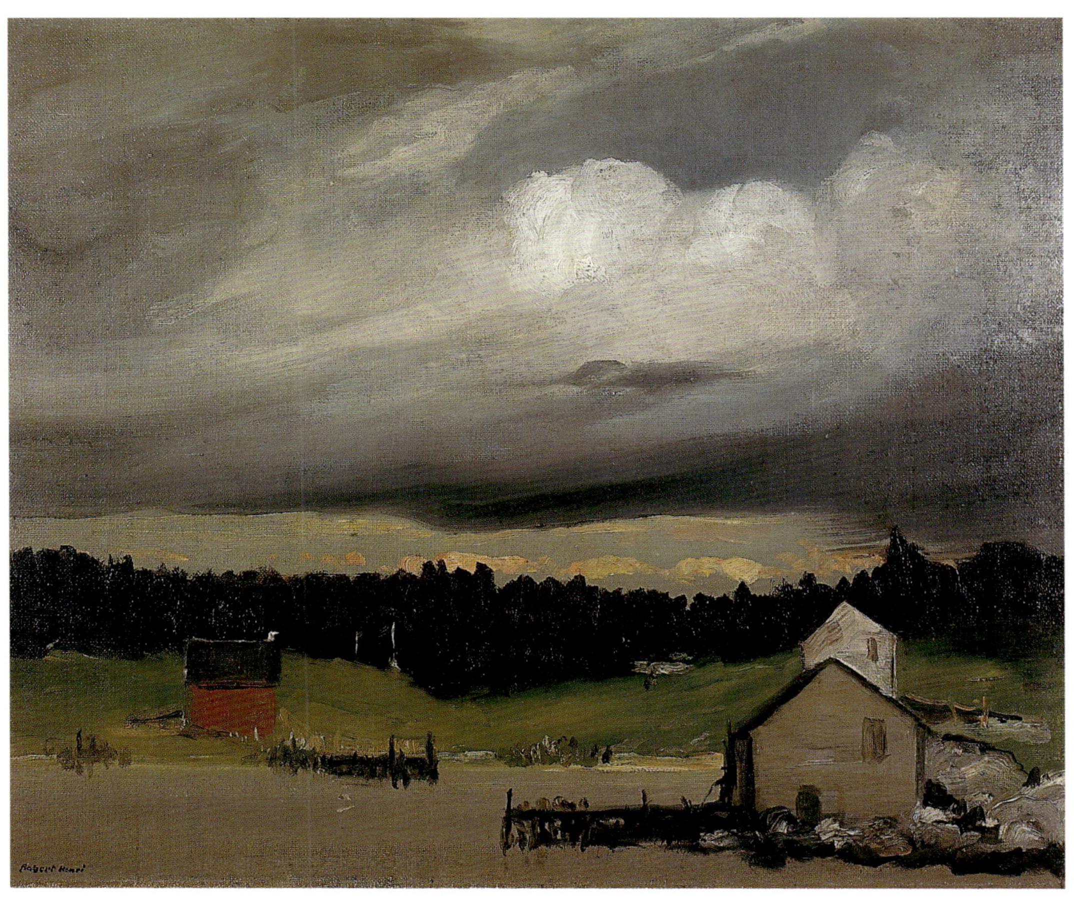

Robert Henri, *Boothbay Harbor,* 1910, oil on canvas, 26 x 32 in.
Sheldon Memorial Art Gallery and Sculpture Garden, University of Nebraska-Lincoln, UNL-Gift of Olga N. Sheldon

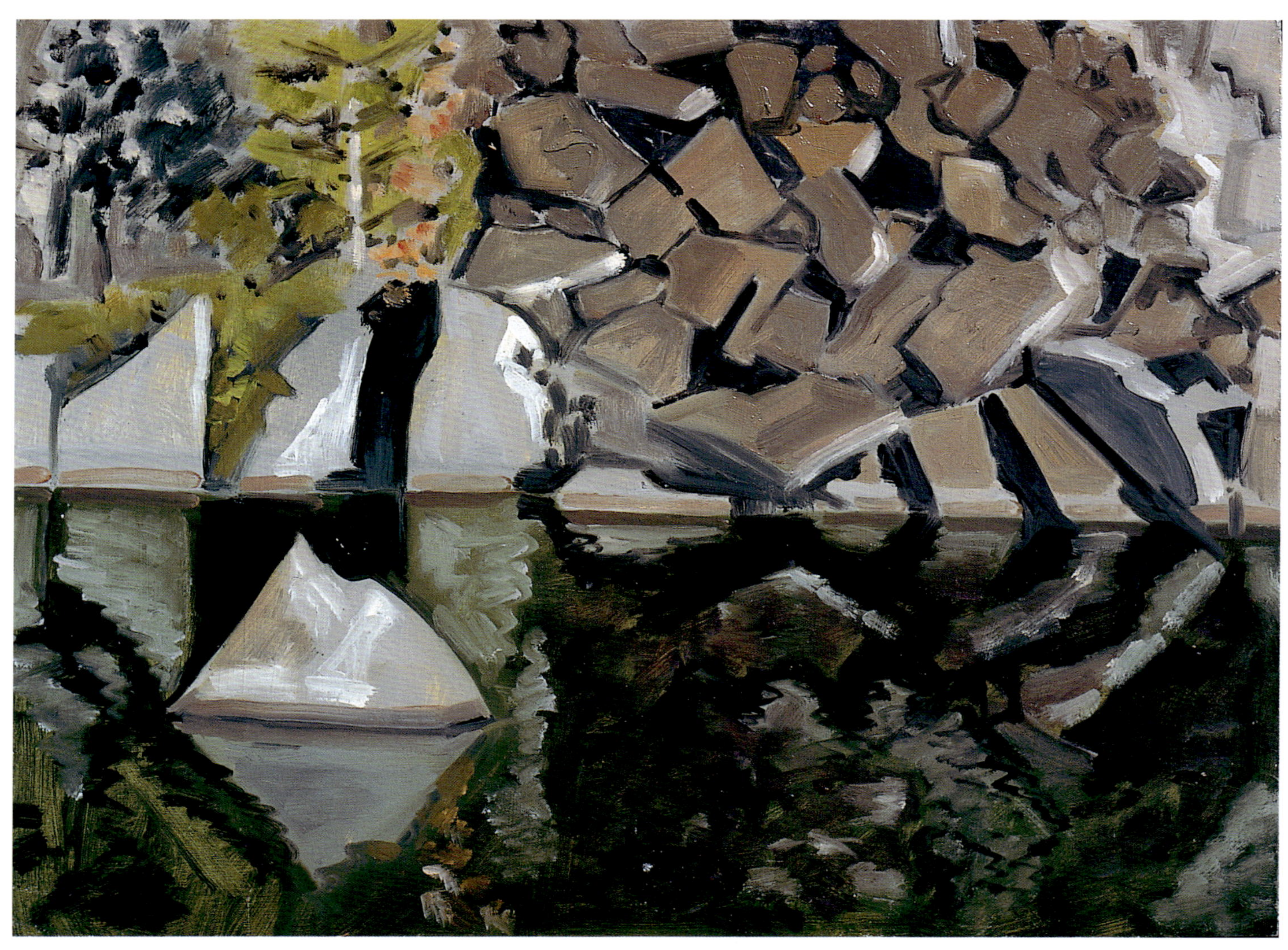

Lois Dodd, *Quarry, Green Water,* 1995, oil on masonite, 11 x 15 in., private collection

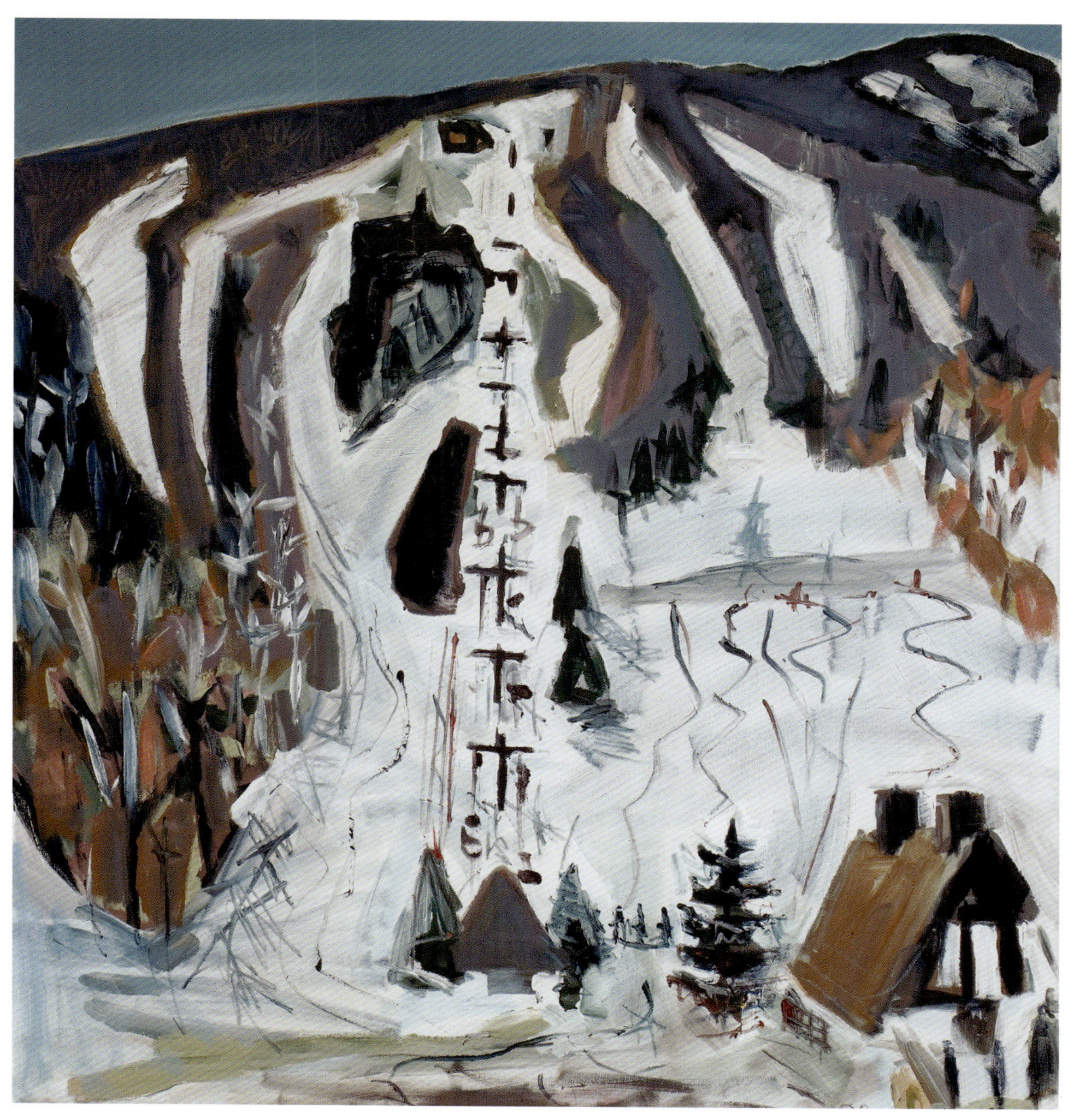

Richard Saltonstall, *Camden Snow Bowl*, 2002, acrylic on canvas, 50 x 44 in.
Photograph courtesy Caldbeck Gallery

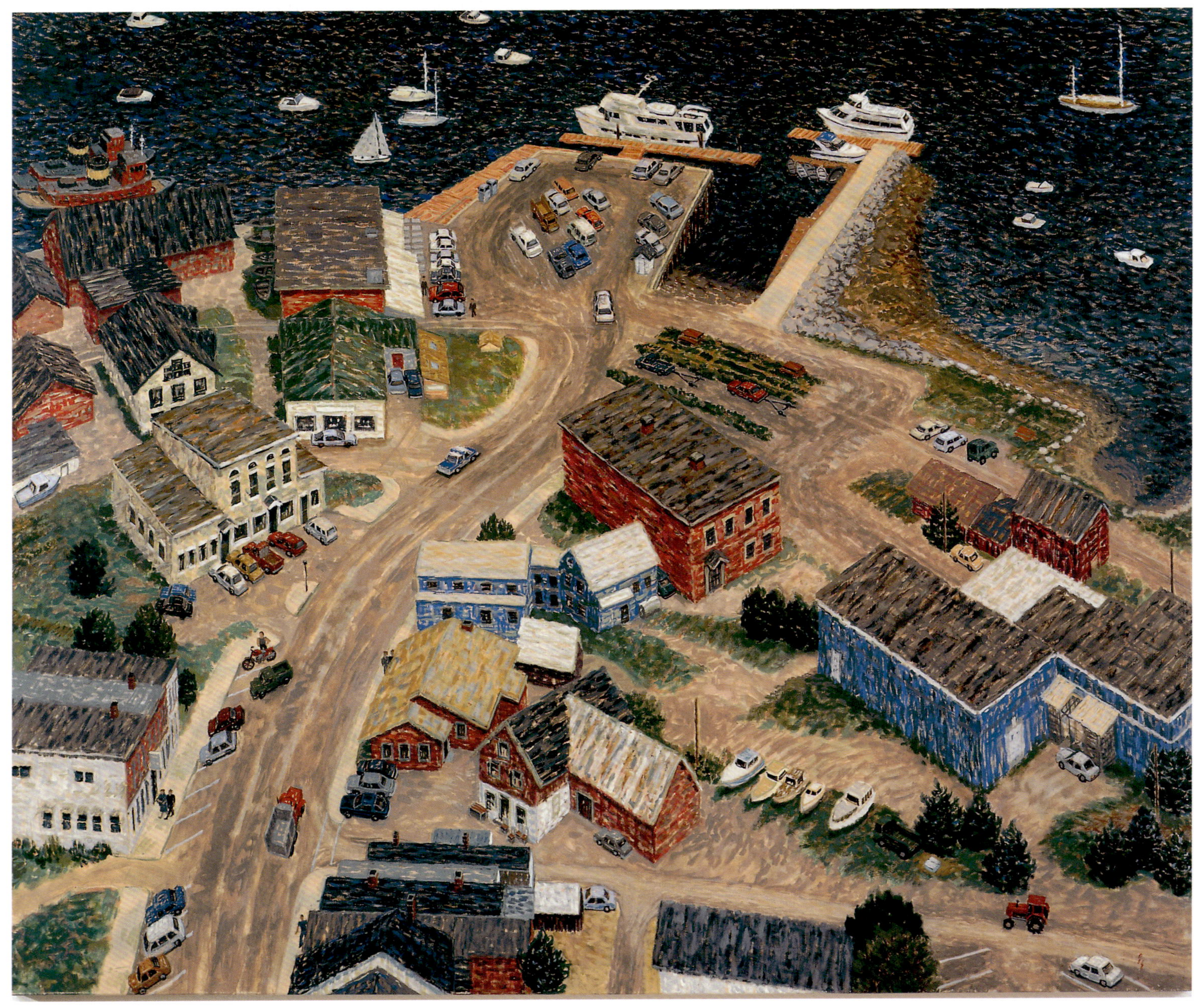

 Yvonne Jacquette, *Waterfront of Belfast, Maine,* 1990, oil on canvas, 84 x 70 in., courtesy DC Moore Gallery, New York

July is the month when people enjoy the outdoors. Maine bays and coves are white with sails. People are tenting and camping. Fishermen go to the bay for mackerel and to the brooks for salmon. . . . Hal Borland described it best when he called [July] "concentrated summer."

—Esther Wood, *Saltwater Seasons,* 1980

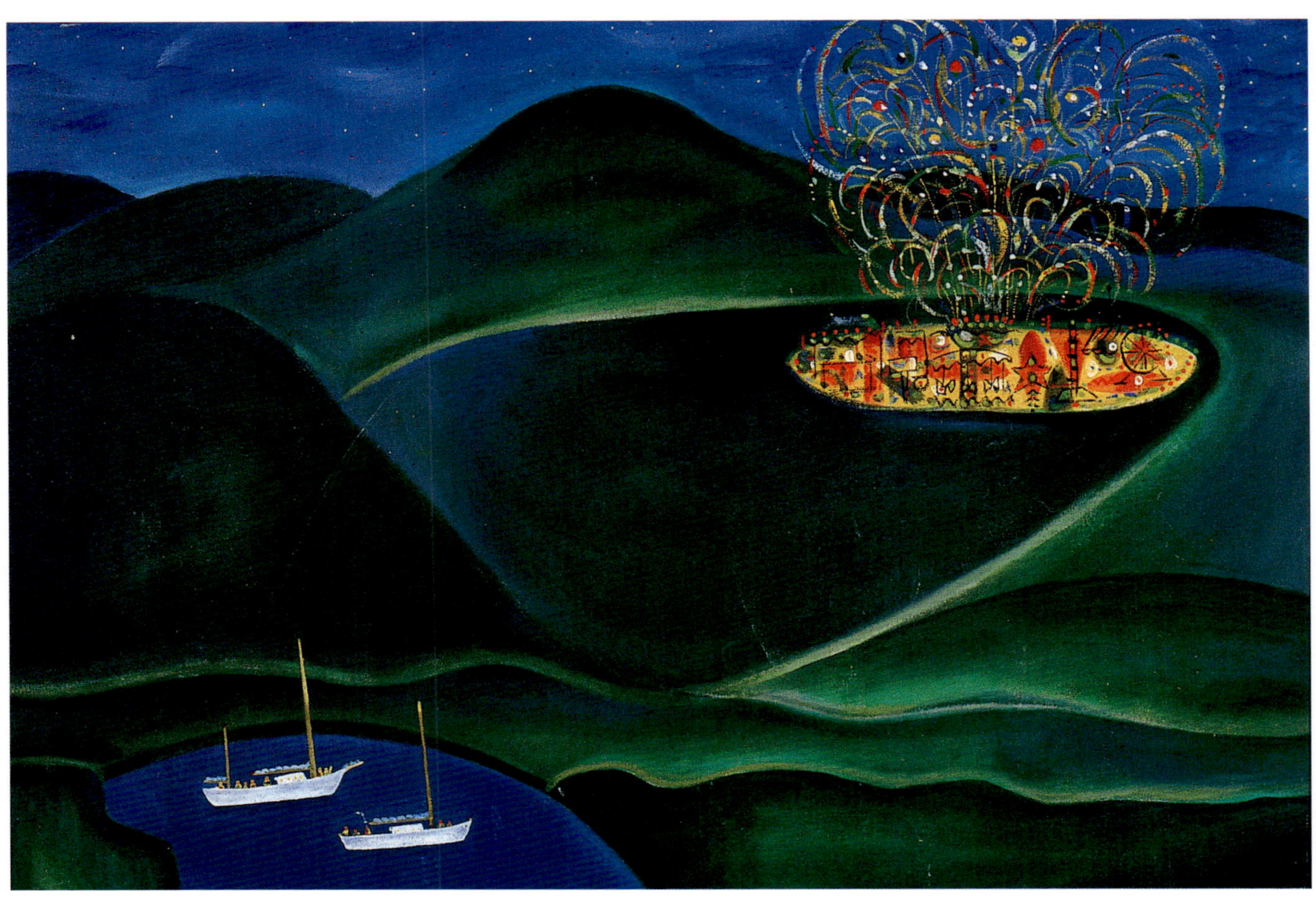

Francis Hamabe, *Fireworks, Blue Hill,* c. 1980, oil on canvas, 22 x 30 in., collection of Juliana P. Little

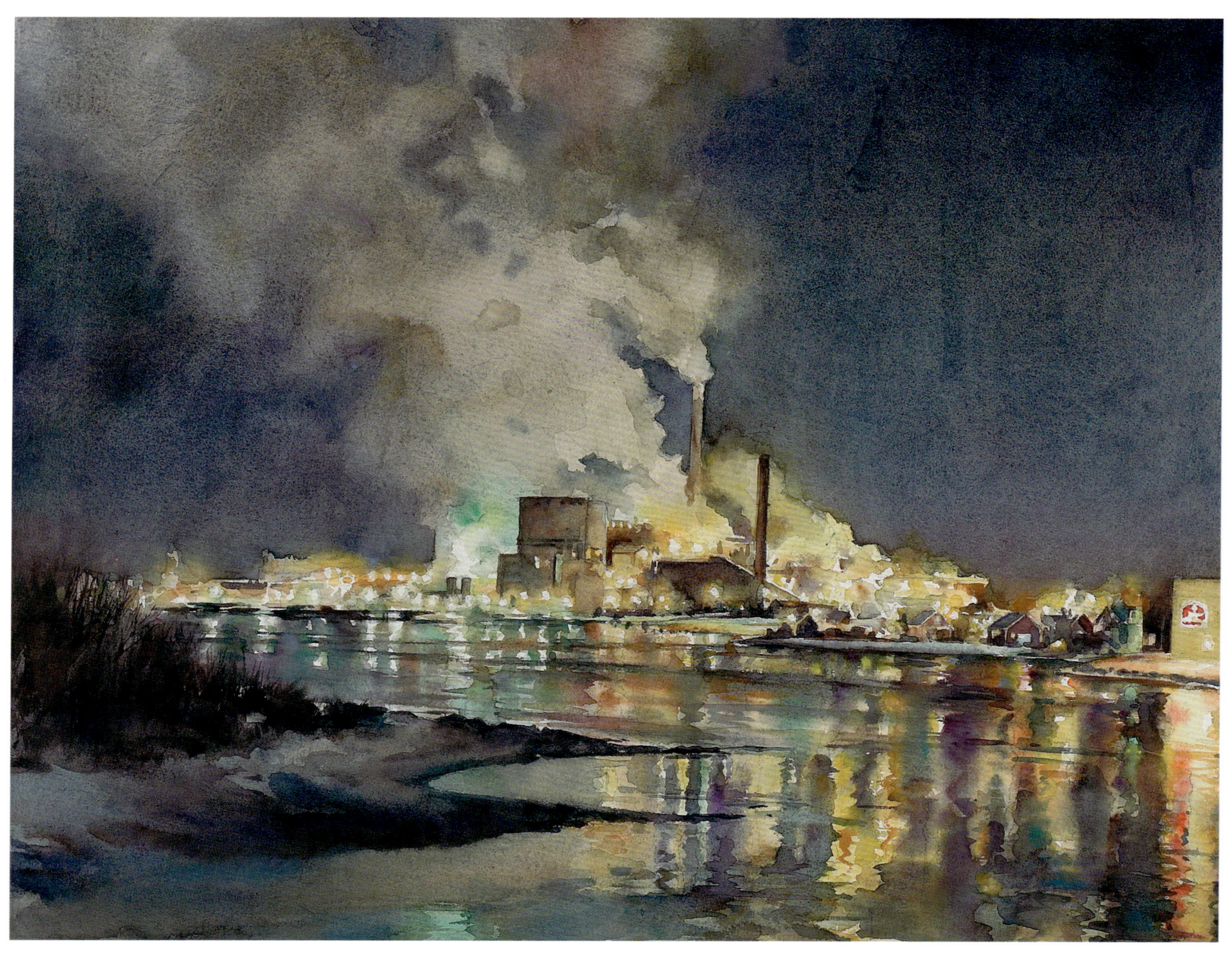

Paul Rickert, *Bucksport Mill,* 2004, watercolor on paper, 22 1/2 x 30 in., collection of the artist

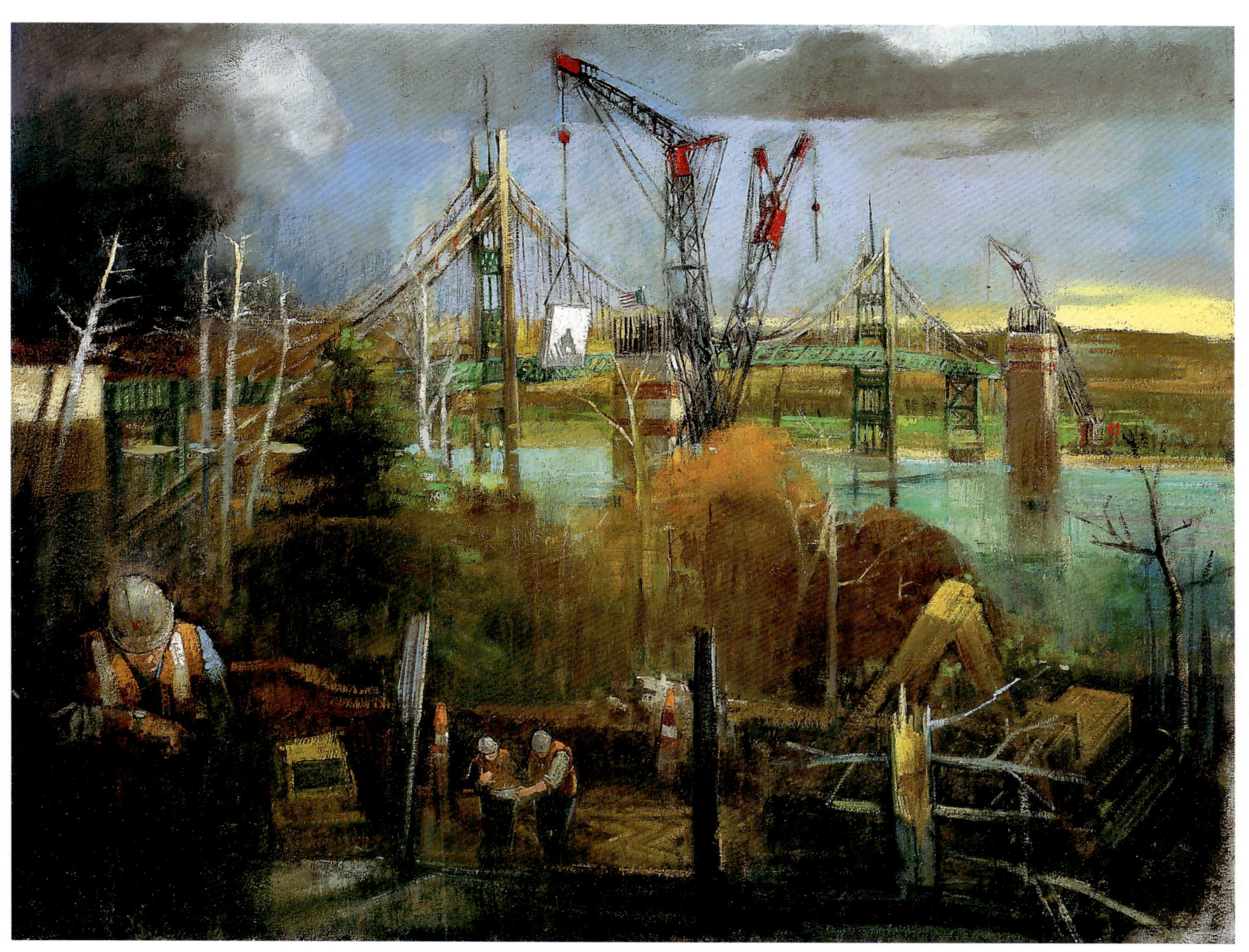

Nancy Morgan-Barnes, *Building the Waldo Hancock Bridge,* 2005, oil on board, 24 x 32 in., collection of the artist

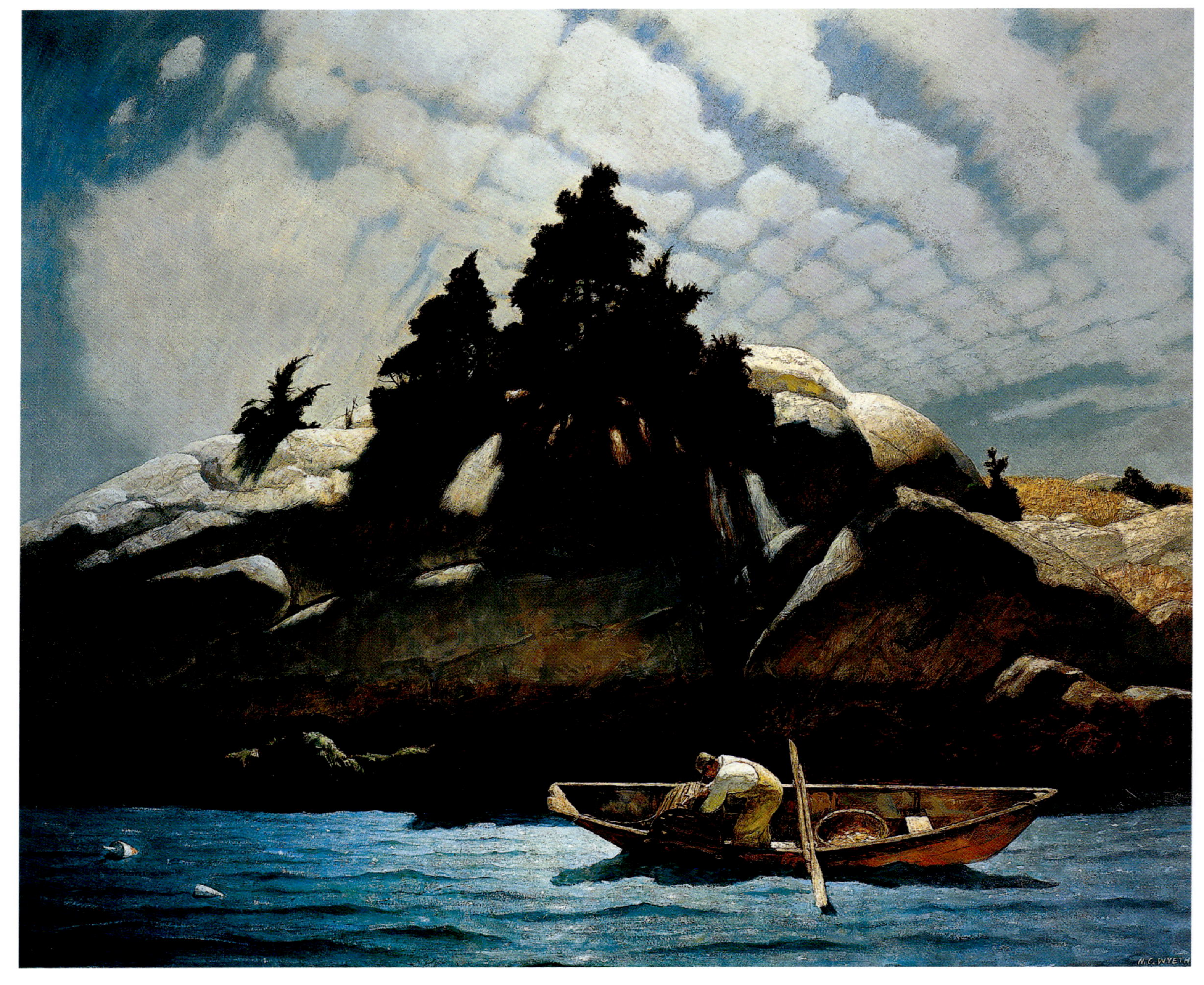

N. C. Wyeth, *Black Spruce Ledge,* 1941, tempera and oil on Renaissance panel, 42 x 52 in., collection of Linda Bean

A Handful of Maine Islands

"Of all the Maine islands," wrote novelist and historian Martin Dibner, "I favor Monhegan, a solitary whale couchant in a blue field of sea, sixteen miles distant with nothing beyond but more sea and the coast of France."

It seems that every artist who steps foot on Monhegan's remote shores falls under its spell. Indeed, the history of American art can be traced through images of the island, from the Hudson River school to Abstract Expressionism. In the sea-level view by Boston marine painter William Edward Norton (1843–1916), Monhegan's bold headlands encroach on the straight horizon.

While James Fitzgerald (1899–1971) came into his own as a painter in Monterey, California, in the 1930s, hobnobbing with the likes of John Steinbeck, he reached artistic fulfillment on Monhegan, to which he moved in 1943. His bold watercolor technique proved ideally suited for a vivid sunset view of Manana, the "nursling" isle that protects Monhegan's small harbor.

Monhegan Island lobstermen setting out in January, the beginning of their hauling and harvesting season, appreciate the windbreak a snow-streaked Manana provides them. In his paintings, Andrew Winter (1893–1958), who, like Fitzgerald, lived year-round on Monhegan, paid many tributes to these hard-working men casting their fate on the deep, chill waters of the Gulf of Maine.

Rockwell Kent, who first came to Monhegan in 1905, envied those island men who knew the sea so intimately. "Standing upon a headland," Kent (1882–1971) wrote in his autobiography *It's Me O Lord* (1955), "I'd look down at the lobstermen at work, their dories almost in the back-wash of the surf. God, how I envied them their power to row! To pull their heavy traps!"

Michael Torlen (b. 1940) also admires the fishers of the sea. Early in his life, he worked alongside his Norwegian-born father, a commercial fisherman, on a tuna clipper off the coast of Southern California. Torlen has been painting on the Maine coast for more than twenty-five years, leaving his home in Purchase, New York, to find yearly refuge on the islands, including Monhegan.

In one of his signature watercolors, Donald Holden (b. 1931) presents a nameless wooded island floating in a reddish haze. Holden distills the essence of an island without resorting to topographical particulars. He once told an interviewer, "I like the Japanese idea that the artist starts the painting and the viewer completes it."

All three generations of Wyeth painters have had a special affinity for the Maine islands, starting with Nathaniel Convers (1882–1945), who explored the coast around the family home, "Eight Bells," in Port Clyde. N. C. Wyeth's *Black Spruce Ledge* reminds us that hauling lobster traps, a labor-intensive task even with today's equipment, was extra arduous from an open dinghy back in the day.

As a child at Port Clyde, Andrew Wyeth (b. 1917) would row out to Little Caldwell Island, part of the St. Georges archipelago. Looking at Wyeth's tempera painting of this diminutive isle, one senses the special solitude a youngster might find on its rocky, kelp-strewn shore. Wyeth passed on his love of Maine islands to his son, Jamie Wyeth (b. 1944). Since 1990, the latter has lived seasonally in the Tenants Harbor Light on Southern Island, the setting for his watercolor *Lighthouse Garden*.

Penobscot Bay offers artists an exceptional array of islands to choose from. On a trip to the coast in 1916, George Bellows found his way to Matinicus, one of Maine's most remote islands. Nearly a hundred years later, Georgia-born Bo Bartlett (b. 1955) took up part-time residence on Wheaton Island just off Matinicus. "I love being one with the rhythms of nature," he has stated, "controlled by the tides, going to bed when the sun sets, and waking up really early when the lobstermen are setting out."

When Marsden Hartley (1877–1943) returned to his native state in the 1930s, he set out to establish himself as the painter from Maine. In addition to Mount Katahdin, Hartley painted along the coast, with productive stays at

Georgetown and Corea and on the island of Vinalhaven. His view of the latter recalls these lines from Harold Vinal's "The Quest":

We heard the dynamo sea below, we heard
Waves leaping under the night-hawk firs,
And knew there was no rest for us, that ever
We would be wanderers.

William Kienbusch (1914–1980) often hitched a ride with a local lobsterman when he set out to explore Maine islands. Fay Dyer, a Vinalhaven fisherman, ferried him to Hurricane Island in late June 1955, his first visit to the "haunted ghost island," where the ruins of abandoned quarries enchanted him.

Poet Elizabeth Bishop once referred to North Haven as "approximately my idea of heaven." The island has been the base of painting operations for Eric Hopkins (b. 1951) for much of his life. Hopkins started taking flying lessons in 1983, giving him a new and exciting vantage point that inspired him to consider the relationships between land, water and sky—considerations he has consistently translated into bold paintings.

When Brita Holmquist (b. 1950) looks out across the waters of Penobscot Bay around Islesboro, she finds color and pattern. Her senses are activated by her surroundings, as is her brush. "In Maine," Holmquist has said, "any turn in the road brings a possibility to encounter overwhelming beauty."

Gretchen Dow Simpson (b. 1939) first visited a Maine island—Vinalhaven—in 1956 and was hooked. She went on to explore Monhegan and Islesboro, drawn to their architecture and landscapes. Her painting of a rocky point of land on the latter island seems surreal, as if we had reached the outer edge of the world.

Most summers, painter Fairfield Porter (1907–1975) retreated to his family's home on Great Spruce Head Island. His *Cliffs of Isle au Haut,* 1974—commissioned by the U.S. Department of the Interior as part of the 1976 Bicentennial celebration—is a bold rendering of this mountainous Maine island with sun-struck cliffs.

An architect, painter and novelist, Emily Lansingh Muir (1903– 2002) summered in Stonington as a child and then settled there with her husband, sculptor William Muir, in 1939. Her vignettes of island life include a view of the town's main street, which maintains its curve to this day. Muir's passion for her surroundings was further borne out through actively seeking to preserve Penobscot Bay.

Stephen Pace (b. 1918) first came to Maine in 1953 to visit fellow abstract painter Michael Loew on Monhegan Island. Twenty years later, he and his wife Pam purchased a turn-of-the-century sea captain's house down the road from the Muirs. Pace's island watercolors are marked by a respect for the fishermen and a passion for this special haven away from his other home in New York City.

About Deer Isle, Jill Hoy (b. 1954) has stated, "In the realm of the place, it is the most powerful root in my life." Her wide-angle view of the island shoreline includes a neighbor's newly painted pram—not a baby carriage but a sailing dinghy used for venturing around the harbor.

William Irvine (b. 1931) moved to America from his native Scotland in the late 1960s, finally settling in Blue Hill. He bought an island off Jonesport and pitched a tent there among blue iris, wild raspberries, pine and bayberry. "Whether there were storms that pushed the horizon closer or blue-domed skies that held the silence of a cathedral," he recalls, "it was this balance between the dynamic and the spiritual that I found so powerful in nature."

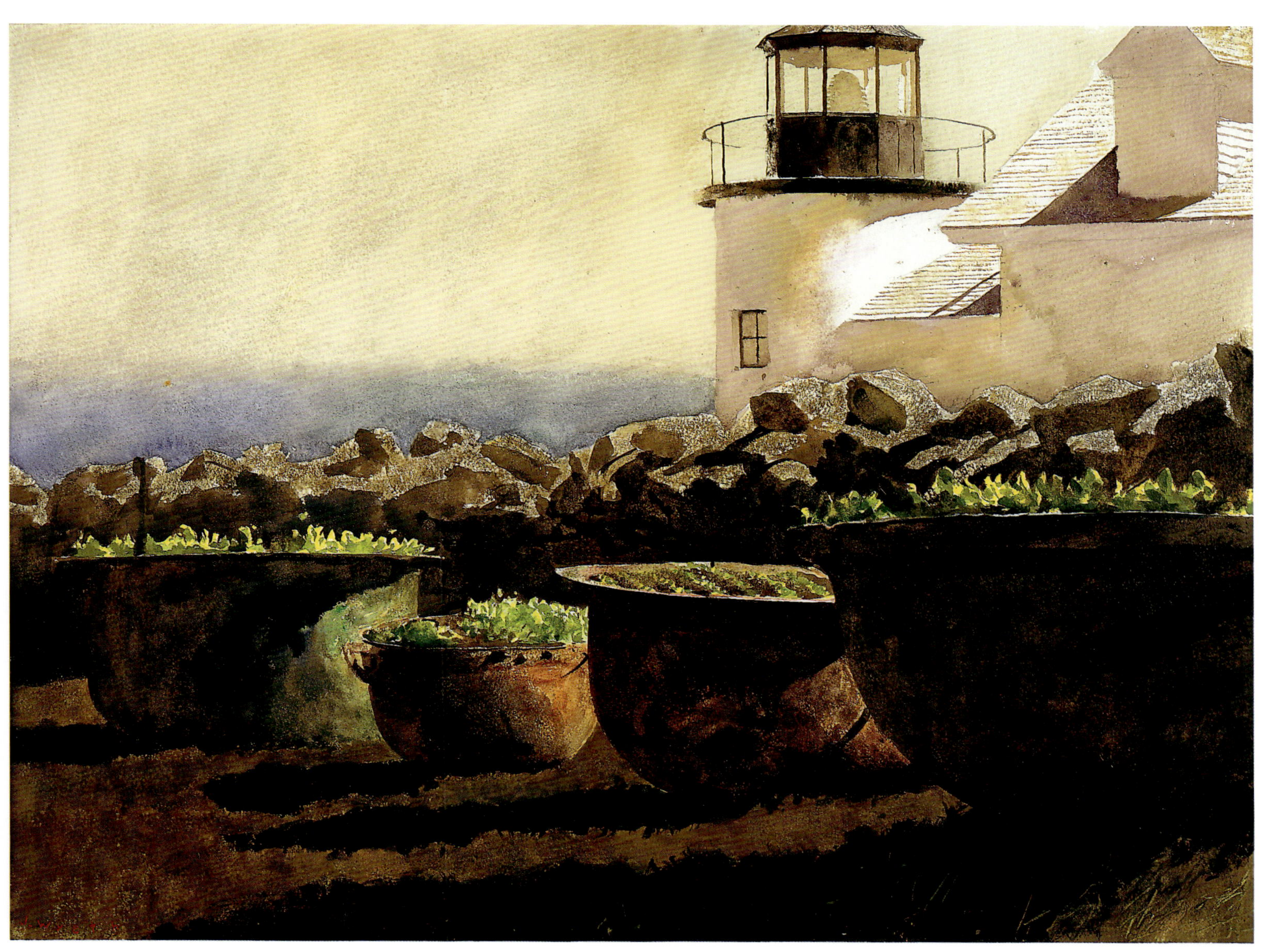

Jamie Wyeth, *Lighthouse Garden,* 1993, watercolor on paper, 20 3/4 x 28 1/4 in., private collection, © Jamie Wyeth

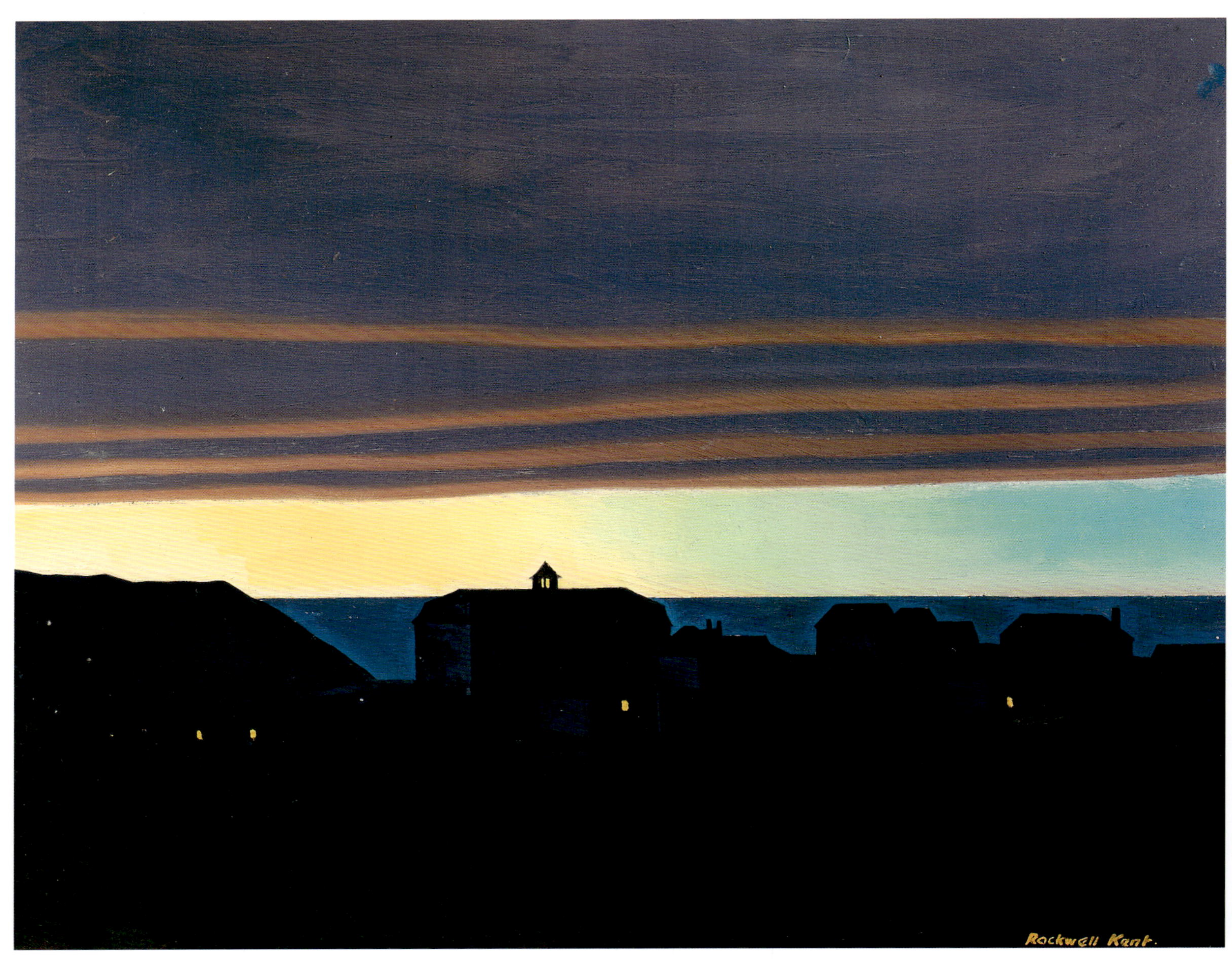

Rockwell Kent, *The Village at Night, Monhegan,* c. 1950, oil on panel, 12 x 16 in., collection of Remak Ramsay

A man working the sea has no friend more steadfast than a lighthouse. Day or night it gives him his bearings, constant warning of danger, reassuring comfort to his chilled bones. He depends on it as he does his compass and engine or sail.

—Martin Dibner, *Seacoast Maine: People and Places,* 1973

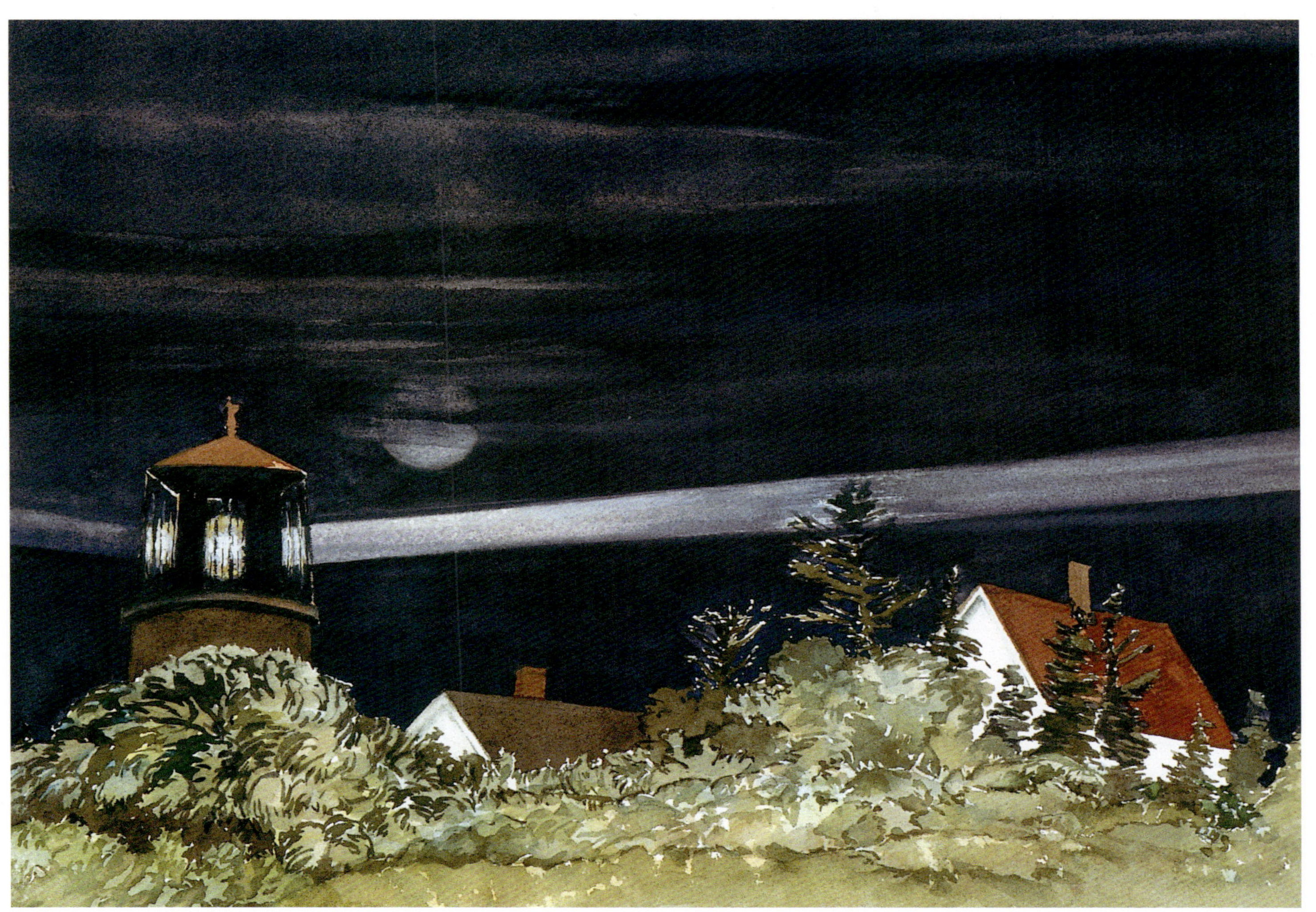

Michael Torlen, *Moon over Monhegan Light (from "Songs for My Father"),* 2000
Watercolor and gouache on paper, 9 x 13 in., private collection

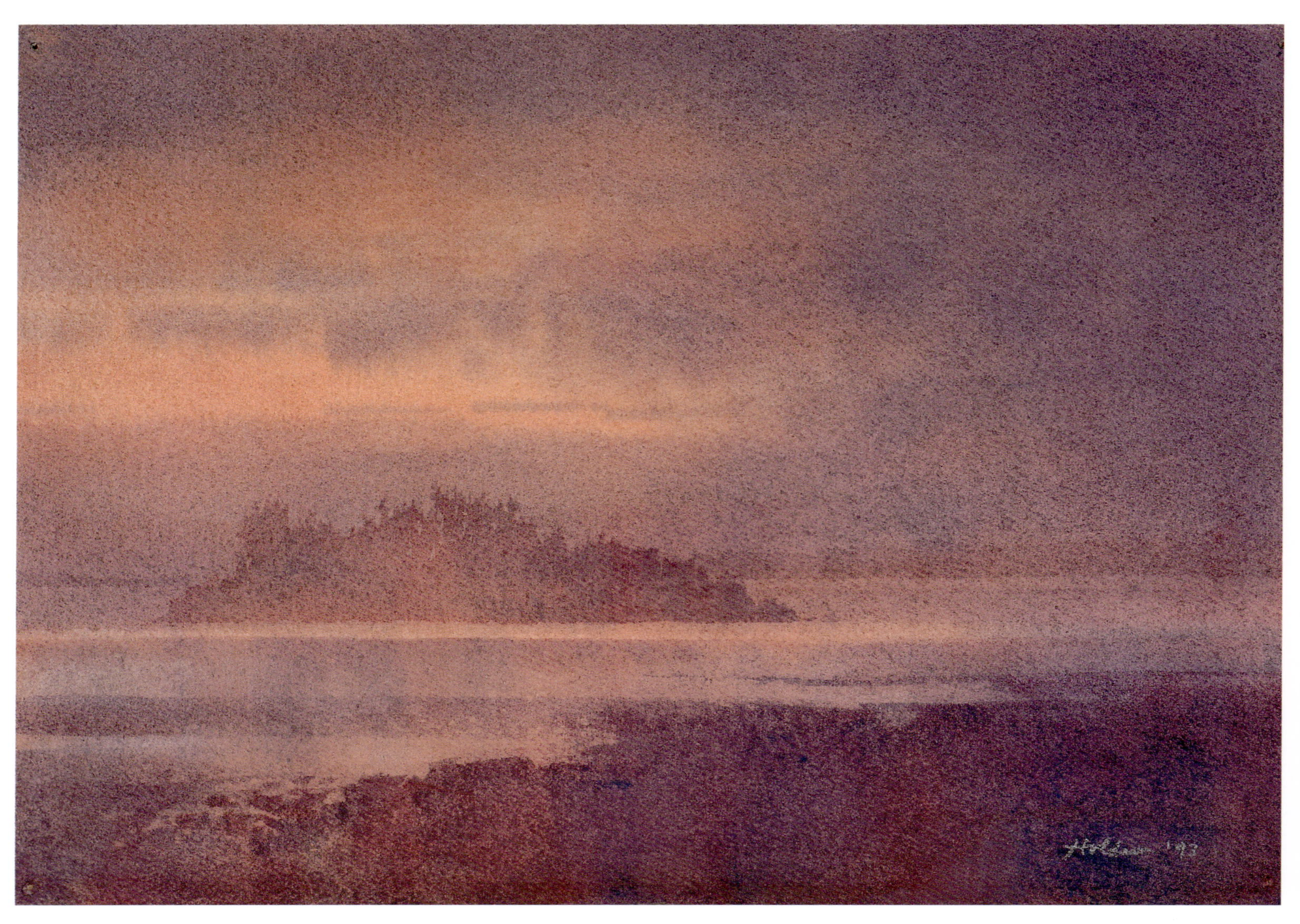

 Donald Holden, *Wooded Island,* 1993, watercolor on paper, 7 1/4 x 10 3/4 in., collection of Blake and Wendy Holden

When we returned from our exploration of the islands of the Penobscot and Mount Desert, we sighted the island [Monhegan], the morning sun playing on its top bathed it in light; amid a peaceful ocean it looked like an island of the blessed; anon the lighthouse and then, as with glowing sail we neared it, houses and then windows could be made out. The wind was fair, but on my suggestion that this could be hallowed ground, the germ of New England, we hauled up a little closer to the wind and dashed up to the head of the harbor, tacked and stood off on our course, westward ho! We had seen the cradle of New England.

—Charles Levi Woodbury

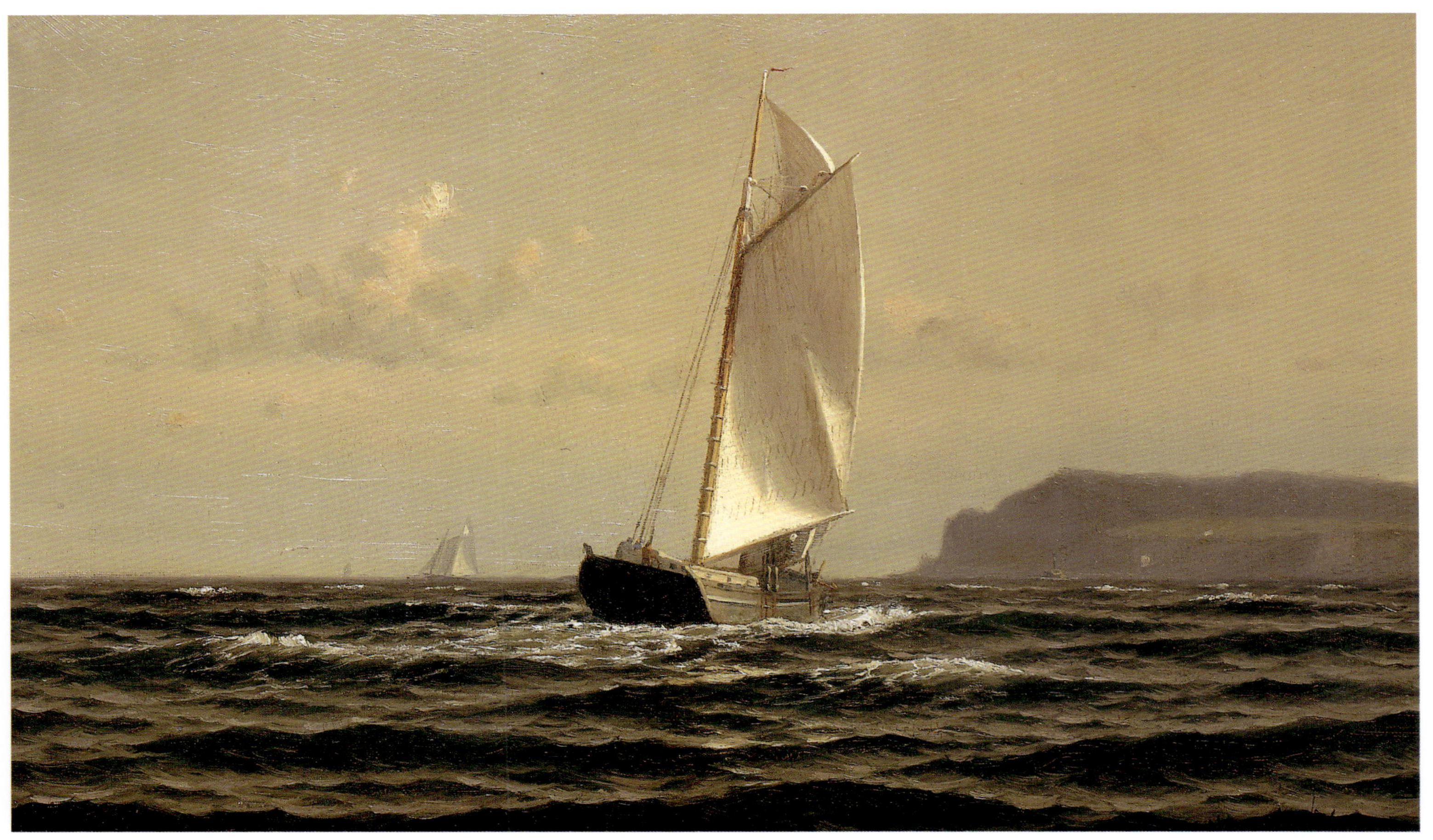

William Edward Norton, *Off Monhegan,* 1876, oil on canvas, 12 x 20 in., collection of Remak Ramsay

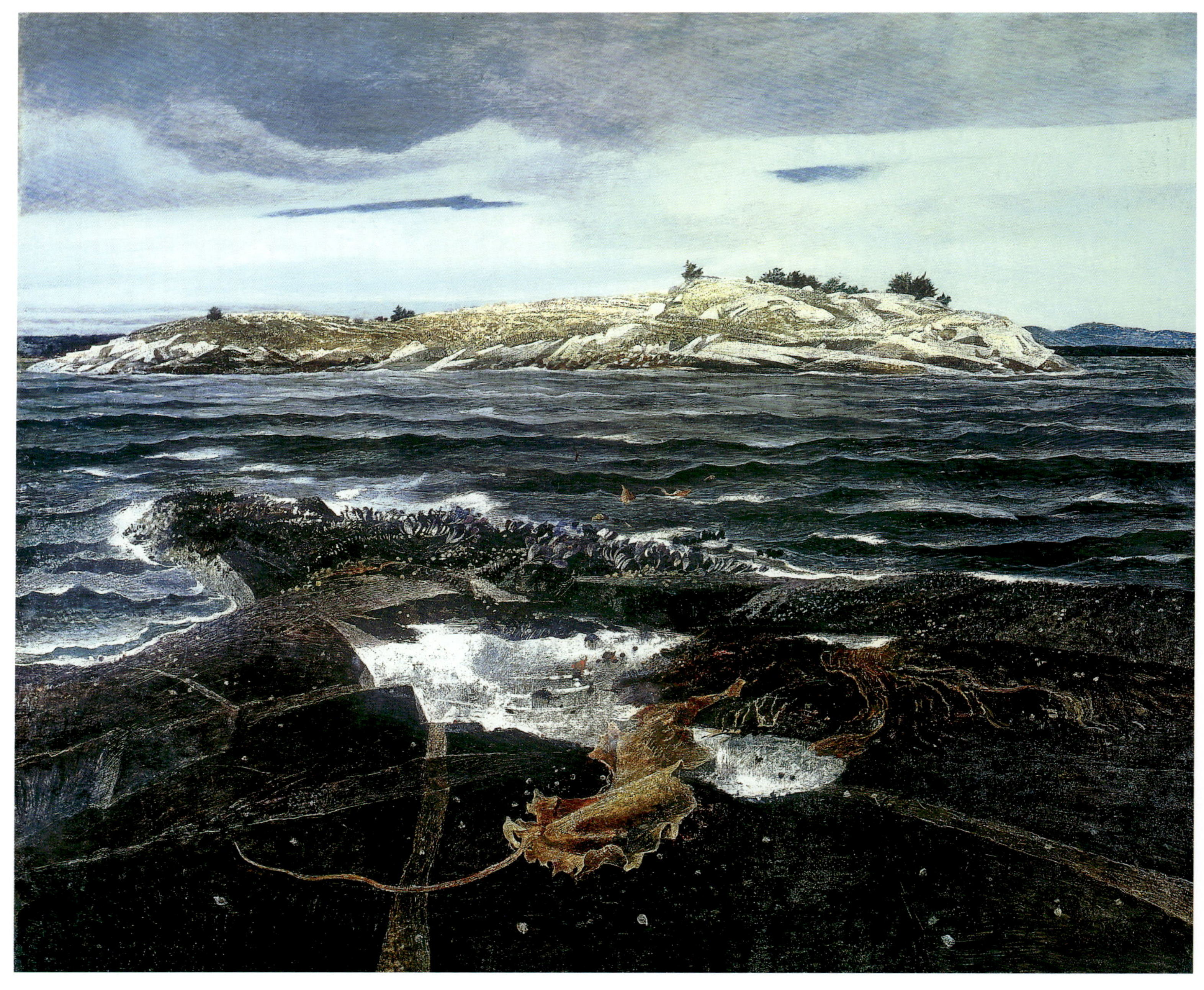

 Andrew Wyeth, *Little Caldwell's Island,* 1940, tempera on panel, 32 x 40 in., Cawley Family Collection, © Andrew Wyeth

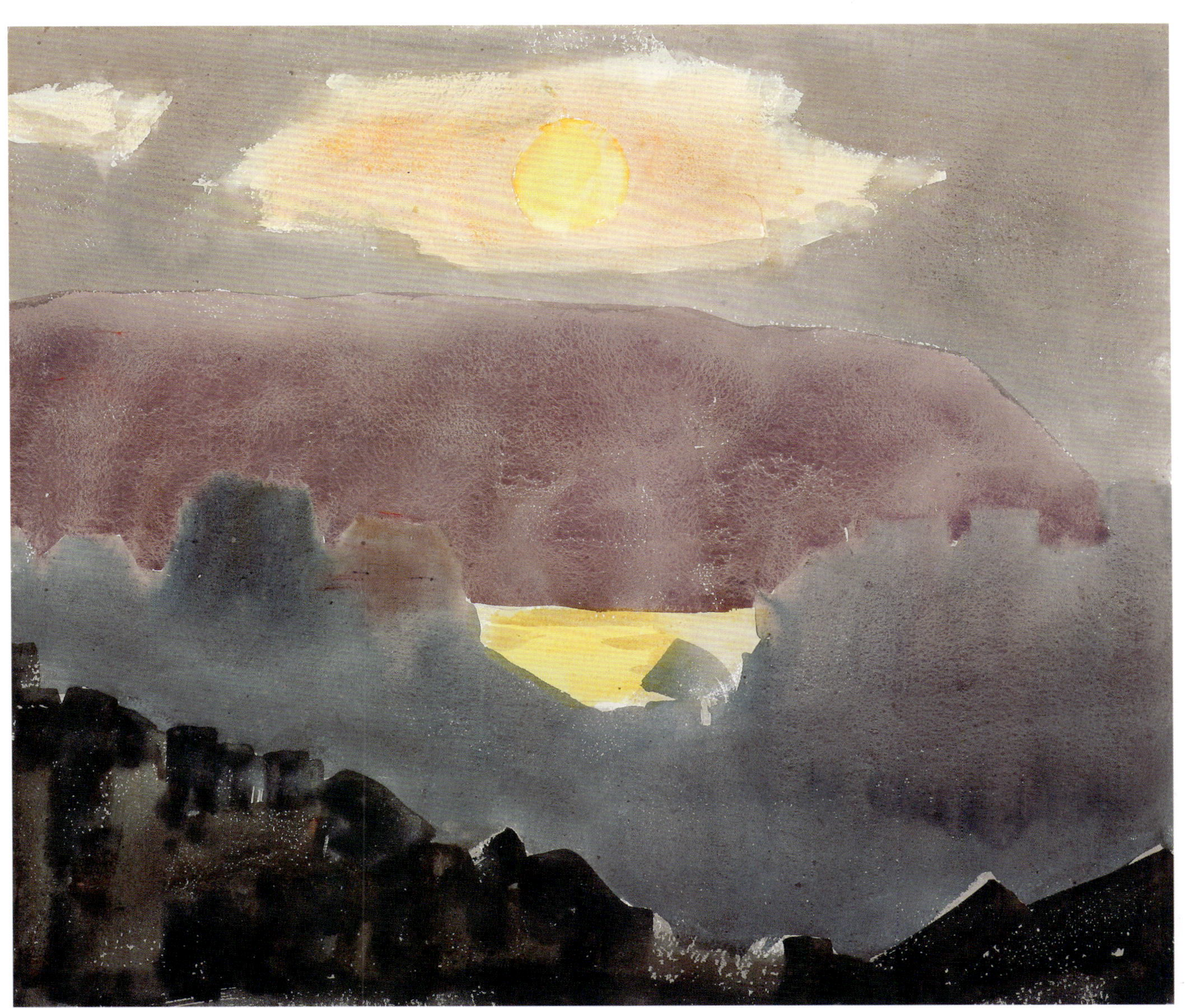

James Fitzgerald, *Sunset Manana,* n.d., watercolor on paper, 20 x 24 in., collection of Robert and Carol Stahl

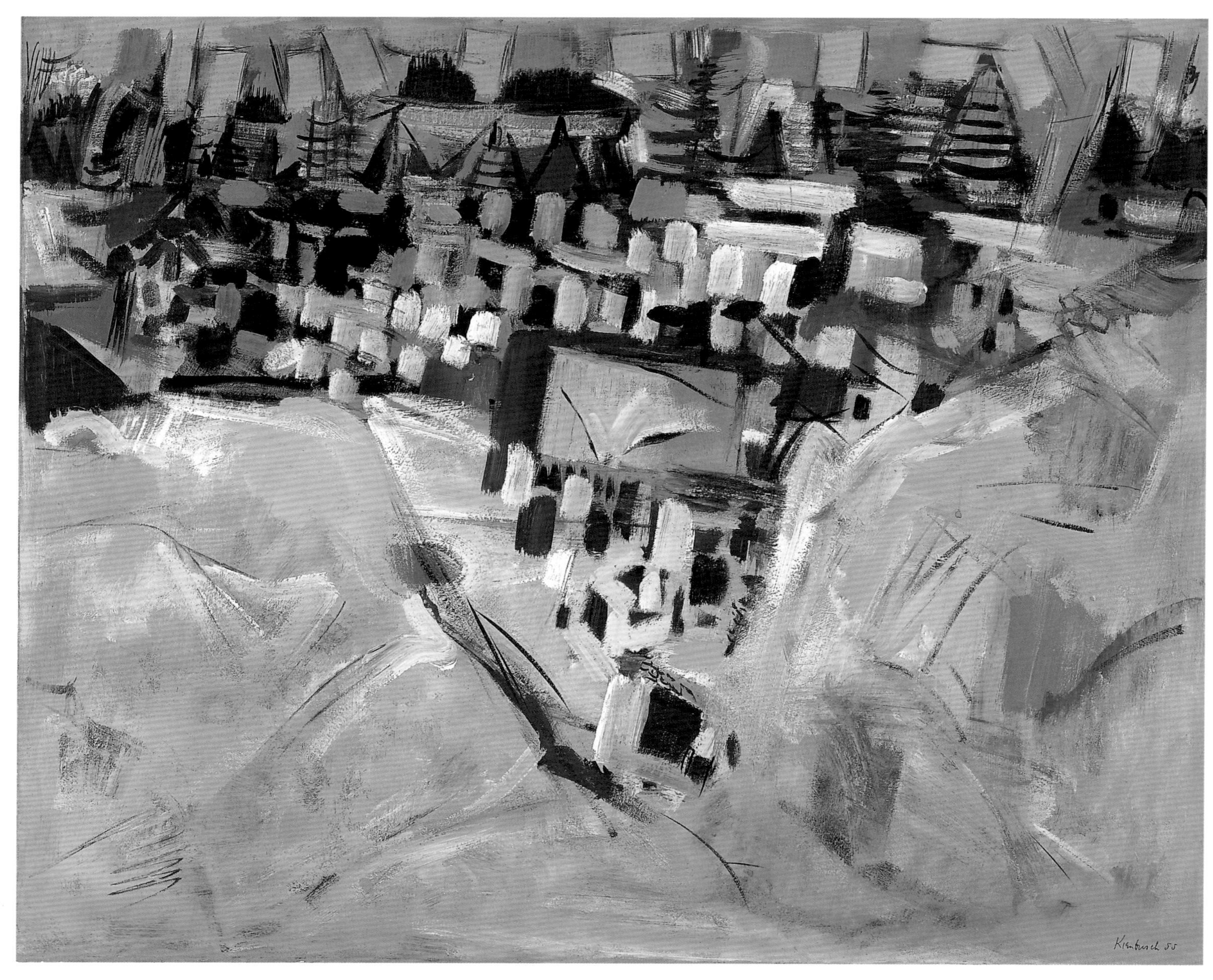

William Kienbusch, *Quarry Hill, Hurricane Island,* 1955, casein on paper, 21 1/2 x 27 3/8 in.
Collection of the Farnsworth Art Museum, Bequest of Mrs. Elizabeth B. Noyce, 1997 (97.3.26)

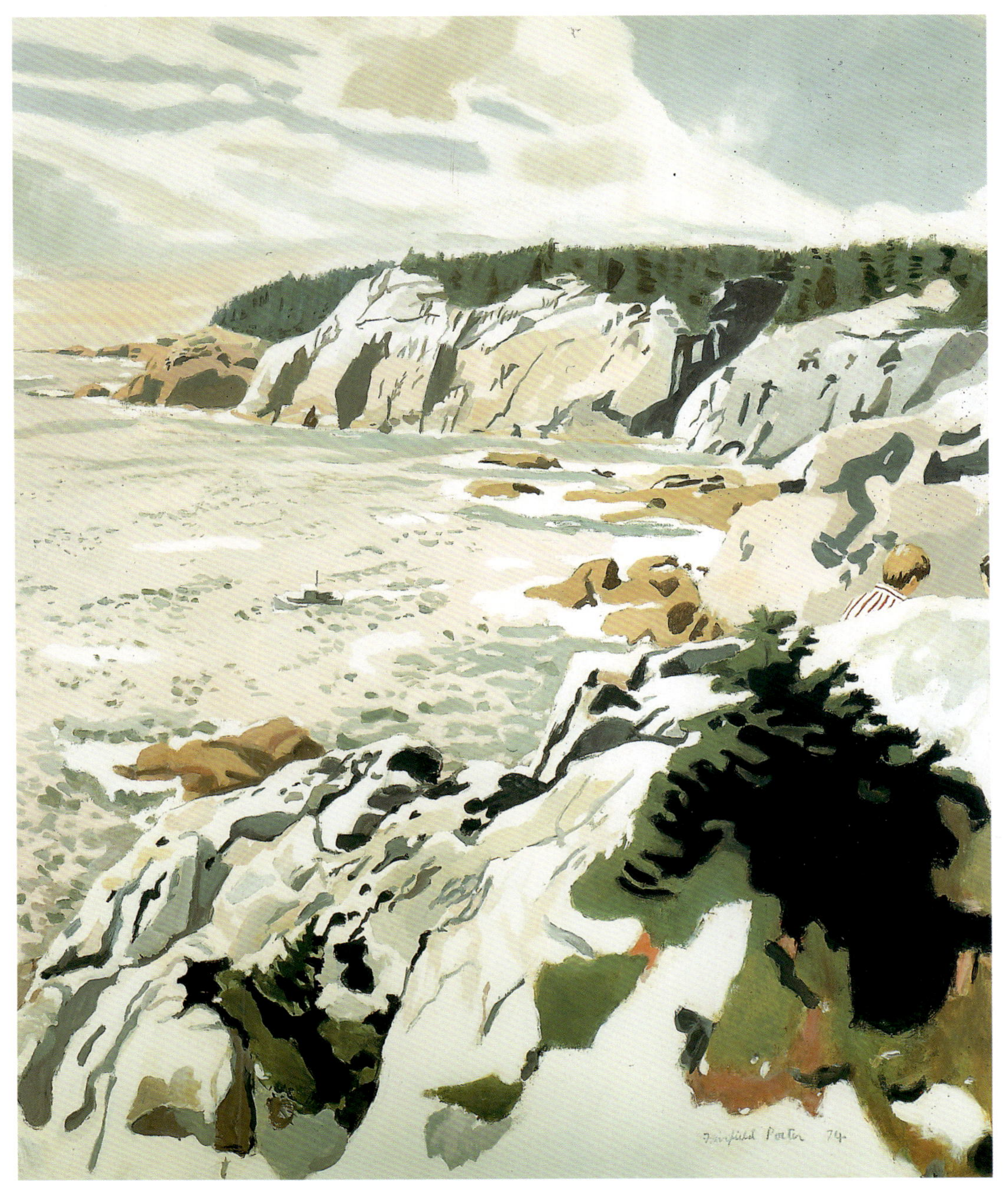

Fairfield Porter, *The Cliffs of Isle au Haut,* 1974, oil on canvas, 72 x 62 in.
Collection of Mr. and Mrs. Graham Gund

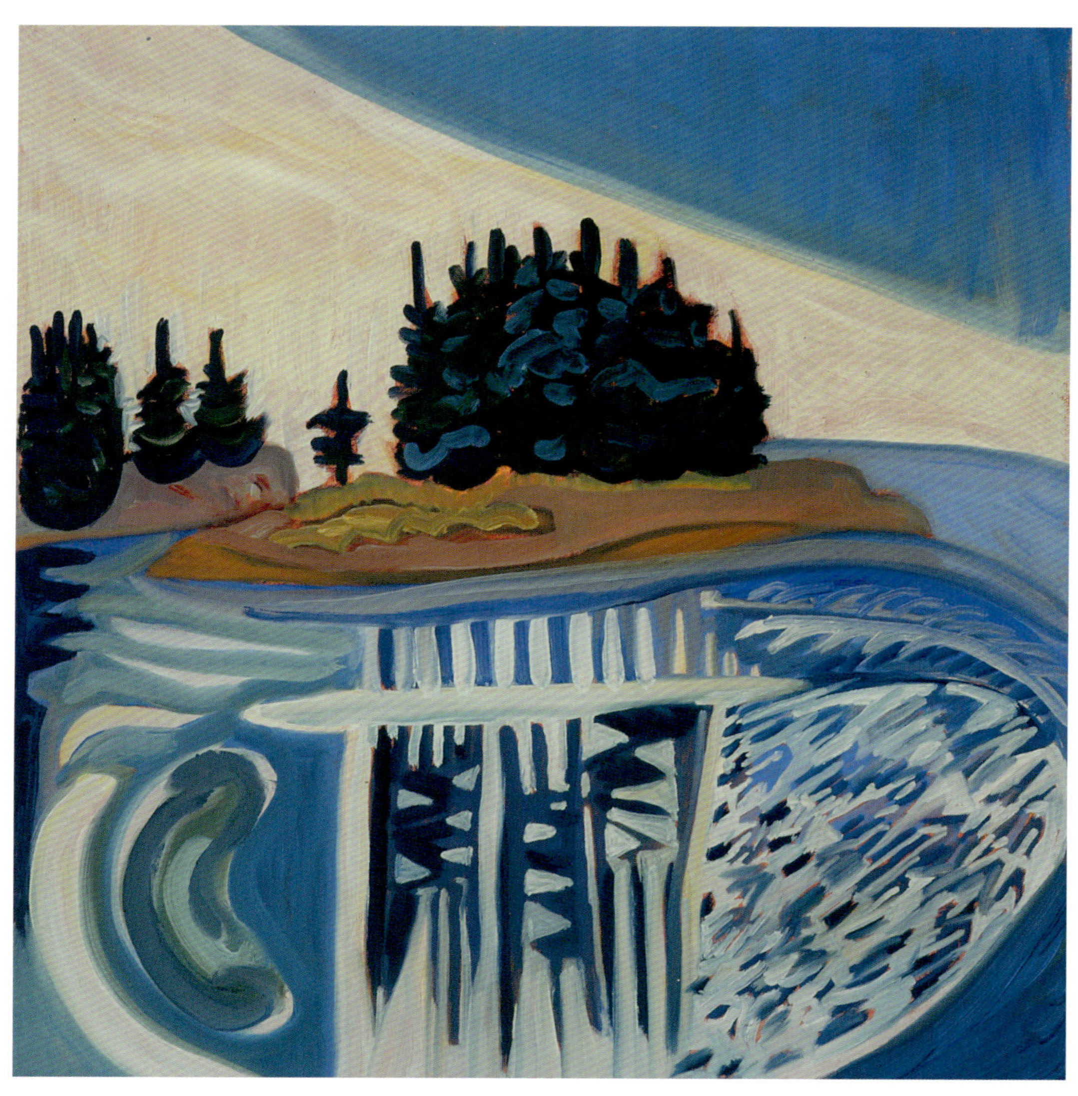

Brita Holmquist, *Wind Gate, Barred Island,* 2005, oil on canvas, 18 x 18 in., private collection

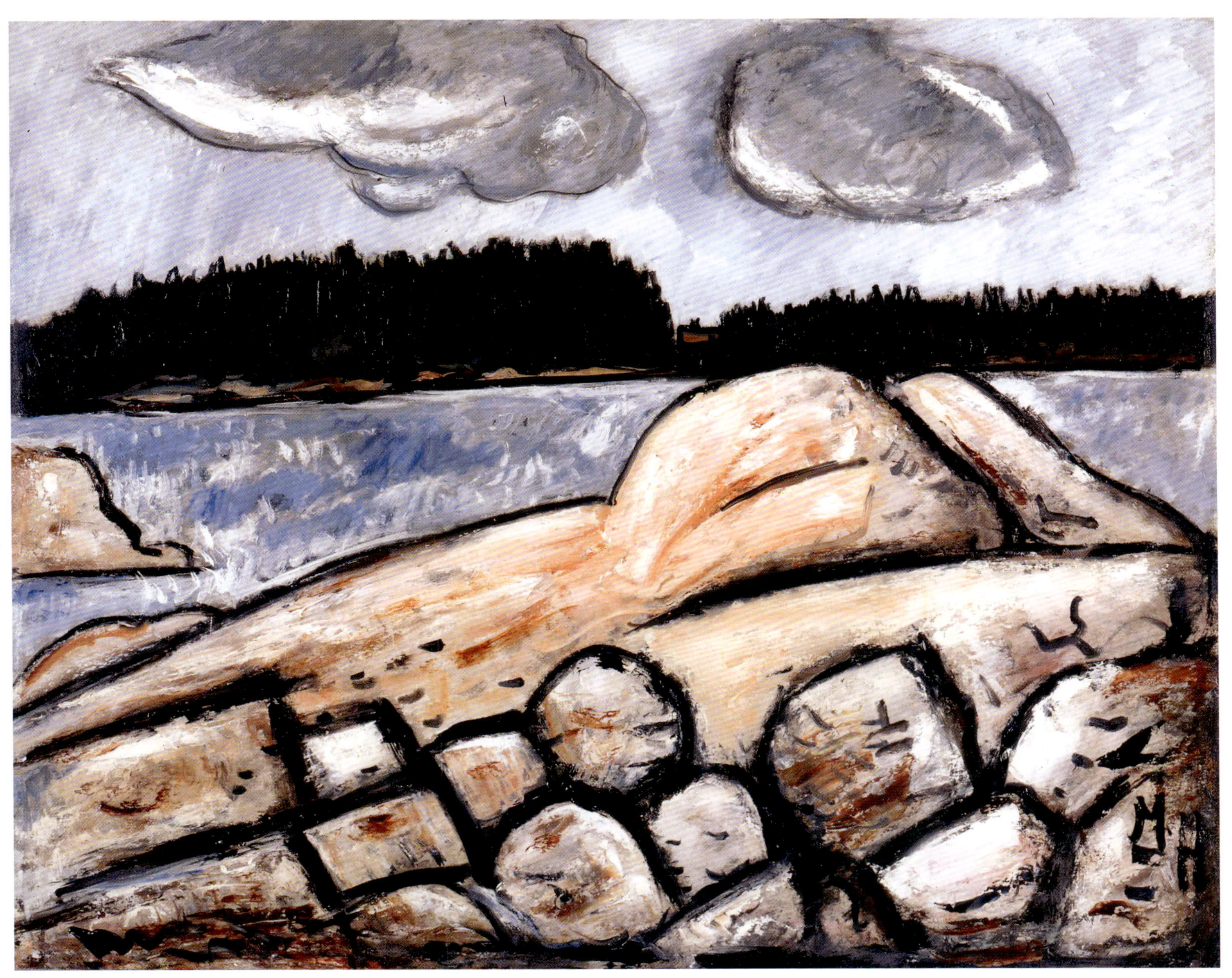

Marsden Hartley, *After the Storm, Vinalhaven,* 1938–39, oil on Academy Board, 22 x 28 in.
Bowdoin College Museum of Art, Brunswick, Maine, Gift of Mrs. Charles Phillip Kuntz

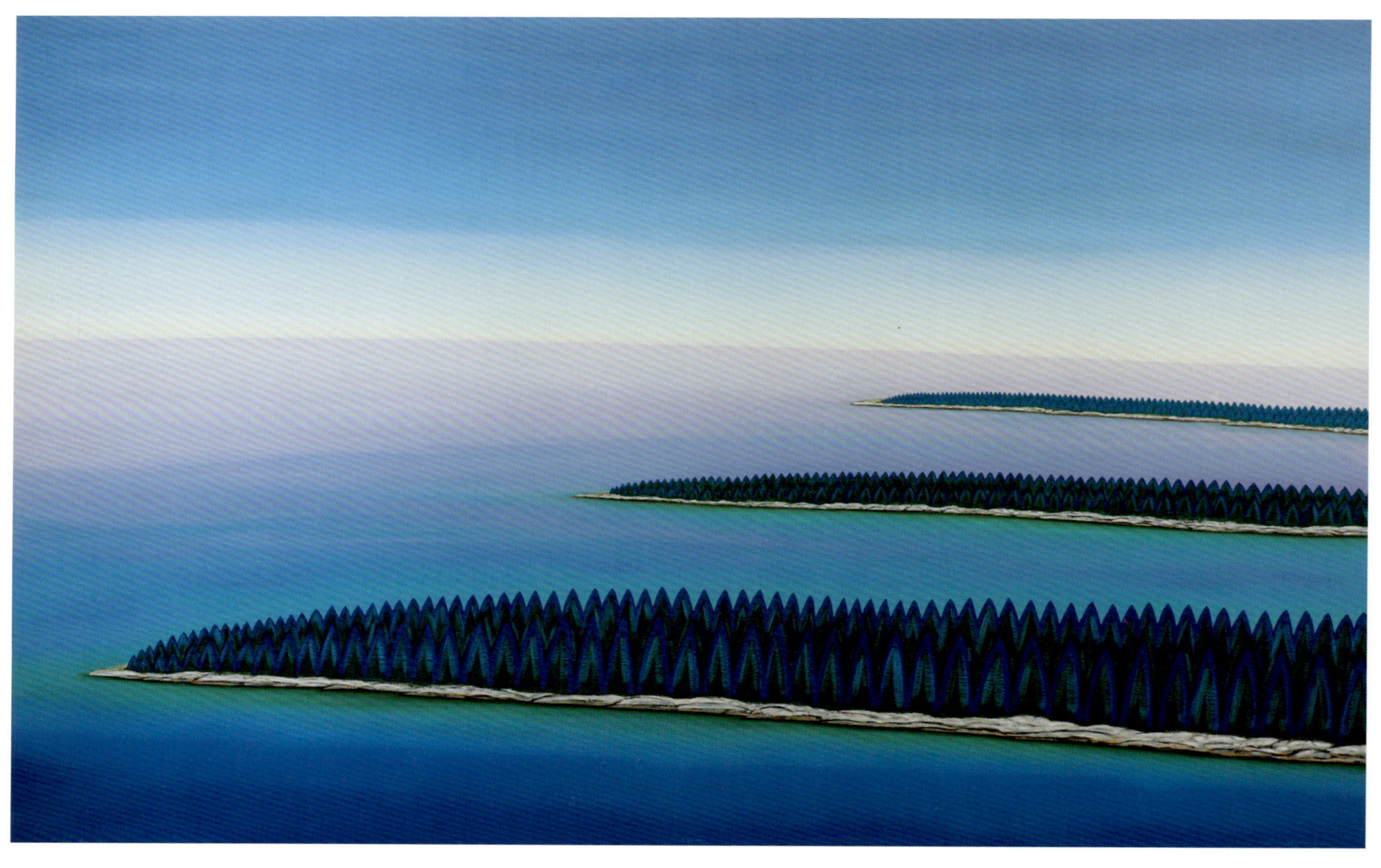

Where North is West of North, not true, he pilots
best who feels the coast for standpipe, spire,
tower, or stack, who owns local knowledge of shoal
or ledge, whose salt nose smells the spruce shore.

—Philip Booth, from "'Chart 1203' Penobscot Bay and Approaches"

Eric Hopkins, *Three Points,* 2003, oil on canvas, 62 x 100 in., collection of the artist

To Mainiacs, Maine is not merely a place. It is a spiritual home and shelter as perfectly fitting and comfortable and natural as its shell is to a snail; which, like snails, they carry with them wherever they may go. To them, Maine is a state of mind and a way of life inseparable from the geography and topography of the area and from their own bones and blood and thoughts and dreams. It is an element, as necessary to them as water is to fish. It is almost a religion.

—Louise Dickinson Rich, *State O' Maine,* 1964

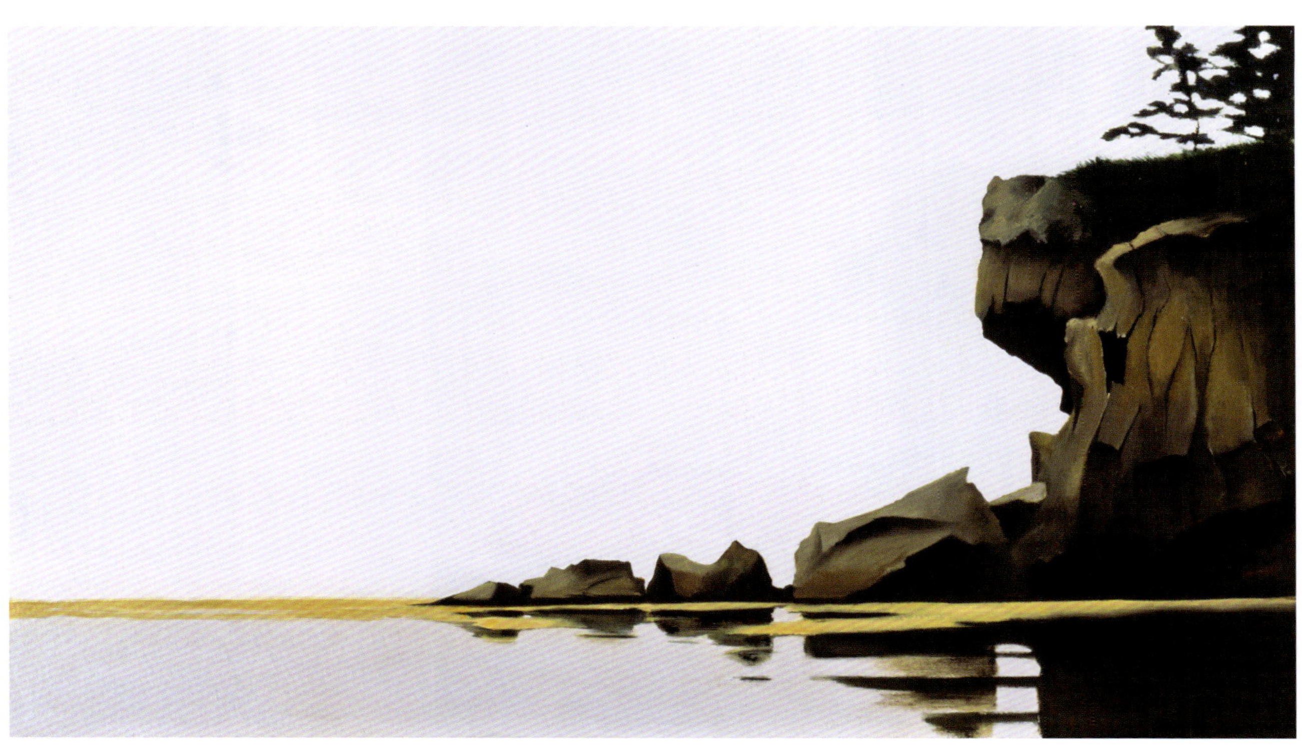

Gretchen Dow Simpson, *Islesboro II,* 2001, oil on linen, 12 x 22 in., private collection

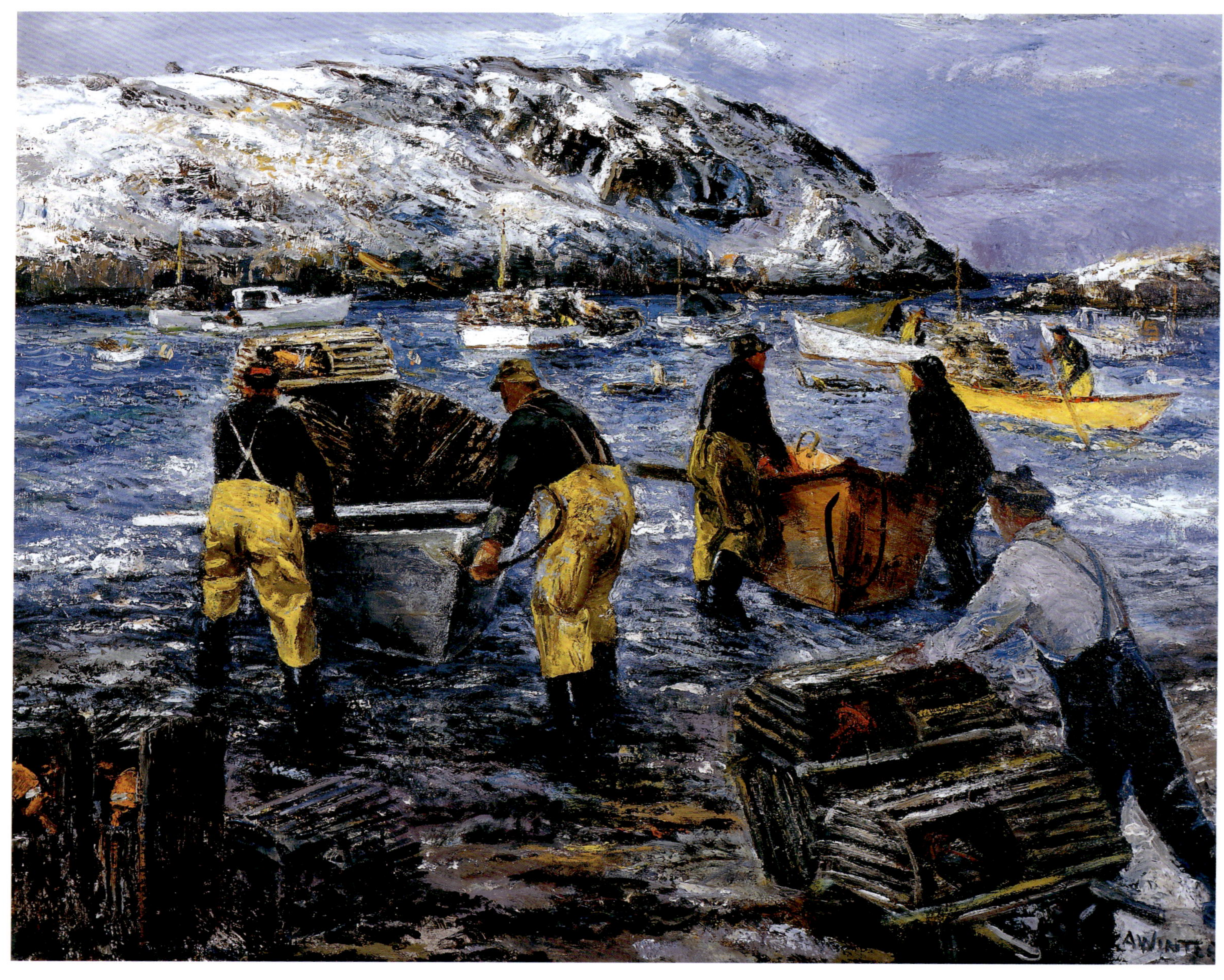

Andrew Winter, *Trap Setting Day,* c. 1940, oil on board, 22 x 28 in., courtesy Wiscasset Bay Gallery

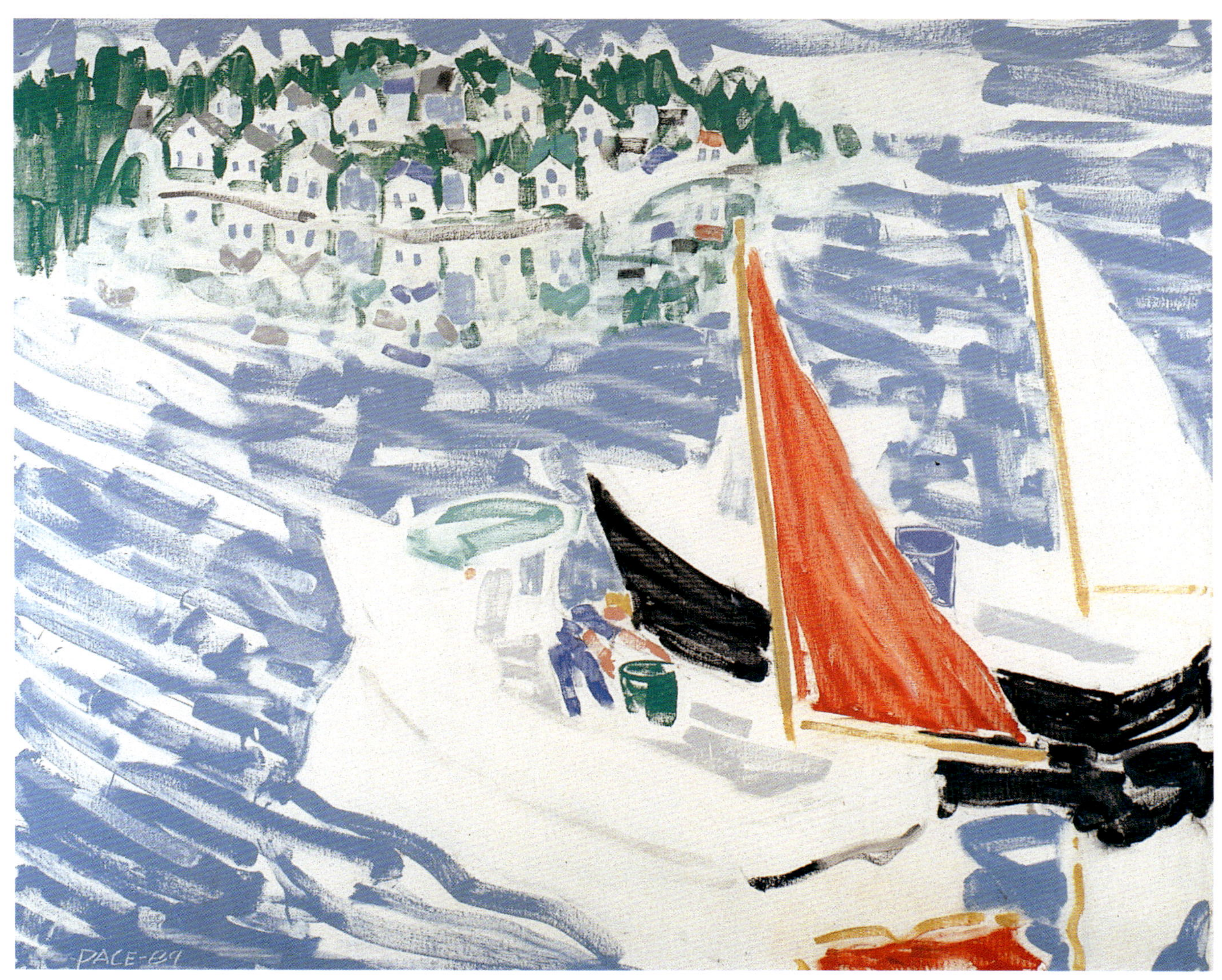

Stephen Pace, *Lobster Boats, Greenland,* 1989, oil on canvas, 48 x 60 in., courtesy Katharina Rich Perlow Gallery

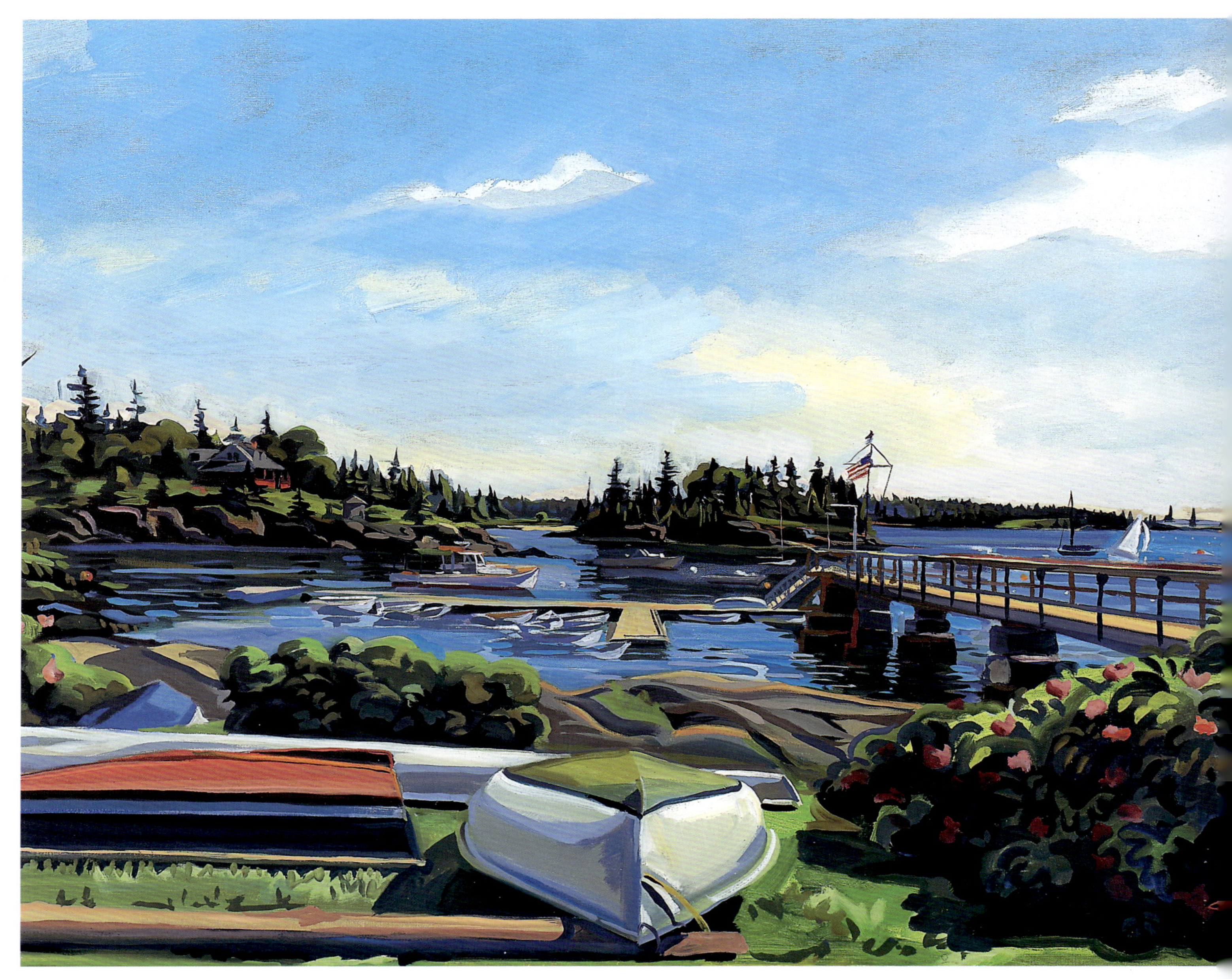

Jill Hoy, *Betty Brown's Freshly Painted Pram,* 2004, oil on canvas, 30 x 50 in., private collection

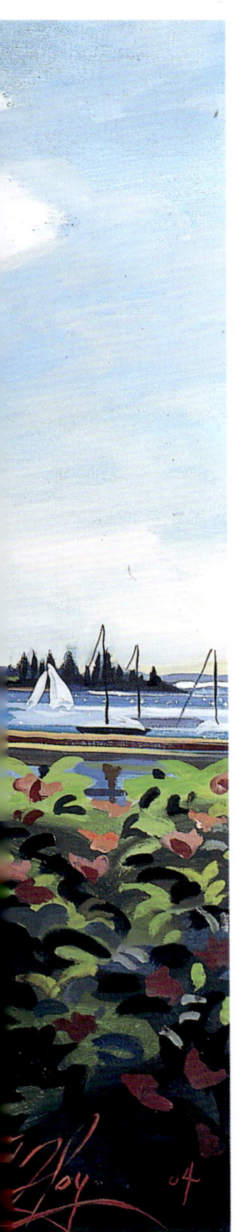

Manners or Something You Should Know If You Go There

In Stonington Maine
fishermen and women
stand up to the world
the way they stand
to buck their motor
boats out of the harbor
before the light of day.

Face the world
the way stoning
people brace
to work rock. Try
pitting your living
against granite *and* The Atlantic
you'll see what they mean.

Don't block their road
when it's time to go home.

—Patricia Ranzoni

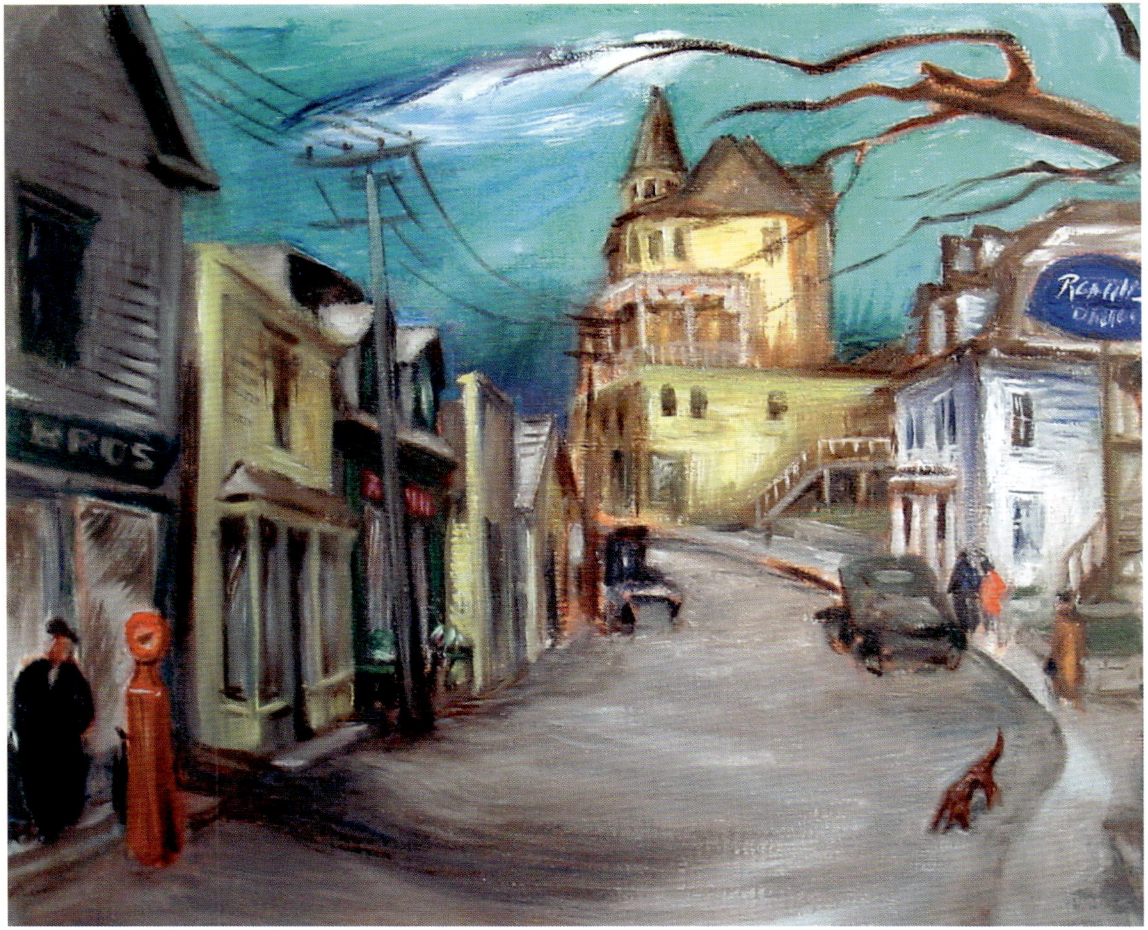

Emily Lansingh Muir, *Main Street, Stonington,* c. 1940, oil on canvas, 20 x 25 in.
Photograph courtesy Gleason Fine Art

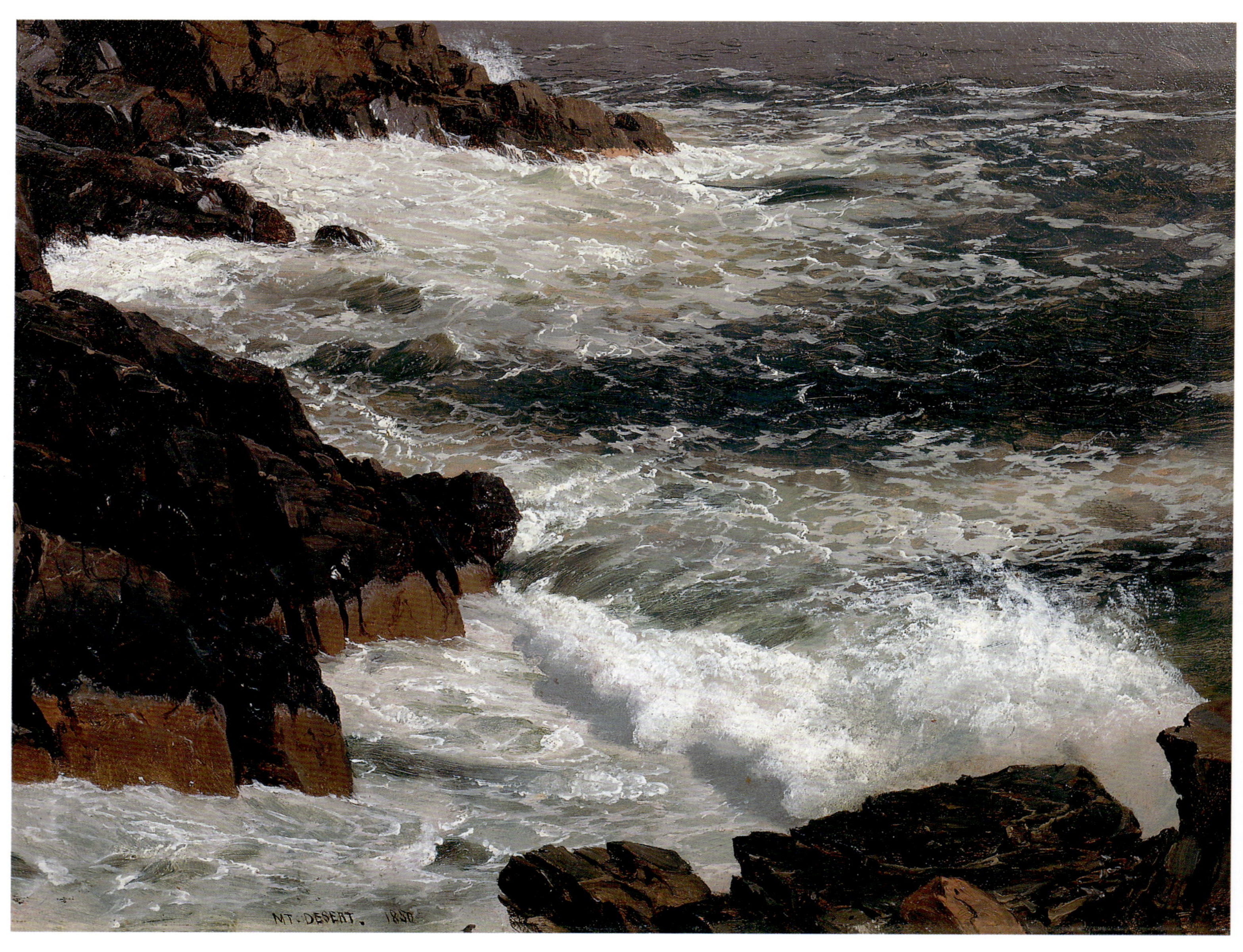

Frederic E. Church, *Rough Surf, Mount Desert Island, Maine,* 1850, oil on paper mounted on wood, 12 1/2 x 16 1/4 in.
Private collection, courtesy Berry-Hill Galleries, New York

Mount Desert Island and Beyond

Mainiacs away from Maine are truly displaced persons, only half alive, only half aware of their immediate surroundings. Their inner attention is always preoccupied and pre-empted by the tiny pinpoint on the face of the globe called Down East. They try to live not in such a manner that they will eventually be welcomed into Paradise, but only so that someday they can go home to Maine.

—LOUISE DICKINSON RICH, *STATE O' MAINE,* 1964

Maine's reputation as one of the preeminent artist destinations in America began in the mid-1800s, when a number of landscape painters made their way "down east" in search of the sublime. They were mightily impressed by what they found on Mount Desert Island.

Fitz Henry Lane (1804–1865), arriving by boat from Gloucester, chose to focus on harbors, ships and coastal landmarks. The picture-perfect quality of his view of Southwest Harbor is echoed more than a century and a half later by a panoramic island view by Bar Harbor resident Ernest McMullen (b. 1942). The two boats in McMullen's *View from Flying Mountain* leave attenuated wakes—like watery contrails—across the mouth of Somes Sound.

Frederic E. Church (1826–1900) also made the trip. When shown in New York City and elsewhere, Church's paintings of Mount Desert Island served to introduce the spectacular scenery of the northeasternmost state to the wider world, consequently inspiring city dwellers to extend their tours of Maine beyond its southern coast. The luminism of his landscapes continues to influence today's painters, as witnessed by the fiery view of Cadillac Mountain by Arthur Chartow (b. 1951).

On leave from service in the Union Army in the summer of 1864, Sanford Robinson Gifford (1823–1880) went on a painting expedition to Mount Desert Island.

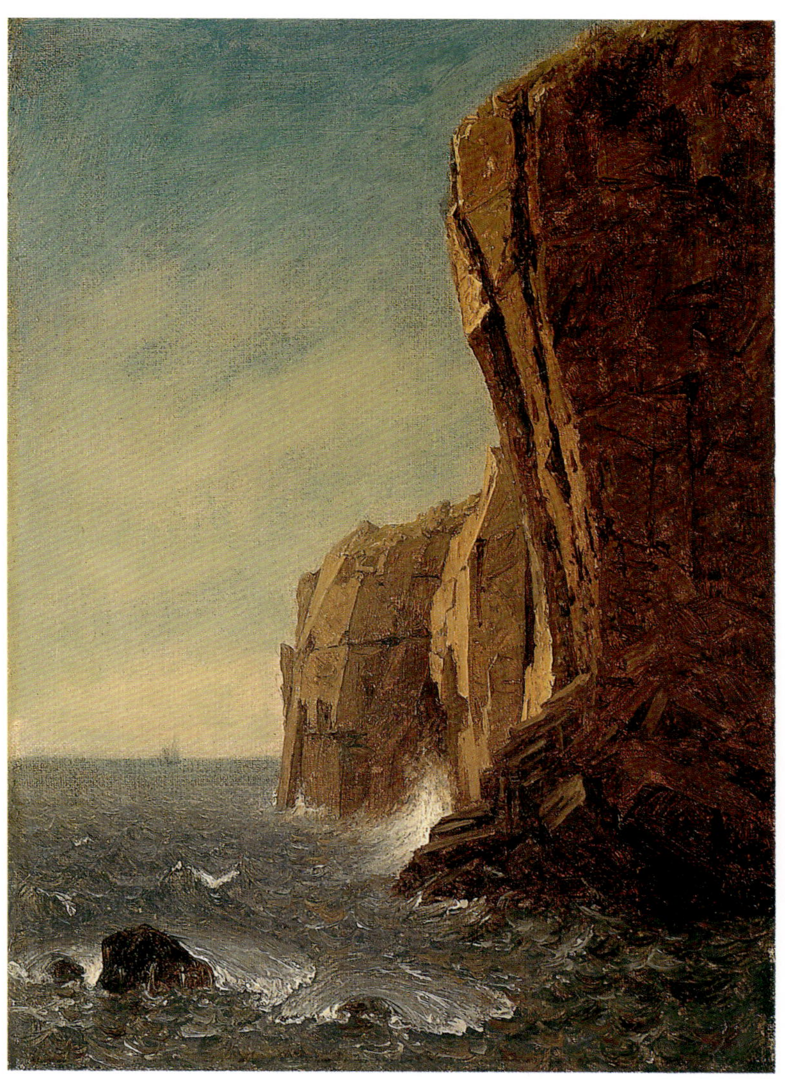

Sanford Robinson Gifford
Rocks at Porcupine Island near Mt. Desert, 1864
Oil on canvas, 12 1/2 x 9 1/8 in.
Collection of the Farnsworth Art Museum
Museum purchase, 1998 (98.7)

A number of memorable canvases resulted, including a dramatic view of the rocky cliffs of Porcupine Island off of Bar Harbor, which might illustrate the opening lines of Harold Vinal's poem "Perpetuity":

The foaming billow and the breaker write
The sea's biography upon the land.

British-born watercolorist S. P. Rolt Triscott (1846–1925) explored the Maine coast before settling on Monhegan (he is said to have been the first artist to live year-round on the island). While visiting Mount Desert Island, he discovered one of its finest views, Little Long Pond in Seal Harbor. Thanks to the conservation efforts of the Rockefeller family, this scene has hardly changed since Triscott's time.

The Rockefellers played a key role in the creation of Acadia National Park, inspired by George Dorr and other visionary conservationists. On a hike in the park, Diana Roper McDowell (b. 1952) from Lamoine was struck by the configuration of balanced rocks made by the Bates cairn atop Gorham Mountain. Acadia offers an artist-in-residence program for painters, writers, dancers and other creative individuals from across the country.

The Beech Mountain cliffs as viewed from the Appalachian Mountain Club at the southern end of Echo Lake have been an obsession for Bar Harbor painter Robert Phipps (b. 1933), representing, in a manner of speaking, his Mont Ste-Victoire. He has painted them in all seasons, fascinated by the changes wrought by snow, sun and autumn hues.

Nearby Beech Hill served as the setting for a family portrait by the master of stained glass, Louis Comfort Tiffany (1848–1933). The fields he painted are still there, but have given over to blueberry bushes, to lupine, and to Beech Hill Farm—an organic farm run by the College of the Atlantic in Bar Harbor.

The millpond next to the library in Somesville, the oldest settlement on Mount Desert Island, shimmers under clear summer skies in Sarah Knock's painting. Knock (b. 1947), from Freeport, shares a sense of the intimate with Phyllis Rees (b. 1926) of Trenton, who is especially devoted to lake- and streamside motifs in and around Acadia National Park. Rees is a conservationist; her paintings encourage us, in her words, to "take care to love what we see."

Many artists know that the best views of Mount Desert Island are found on the Cranberry Isles, a cluster of five islands that has sustained many artists over the past century. Joellyn Duesberry (b. 1944), who travels from Denver every summer to paint down east, sets up her easel on Great Cranberry Island to paint the full-bodied vista of rolling hills that fill the horizon.

Ashley Bryan (b. 1923), award-winning children's book author and illustrator, first visited the Cranberries while a student at the Skowhegan School in 1946. He ended up settling on Little Cranberry, there to practice his many arts, including puppet making and oil painting—the latter inspired by island gardens, including the dahlia beds of his neighbor, Emerson Ham.

The outermost of the Cranberry Isles, Baker's Island is known for its "dancing" rocks—great slabs of granite on its exposed ocean side that shift with storm and tide, and sometimes rock to and fro when stepped on. Ogden M. Pleissner (1905–1983), realist painter known for his watercolors of New England scenes, depicts visitors seated on a natural stone platform taking the sun.

Schoodic Point is a favorite place for artists of all aesthetic stripes. Frank Mason (b. 1921) found the misty coastline custom-made for one of his atmospheric oils. By contrast, Louise Bourne (b. 1959), a Brooklin resident, creates a seascape of stylized rows of waves rearing up on a windy afternoon. "My paintings," Bourne has written, "are attempts at coherent response to situations I find stunning—to times I want to keep looking and feeling."

Through their innovative collaborations, Gayle Fraas (b. 1952) and Duncan Slade (b. 1951) from Edgecomb have been at the forefront of American textile art for more than a

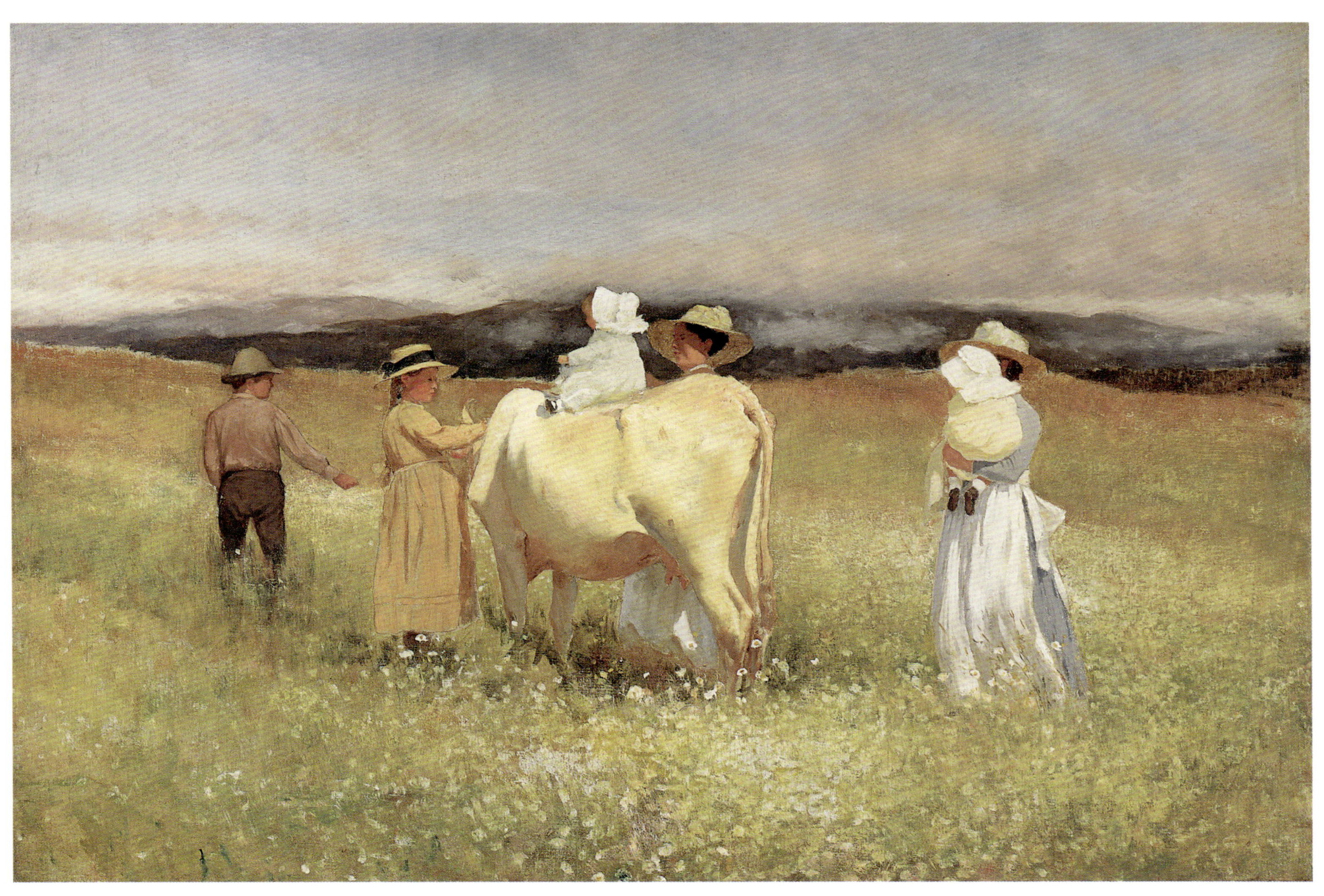

Louis Comfort Tiffany, *My Family at Somesville,* c. 1888, oil on canvas, 24 x 36 in.
The Charles Hosmer Morse Museum of American Art, Winter Park, Florida

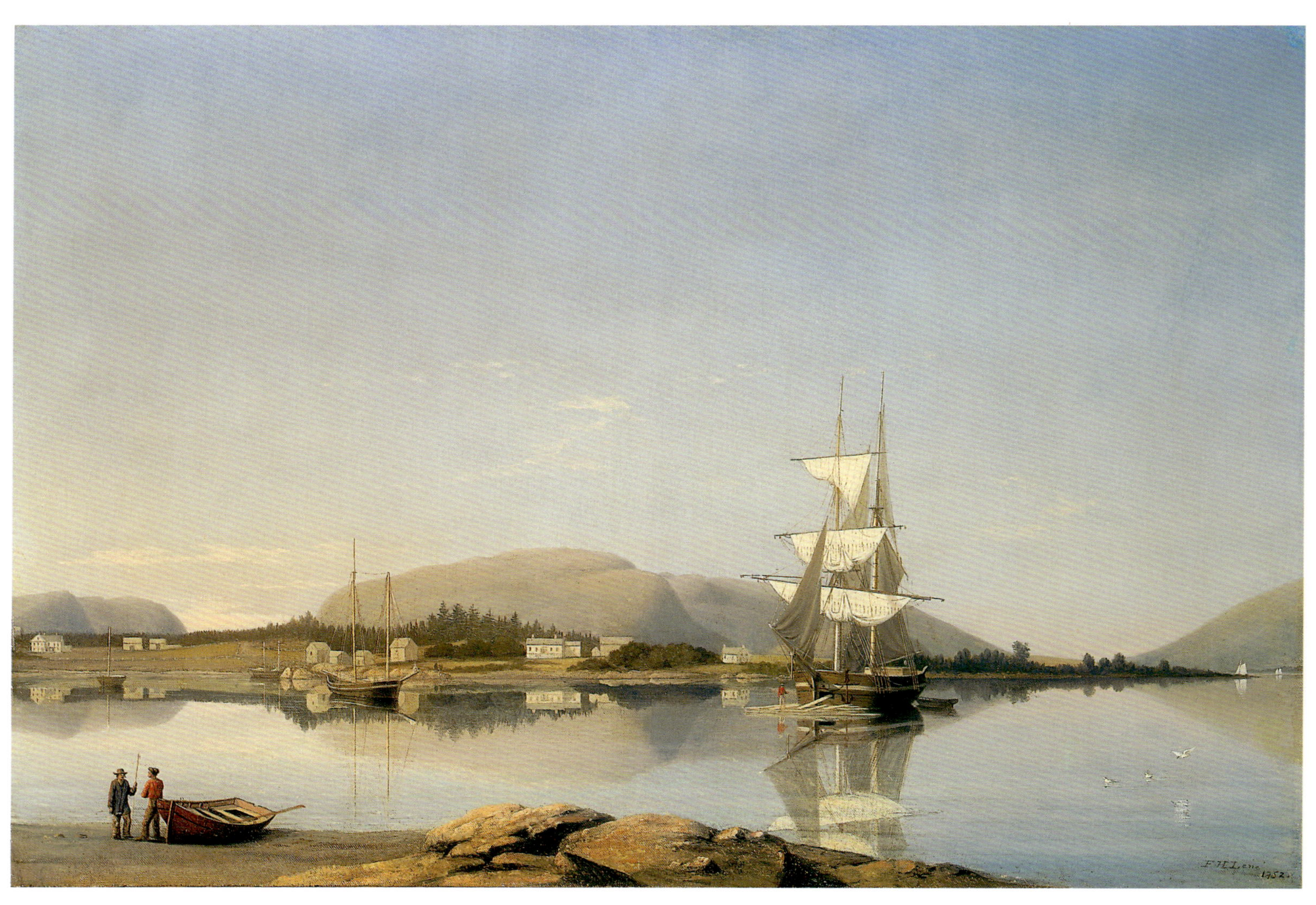

Fitz Henry Lane, *Entrance of Somes Sound from Southwest Harbor,* 1852, oil on canvas, 23 3/4 x 35 34 in., private collection

quarter century. They employed dye painted on hand- and machine-quilted cotton to portray a small island on Donnell Pond, a favorite camping area just northeast of Ellsworth.

Some people feel that Washington County represents the real Maine—small towns, sometimes hard on their luck yet full of gumption. In her view of Jonesport, Carol Raybin (b. 1941) captures a quintessential stretch of down east road made remarkable by a sign for Tall Barney's, a restaurant named for a nineteenth-century resident of the town who stood well over six feet tall.

Born in Latvia in 1913, Hyman Bloom immigrated to Boston. He visited Lubec near the northeastern tip of Maine in the 1950s and subsequently created a series of drawings and paintings related to the primeval forestland he found there. "Bloom is speaking of the woods of life," *Boston Globe* critic Edgar Driscoll wrote in a review in 1965, "with all the perils and pitfalls they hold. Yet somehow through the tangle, a path or clearing, or merely a shaft of light seems to point the way."

Maine seems destined to remain a mecca for painters from all corners of the world, pointing the way to new art. Near the end of the landmark book *Maine and Its Role in American Art* (1963), art historian James Carpenter predicted that "one thesis" would stand the test of time: that artists working in Maine will continue to feel the "impress of a place" and that their works will "bear witness to this."

Carl Little
Somesville, Maine, March 2006

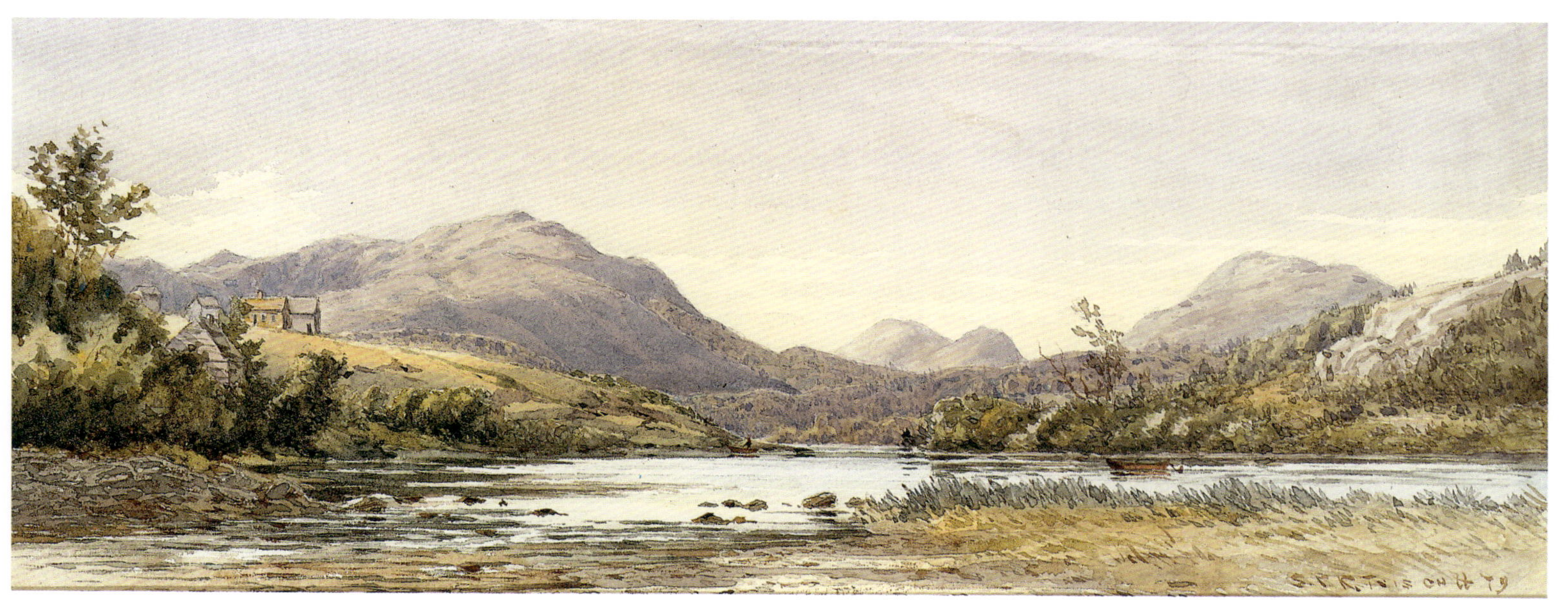

S. P. Rolt Triscott, *Jordan Pond, Northeast Harbor, Mt. Desert, Maine,* 1879
Watercolor on paper, 5 1/4 x 13 3/4 in., collection of Remak Ramsay

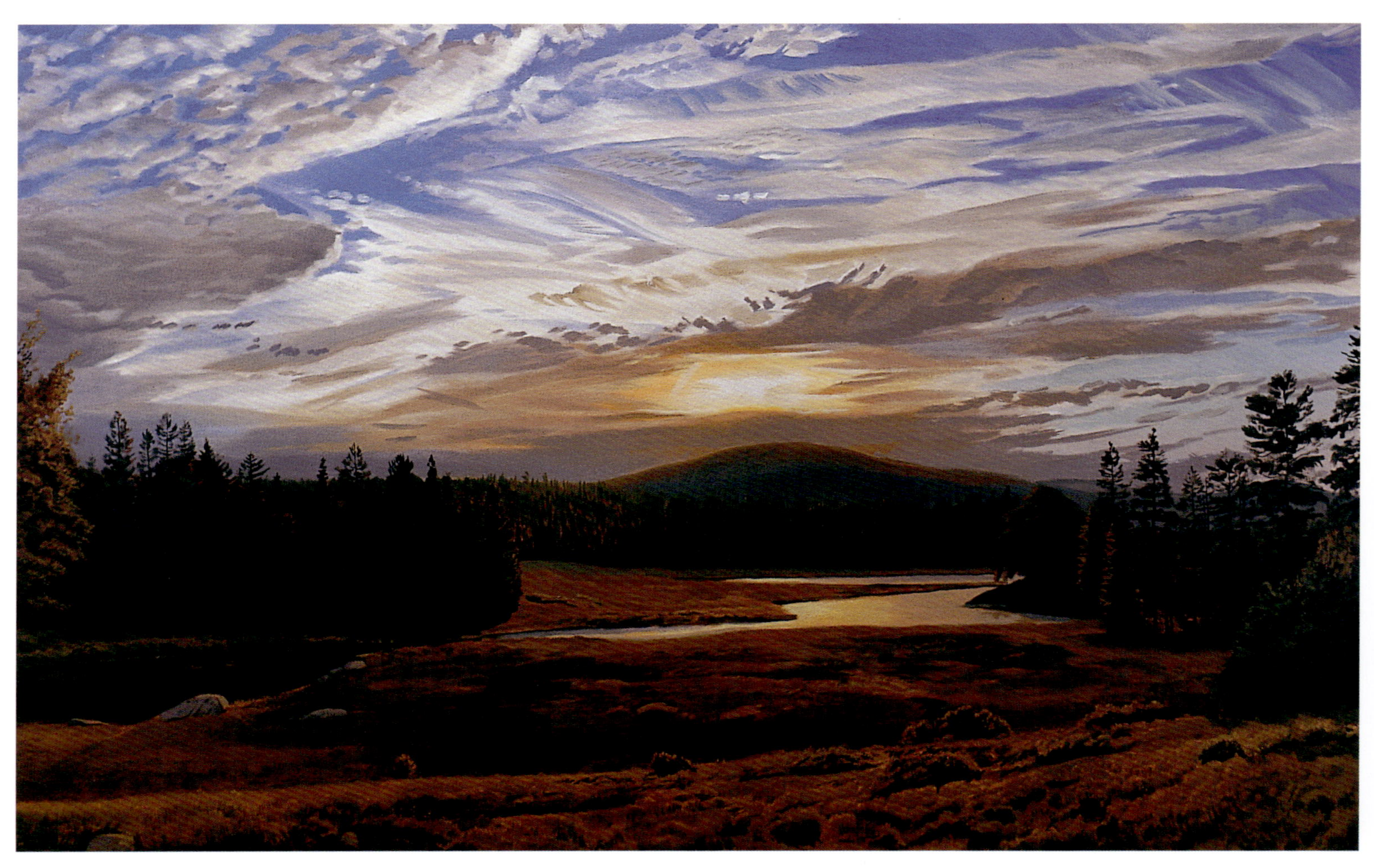

 Arthur Chartow, *Sunup, Cadillac Mountain,* 2001, oil on canvas, 22 x 42 in.,

Aug. 3. Beat out the narrow E. entrance of "Burnt Coat" with very light air, past Long Island and by Long Ledge Buoy up Somes Sound. Shopping at Somesville. Beat down the Sound, and being caught by flood tide and calm anchored off Fernald's Point. Mounted Fernald's Hill [Flying Mt.] in evening. Superb view.

—Charles Eliot

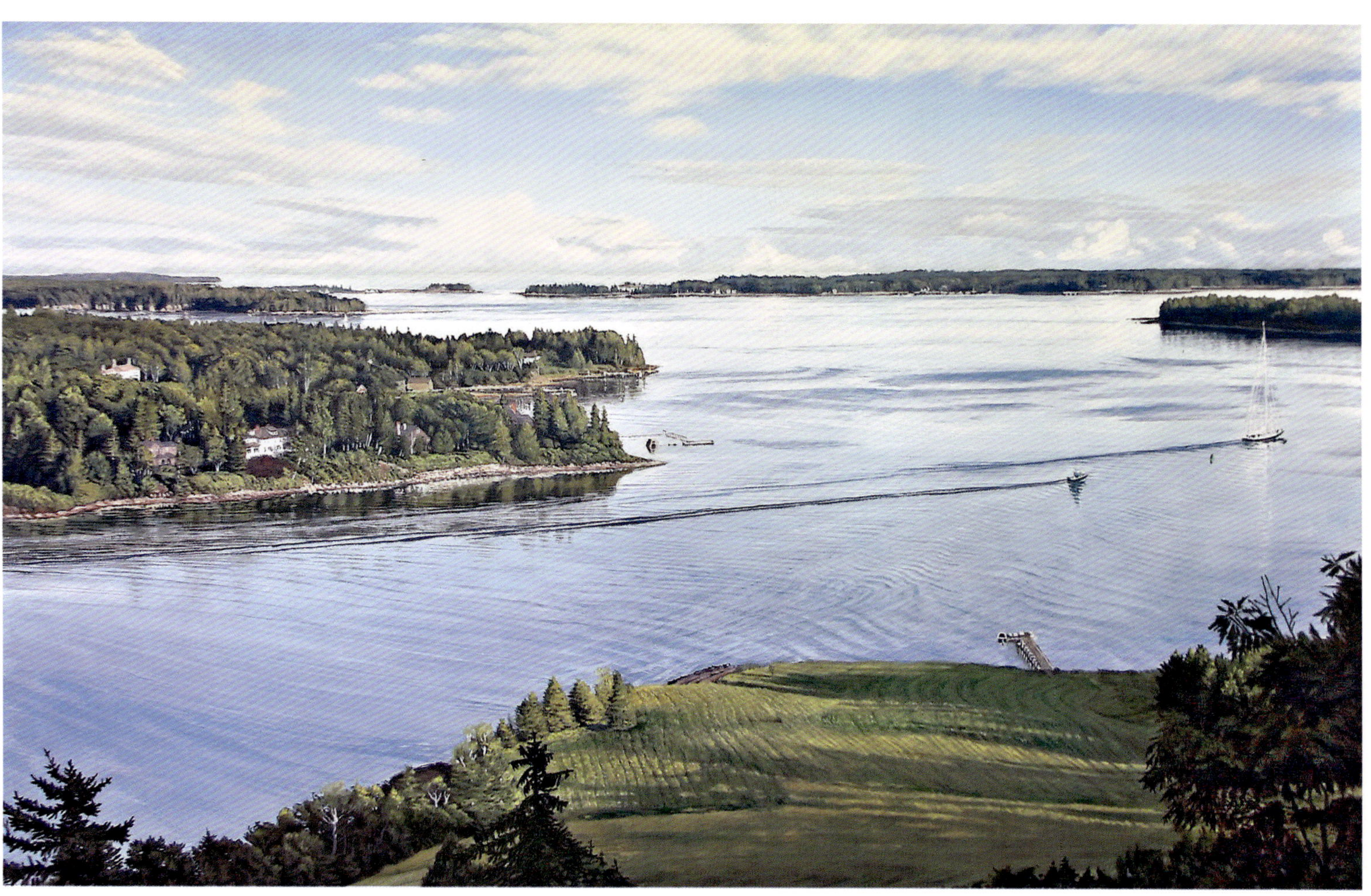

Ernest McMullen, *View from Flying Mountain,* 2004, oil on board, 30 x 44 in., collection of Margot and Boykin Rose

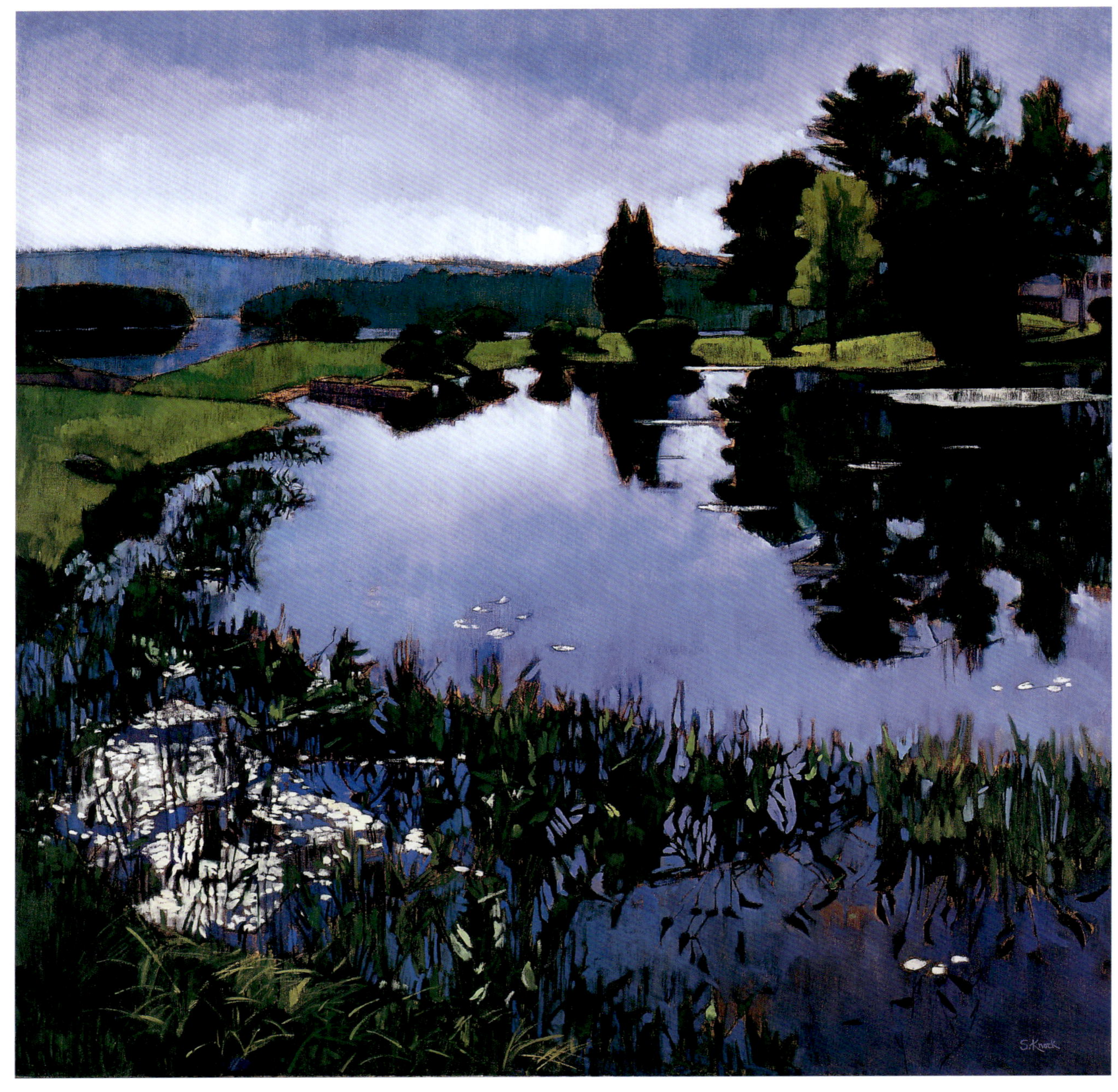

 Sarah Knock, *Somesville, Mt. Desert Island #2,* 1998, oil on canvas, 40 x 50 in., collection of Clifford Blanchard

If what we seem to say
mostly concerns the weather
we can expect Downeast
where tide and undertow
and variable winds
work endlessly together,
it is because our stay
in part, at least, depends
on how opinions mix
in talk that has to do
far more, we've grown to think,
with love than politics.

—SAMUEL FRENCH MORSE

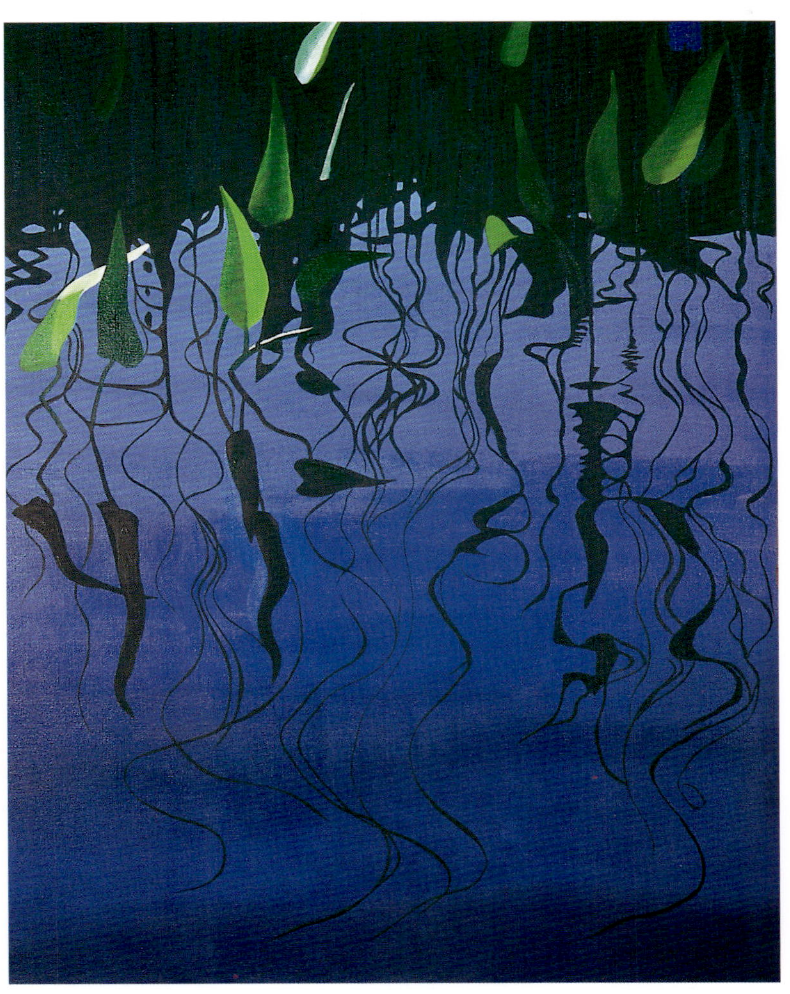

Phyllis Rees, *Seal Cove Pond Pickerel Weed II,* 1996
Oil and acrylic on canvas, 40 x 32 in.
Collection of John Pouwels, Franklin, Maine

Gaze on these rocks, and know how they are worn
Smooth by the iteration of the sea,
Like the smooth cheeks of aged toilers born
Along this coast whose buffetings may be
The secret of the granite hardihood
That makes them look on life and call it good.

—Wilbert Snow, from "Granite"

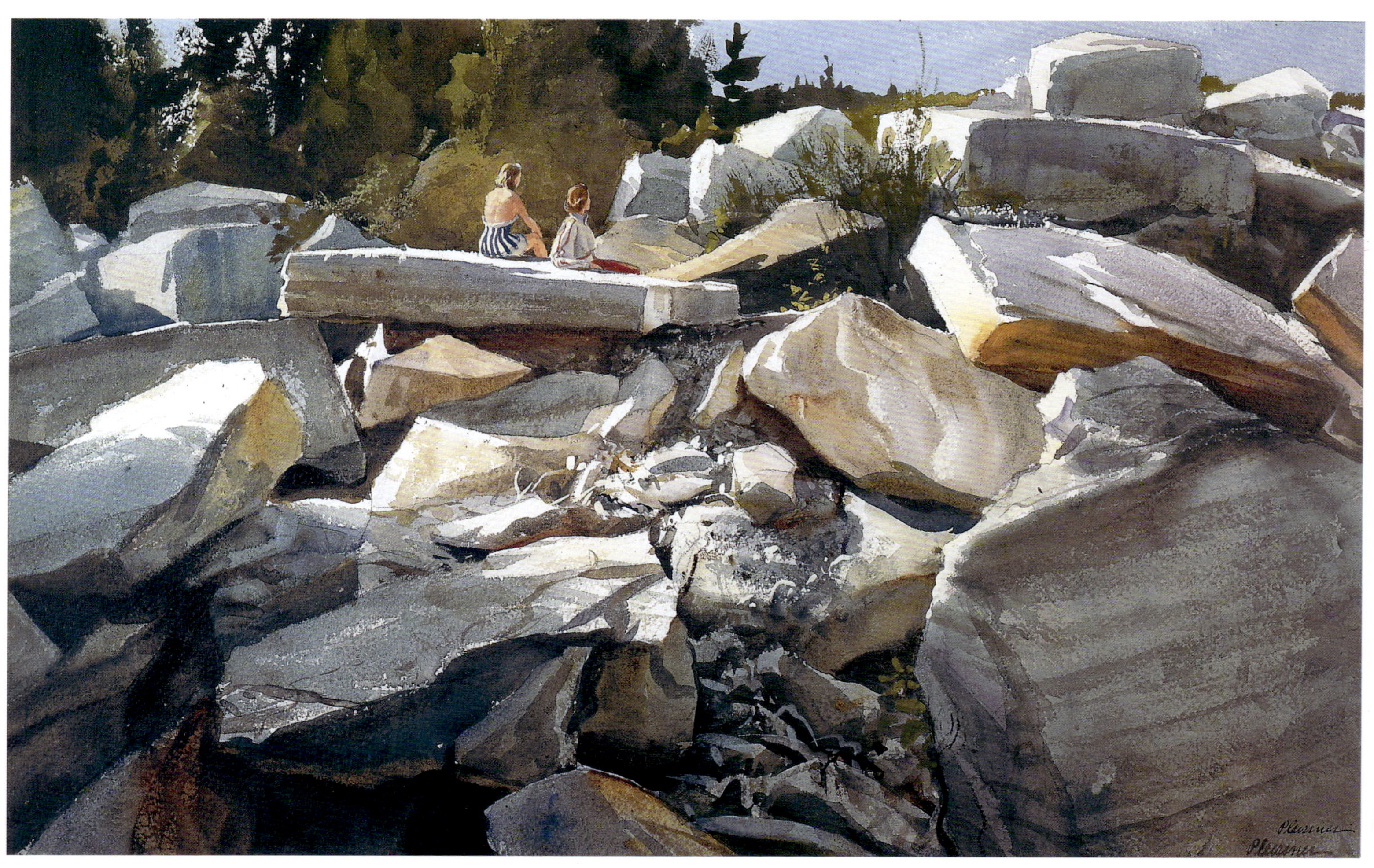

Ogden M. Pleissner, *Sunbathers, Dancing Rocks, Baker's Island, Maine,* 1962
Watercolor on paper, 16 1/4 x 26 1/4 in., collection of Remak Ramsay

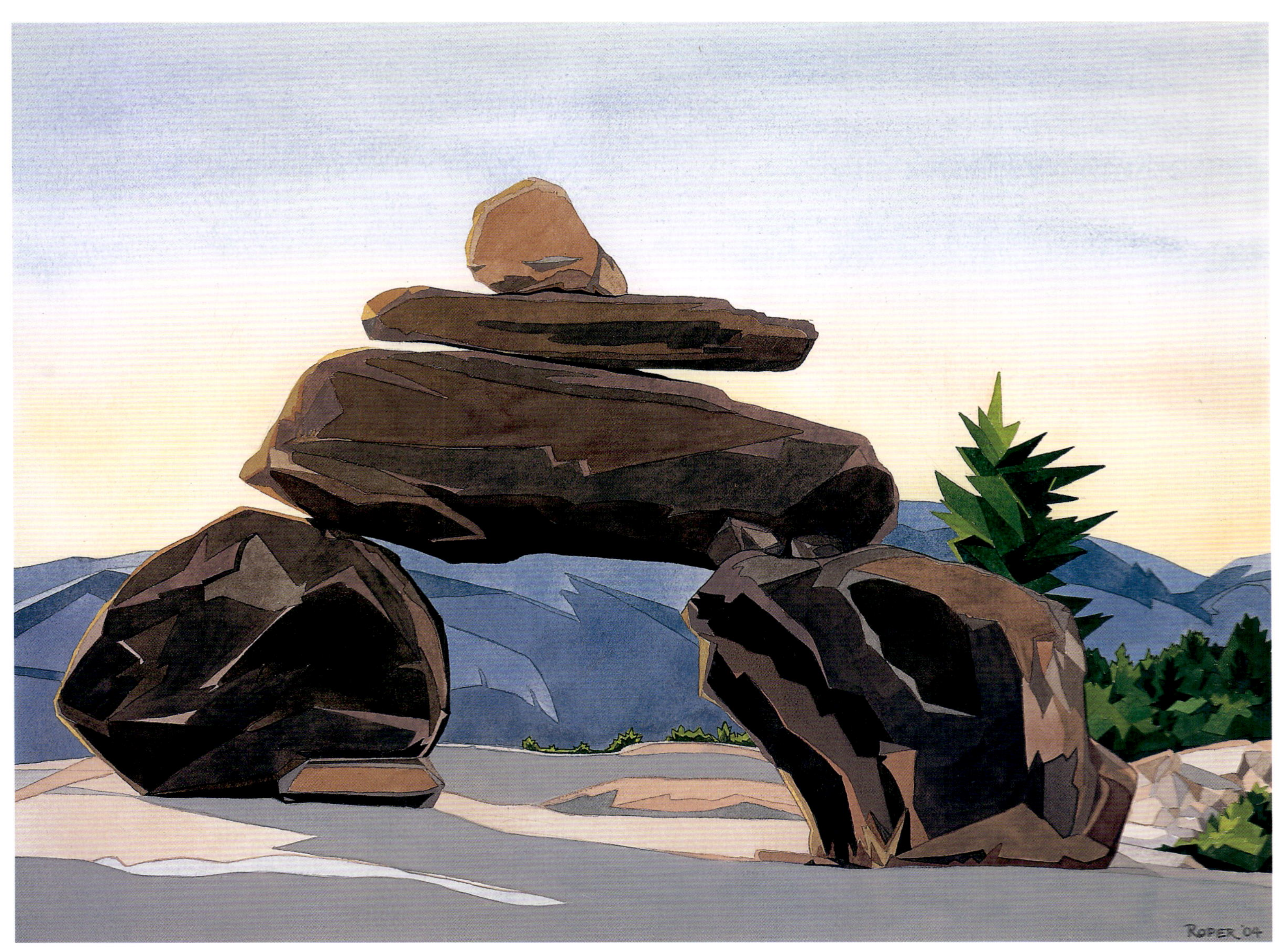

Diana Roper McDowell, *Bates Cairn on Gorham Mountain,* 2004, watercolor on paper, $21\frac{1}{2}$ x $15\frac{1}{4}$ in., collection of the artist

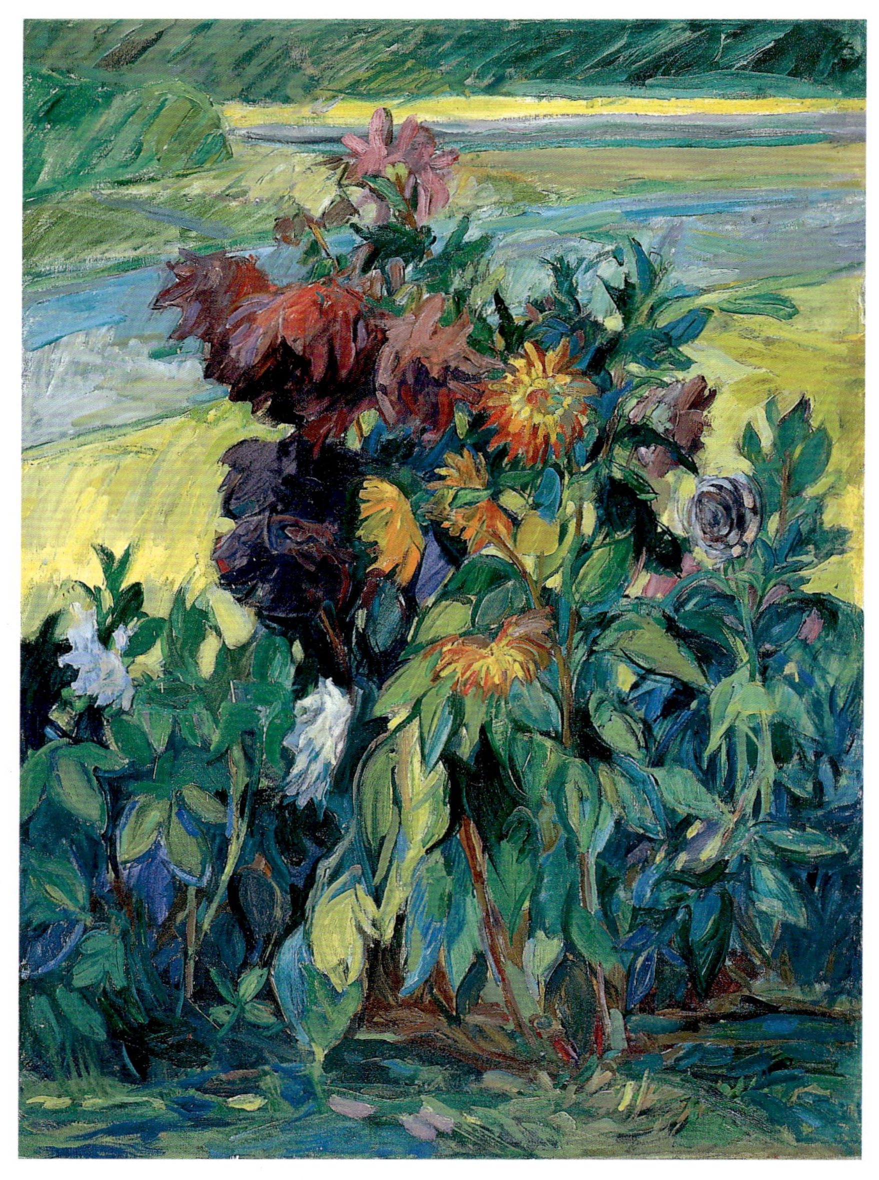

Ashley Bryan, *Emerson's Dahlias,* 1992, oil on canvas, 36 x 48 in.
Collection of Alan Stuart

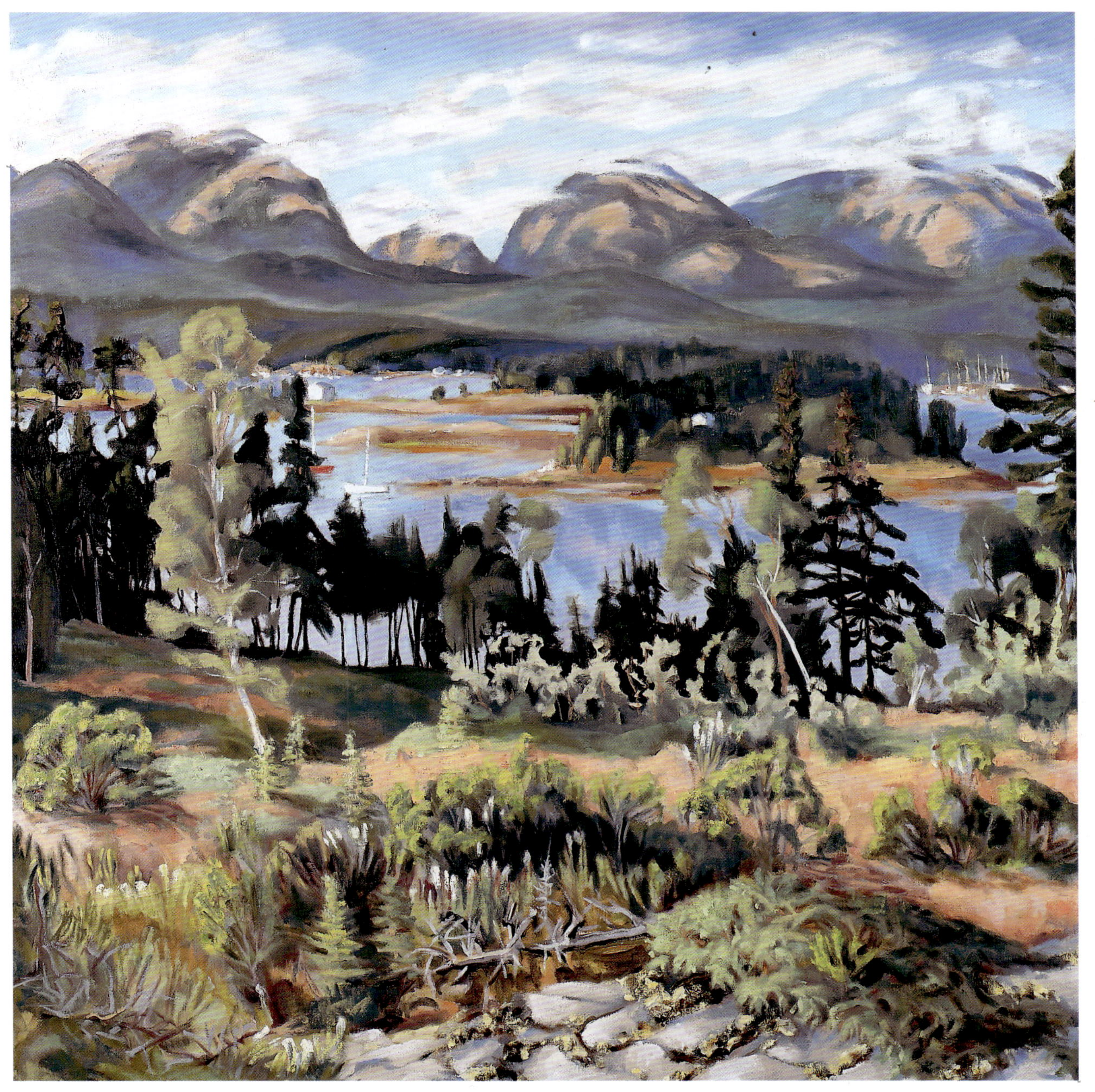

Joellyn Duesberry, *Mt. Desert from Big Cranberry Island,* 2005, oil on linen, 40 x 40 in., collection of the artist

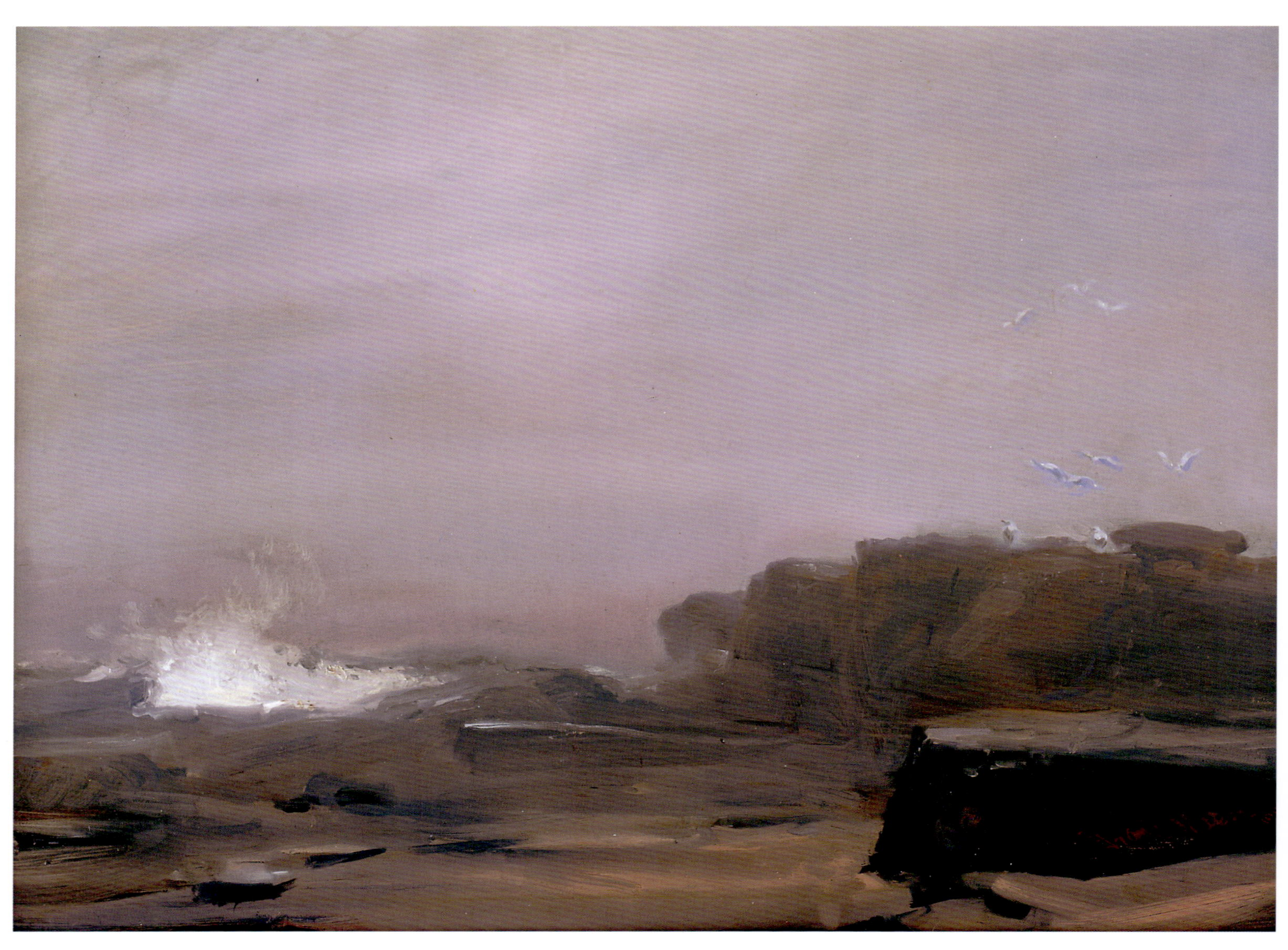

Frank Mason, *Dawn, Low Tide, Schoodic Point, Acadia National Park, Maine,* 1994
Oil on panel, 16 x 22 in., collection of Ms. Peace Sullivan

In endless variation on a theme
The waves come in and lace the rocky shore.
One after one long ripples rise and spread
Until they break in necklaces of foam
Or fountain up in spume, an endless store—
The gentle sea is singing in my head.

—May Sarton, from "Seascape"

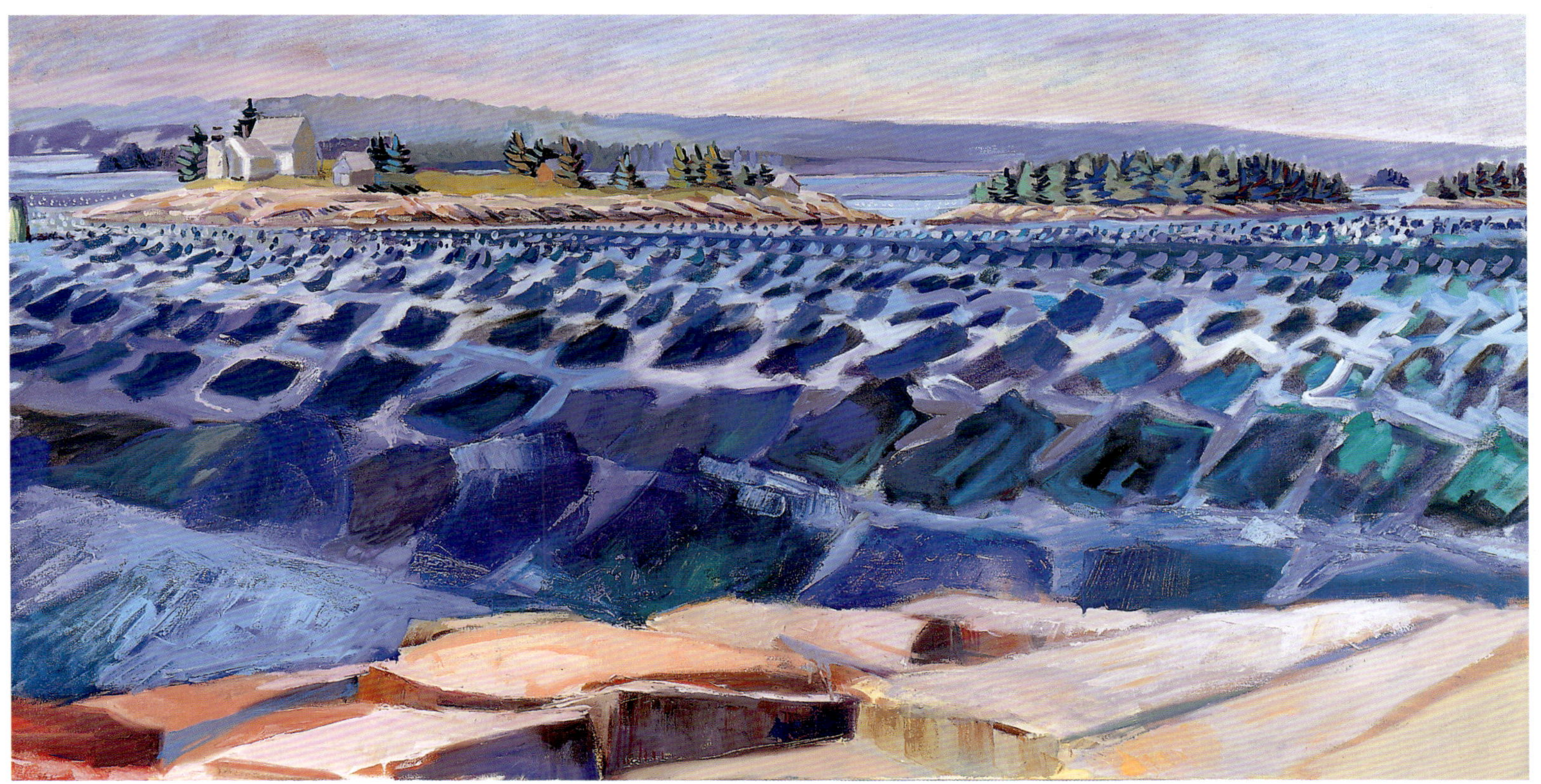

Louise Bourne, *From Schoodic,* 2003, oil on canvas, 24 x 48 in., Galeyrie, Falmouth, Maine

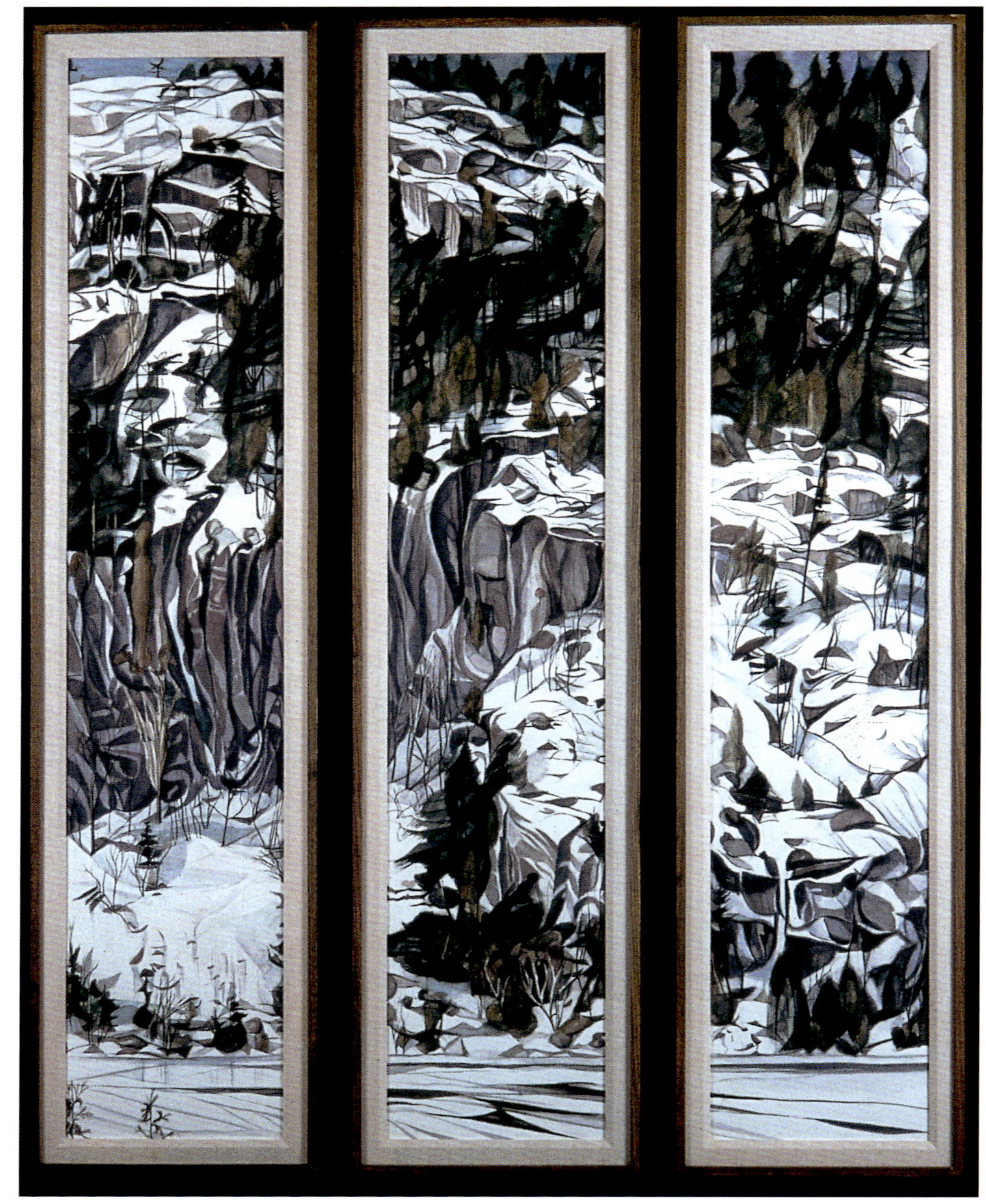

Robert Phipps, *Winter Triptych,* 1984, watercolor on paper, 40 x 60 in., collection of the artist

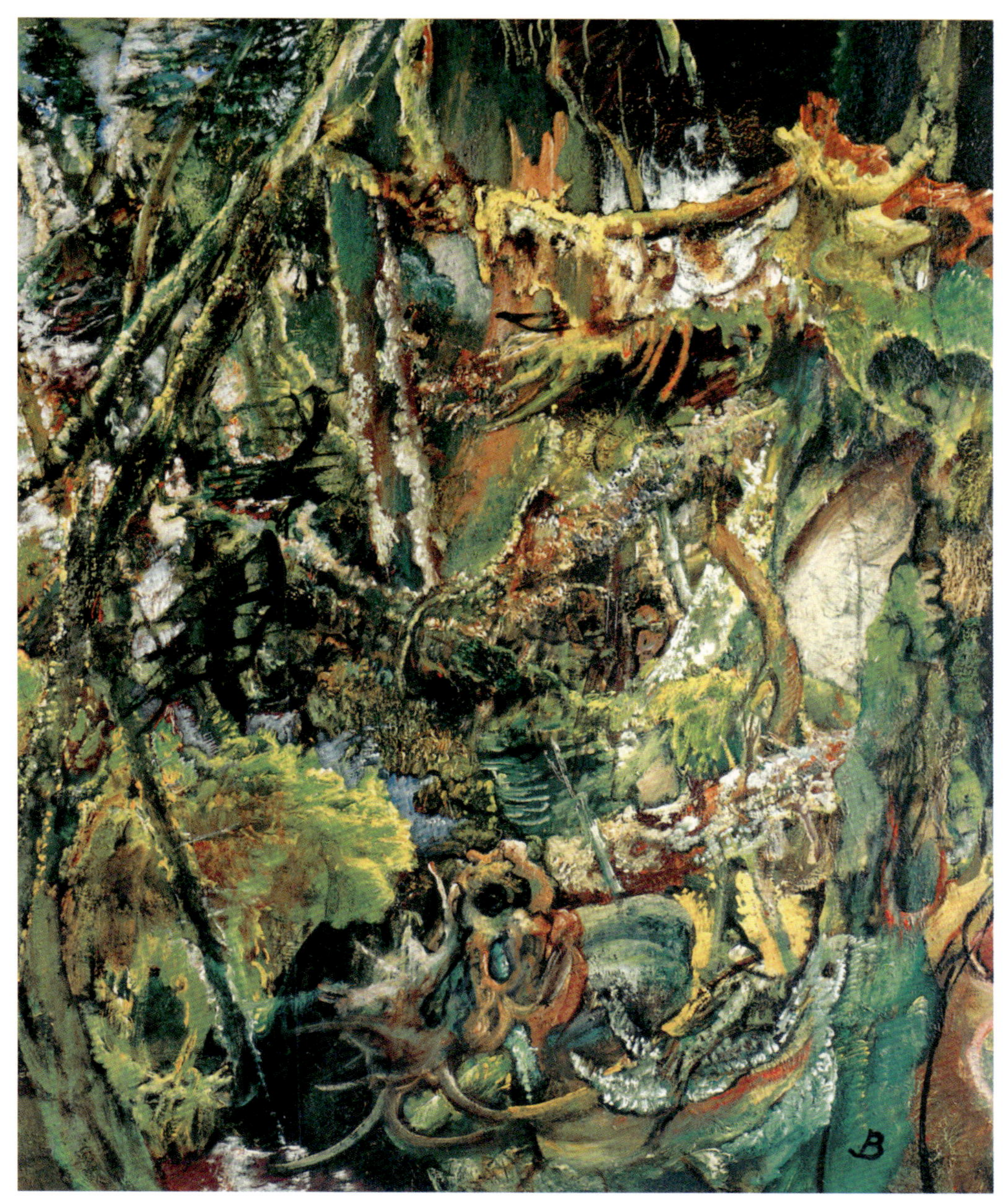

Hyman Bloom, *Woods in Lubec,* 1986, oil on canvas, 30 x 25 in., collection of Merloyd Ludington

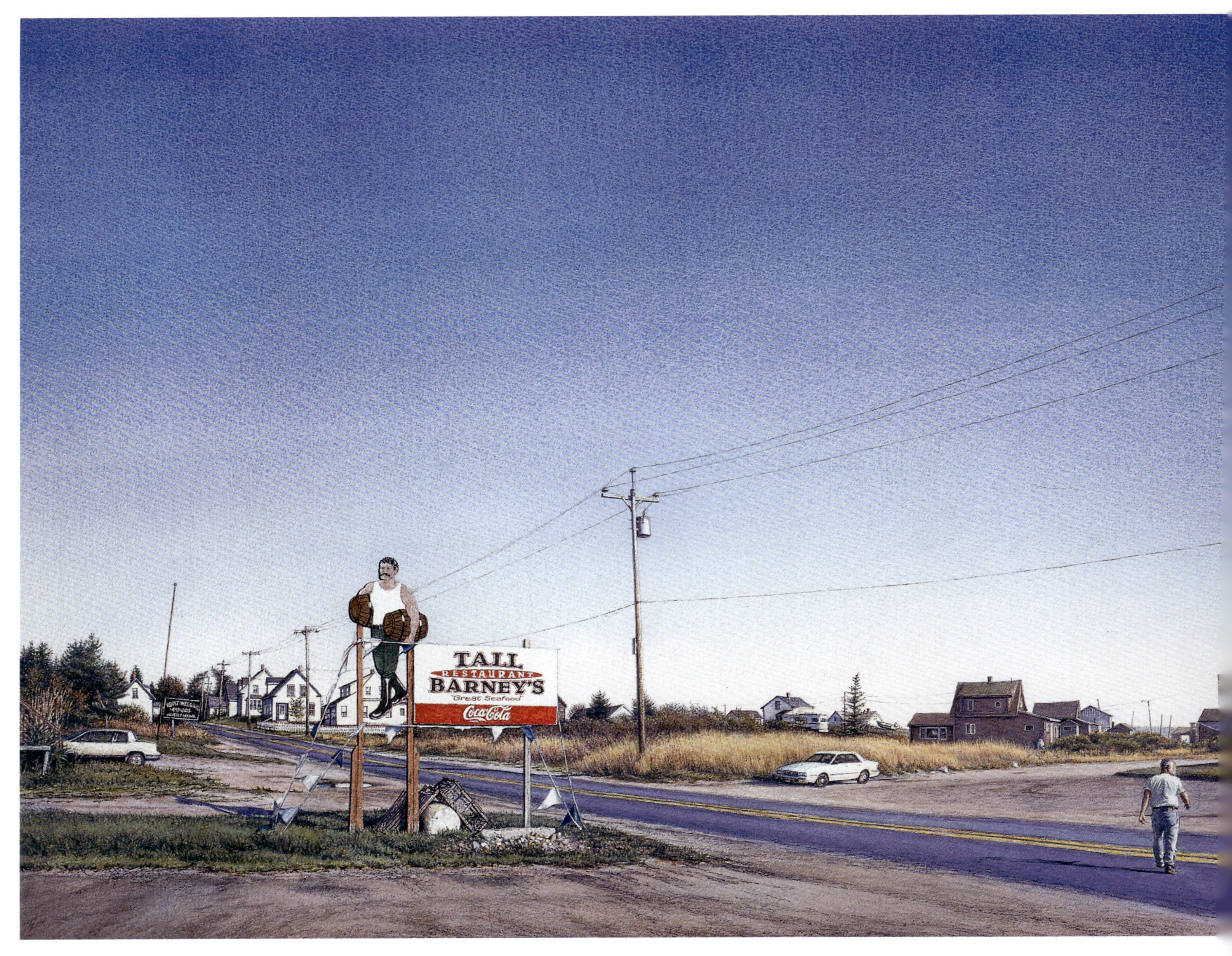

Carol Raybin, *Tall Barney's (Jonesport, Maine),* 2005, watercolor on paper, 22 $^{3}/_{4}$ x 35 in., collection of the artist

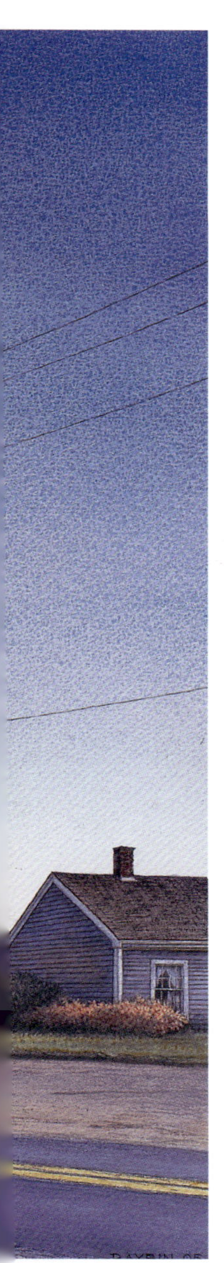

Once I pointed out to a Maine Yankee during a cracker-barrel argument in a coastal general store that he and his kind were a minority. He looked at me with cool amusement. "Ay-up, I guess we be," he said complacently. "So's God, come to that. Don't seem to fret Him none either."

That's the attitude that is typical of Down-easters. It is about the only thing that is typical.

—LOUISE DICKINSON RICH, *STATE O'MAINE,* 1964

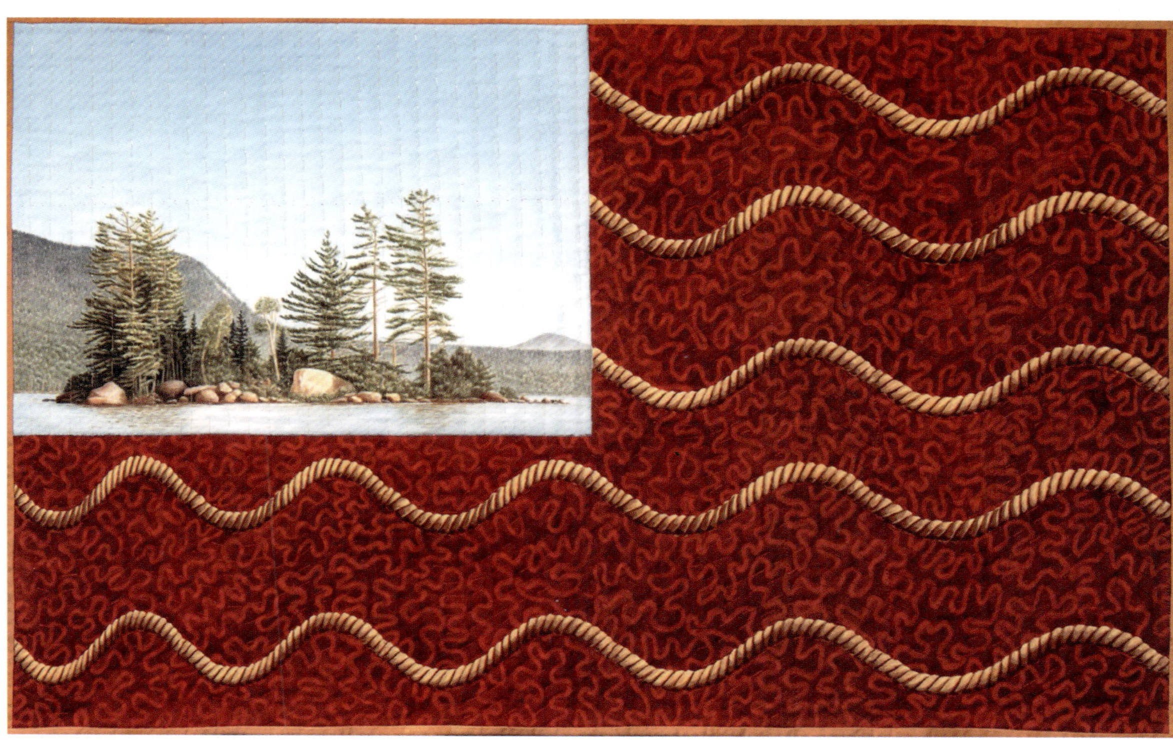

Gayle Fraas and Duncan Slade, *Donnell Pond,* 2005
Dye painted on cotton, machine and hand stitched, 18 by 30 in.
Collection of Gwen and Edward Asplundh; photograph courtesy Gleason Fine Art

List of Artists

Selected Bibliography

Aldridge, Richard, ed. *Maine Lines.* Philadelphia and New York: J. P. Lippincott, 1970.

Booth, Philip. *Lifelines: Selected Poems, 1950–1999.* New York: Viking, 1999.

Carpenter, James, et al. *Maine and Its Role in American Art.* New York: Viking Press, 1963.

Casey, Edward C. *Getting Back into Place: Toward a Renewed Understanding of the Place-World.* Bloomington: Indiana University Press, 1993.

Cole, John. *In Maine.* New York: E.P. Dutton & Co., 1974.

Dibner, Martin. *Seacoast Maine: People and Places.* Gardiner, ME: Harpswell Press, 1973.

Drake, Samuel Adams. *The Pine Tree Coast.* Boston: Estes & Lauriat, 1891.

Eberhart, Richard. *Maine Poems.* New York: Oxford University Press, 1989.

Eliot, Charles. *Charles Eliot, Landscape Architect.* Boston: American Society of Landscape Architects, 1999.

Foster, Elizabeth. *The Islanders.* Boston: Houghton Mifflin, 1946.

Gussow, Alan. *A Sense of Place: The Artist and the American Land.* San Francisco: Friends of the Earth, 1976.

Kimber, Robert. *Upcountry.* New York: Lyons & Burford, 1991.

Maine Speaks: An Anthology of Maine Literature. Brunswick, ME: Maine Writers and Publishers Alliance, 1989.

Morse, Samuel French. *Collected Poems.* Edited by Guy Rotella. Orono, ME: National Poetry Foundation, University of Maine, 1995.

Putz, George. *The Maine Coast.* Secaucus, NJ: Chartwell Books, 1985.

Ranzoni, Patricia. *Settling: Poems.* Orono, ME: Puckerbrush Press, 2000.

Rich, Louise Dickinson. *State O' Maine.* New York: Harper & Row, 1964.

Sarton, May. *Letters from Maine: Poems.* New York: W.W. Norton & Company, 1984.

Snow, Wilbert. *Collected Poems.* Middletown, CT: Wesleyan University Press, 1957.

Vinal, Harold. *Hurricane: A Maine Coast Chronicle and Other Poems.* New York: Steven Daye Press, 1957.

Wood, Esther. *Saltwater Seasons: Recollections of a Country Woman.* Camden: Down East Books, 1980.

Wormser, Baron. *When.* Louisville, KY: Sarabande Books, 1997.

Photography Credits

PHOCASSO/J.W.White 66
Melville D. McLean 2, 54, 55, 96
Jay York 1, 35, 50, 62, 121
David Plakke 23
Dennis and Diana Griggs 22, 47
William O'Connor 119
Peter Scarpaci 45
Anna Held Audette 71
Ken Woisard 15, 83, 85, 117
Ben Magro 70, 100
Susan Byrne 104
Tannery Hill, Topstraw, ME 39
Will Brown 51
Kent Williams 60
Odyssia Gallery 69
Jim Frank 91

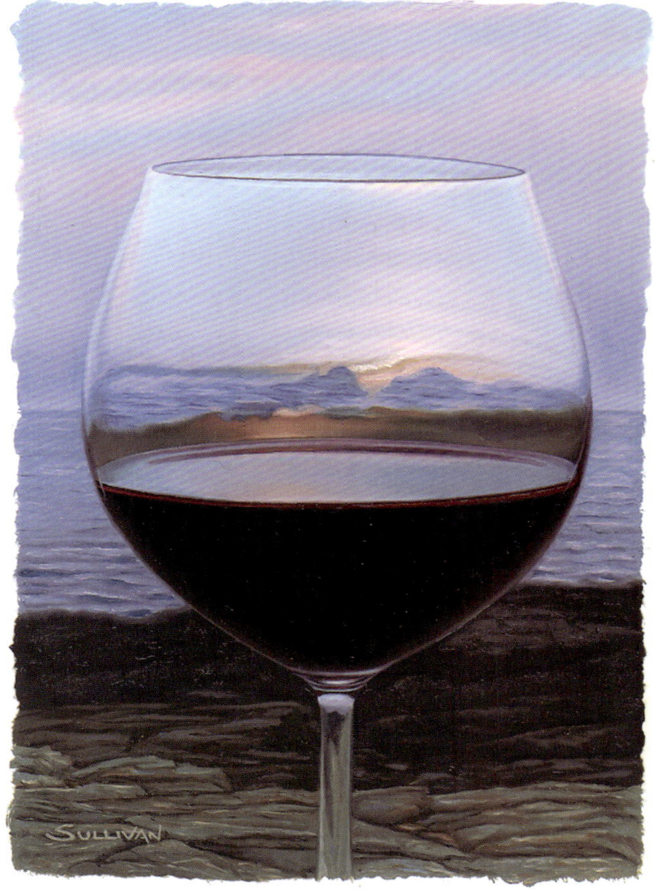

Rob Sullivan, *Two Lights at Dusk (Pinot Noir),* 2005
Oil on rag board, 6 x 4 1/2 in.
Private collection, courtesy Jameson Gallery

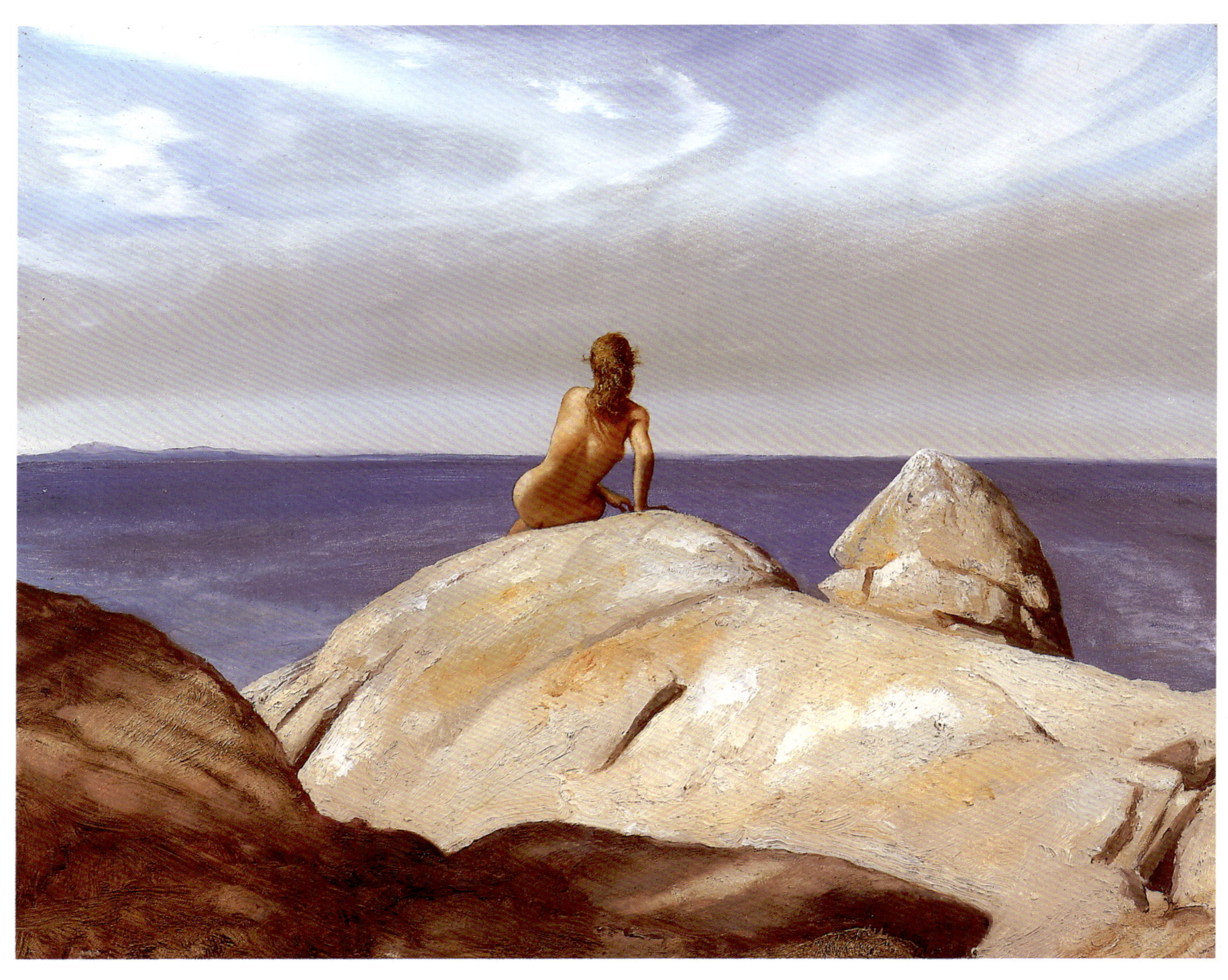

Bo Bartlett, *Siren Song,* 2000, oil on linen, 14 x 18 in., courtesy of the artist and P·P·O·W Gallery, New York